The Invention of Race

For Bobi, Relicque, and Irene

TOMMY L. LOTT

The
Invention
of Race

Black Culture and
the Politics of
Representation

First published 1999

2 4 6 8 10 9 7 5 3 1

Blackwell Publishers Inc.
350 Main Street
Malden, Massachusetts 02148
USA

Blackwell Publishers Ltd
108 Cowley Road
Oxford OX4 1JF
UK

Library of Congress Cataloging-in-Publication Data
Lott, Tommy Lee, 1946–
    The invention of race : Black culture and the politics of
  representation / Tommy L. Lott.
        p.   cm.
    Includes bibliographical references and index.
    ISBN 0–631–21018–0 (acid-free paper). — ISBN 0–631–21019–9 (pbk.
  : acid-free paper)
      1. Afro-Americans—Intellectual life.   2. Afro-American arts.
  3. Afro-Americans in popular culture.   4. Afro-Americans—Race
  identity.   5. United States—Race relations.   6. Racism—United
  States.   7. Racism in popular culture—United States.   I. Title.
  E185.615.L67   1999
  305.896′073—dc21   98–26086
                                                                    CIP

British Library Cataloguing in Publication Data

A CIP catalogue record for this book is available from the British Library.

Typeset in 10½ on 13 pt Meridien
by Graphicraft Limited, Hong Kong
Printed in Great Britain by TJ International, Padstow, Cornwall

This book is printed on acid-free paper

Contents

Acknowledgments   vi

Introduction   1

1   Racist Discourse and the Negro-ape Metaphor   7

2   Slavery, Modernity, and the Reclamation
of Anterior Cultures   14

3   Frederick Douglass on the Myth of the Black Rapist   27

4   Du Bois on the Invention of Race   47

5   Black Consciousness in the Art of Sargent Johnson   67

6   Black Vernacular Representation and Cultural
Malpractice   84

7   Marooned in America: Black Urban Youth Culture
and Social Pathology   111

8   Black Marxist in Babylon: Bayard Rustin and
the 1968 UFT Strike   127

9   A No-theory Theory of Contemporary Black Cinema   139

10   Prime-time Blackness   152

Notes   167

Select Bibliography   213

Index   222

Acknowledgments

Introduction

Several overlapping social and political themes related to race and representation are explored in these essays. The title is derived from remarks by W. E. B. Du Bois to the Negro Academy in 1897.[1] I exploit the ambiguity of Du Bois's term "invention" to suggest that, along with the general idea that all races are political inventions, black people have a right to invent themselves for political purposes. My use of this notion of race takes for granted the existence of African elements in many black cultural traditions, and recognizes that these traditions developed partly in response to a dominant racist culture. There are, of course, many different black cultures in various parts of the world. I use the term "black culture" with an African-American paradigm in mind to discuss a host of issues pertaining to racist discourse and racial mythology in Modern Western thought, ideas about modernity and Africa in nineteenth- and twentieth-century black thought, race uplift and the role of aesthetics, representations of black vernacular culture during the Harlem Renaissance and in recent hip-hop culture, black urban poverty and the culture-of-poverty thesis in recent black social thought, Marxism and the race-class debate in the civil rights movement, independent black cinema and the Third Cinema movement, and multicultural images of black people on prime-time television in the 1980s. Each essay is autonomous, with several intersecting ideas regarding black culture and black identity.

In the opening chapter "Racist Discourse and the Negro-ape Metaphor," I briefly trace a history of scientific views that influenced racist discourse since the early Modern era. Along with the historical development of philosophic-scientific racism, Negro-ape mythology flourished for centuries in popular culture and the arts. Many contemporary works of art and entertainment by black artists, however, contest this mythology. They have used black popular culture and mass media to "demythify" the Negro-ape metaphor.

The significant role racist symbolism has played in the subjugation of black people is important to consider in connection with questions related to slavery and lynching. My aim is not to present these nineteenth-century issues from a wholly historical perspective, but rather to provide an historical grounding for contemporary issues of gender, race, and class. Questions regarding the extent to which the anterior culture of African Americans was erased by slavery, for instance, are central to a current controversy between proponents of Afrocentrism and their detractors.[2] In "Slavery, Modernity, and the Reclamation of Anterior Cultures" I consider Paul Gilroy's criticism of Molefi Asante's Afrocentric view. I cite key elements of nineteenth-century African-American thought regarding the place of Africa in the modern world to contextualize their debate.[3] I point out that, although Gilroy rightfully insists that we need a notion of transformed African retentions to account for black cultural practices, he nonetheless presupposes a model of African-European hybridity that leaves open conceptual and empirical questions regarding the strength of the African element in New World black cultures.

Some of the current debates in feminist thought also have a historical grounding in the nineteenth century.[4] Frederick Douglass and Ida B. Wells-Barnett were well known for their early involvement in the antilynching campaign. In "Frederick Douglass on the Myth of the Black Rapist" I critically examine Douglass's account of the institutionalized practice of lynching black men accused of raping white women. Both Douglass and Wells-Barnett sought to expose the political use of racist sexual mythology by advocates of lynch law. They argued that false rape accusations were being used, not only to justify lynching, but also to deny social equality to African Americans. The insights they offered in the nineteenth century resonate with recent discussions of rape and racialized sexual politics by feminists writers Bettina Aptheker, Susan Brownmiller, Angela Davis, Joy James, Valerie Smith, and Alice Walker.[5]

Nineteenth-century black intellectuals maintained a variety of views about the social elevation of black people. In "Du Bois on the Invention of Race" I discuss Du Bois's classic argument for the African-American duty to retain a distinct race identity as a means of group progress. The sociohistorical concept of race Du Bois advanced was a key element in Alain Locke's interpretation of this duty. Locke understood Du Bois's injunction to entail an obligation of black intellectuals to retain black folk cultural traditions. As a mentor for several writers and artists, he insisted upon a representation of black folk culture that included "genuine portraiture" (that is, representations that are neither caricature nor Nordicized) in all the various art forms. In "Black Vernacular Representation and Cultural Malpractice" I reconsider Locke's objection to the minstrel image. He was concerned with deliberate misrepresentation. But his accusation against Zora Neale Hurston's representation of southern black folk culture is problematic. I point out that his charge of cultural malpractice involves a judgment regarding Hurston's intention. His criticism of Hurston (who employed the actual speech of black southerners) is inconsistent with his praise of Paul Laurence Dunbar (who relied on a highly suspect literary dialect). I trace this inconsistency to a major shortcoming of Locke's aesthetic view, which fails to accommodate the inherent political ambiguity of minstrelsy. This consideration is extended to a similar charge of minstrelsy in rap music. As in the case of black minstrels, rap artists effectively exploit a politically ambiguous criminal image to conceal a subversive function that critics of hip-hop culture have failed to appreciate.

Rap music has been a frequent source of controversy, not only in mainstream media, but also within the black community. There is a rich history of critical attention to various aspects of black culture since the nineteenth century. Questions regarding aesthetics and politics engaged the thought of Du Bois, Anna Julia Cooper, and Alain Locke, as well as novelists such as Pauline Hopkins and Frances Harper. Many of the concerns expressed in the Harlem Renaissance debate over propaganda and aesthetics in black art remain central issues in cultural studies today.[6] I add to my earlier discussion of rap music a further consideration of the politics of representation in hip-hop that has a direct connection with questions regarding the plight of black urban poor people. The association of hip-hop culture with crime and the so-called "black underclass" has been reinforced through mass media where the neoconservative critique of government intervention has dominated current debates regarding social policy.[7] In "Marooned in America: Black Urban Youth Culture and Social Pathology" I attempt to rectify a shortcoming of William Julius Wilson's response to neoconservatives who maintain a view of black urban youth culture as pathological. Against this widely held view I argue that mainstream values are expressed in rap music. The mainstream values embraced by rap artists appear distorted only because they are often stated in terms that reflect conditions of extreme poverty in black urban environments.[8]

The race-class question is a recurring issue in several essays. In "Black Marxist in Babylon: Bayard Rustin and the 1968 UFT Strike," I focus on a Marxist-nationalist debate from the civil rights era. Bayard Rustin's advocacy of a Social Democratic theory of social change in the context of the black power movement raises some of the earlier concerns of Frederick Douglass and Ida B. Wells-Barnett regarding the viability of interracial political coalitions. More recently, similar concerns have been raised in connection with William Julius Wilson's proposals regarding race-neutral social policy directed towards improving the plight of the black urban poor.[9]

At the turn of the century Du Bois asserted the duty to retain an African-American race identity as a cultural imperative that obligates the black middle class not to seek absorption into the white mainstream. To meet the demands of this cultural imperative Alain Locke developed an aesthetic theory that could be incorporated into a race-uplift social philosophy. Langston Hughes, Claude McKay, and many other Harlem Renaissance writers are well known for having questioned the viability of art and literature as a means of race uplift. In "Black Consciousness in the Art of Sargent Johnson" I reflect on the social implications of Locke's aesthetic theory, well represented in the work of Sargent Johnson, a Harlem Renaissance artist and follower of Locke. Ironically, Locke made only scant comments about Johnson, which were reserved and indirectly critical. I trace this inconsistency to the tension between Locke's notions of folk and fine art, a tension that Johnson sought to resolve in his work. With regard to politics, I indicate the merits and the short-comings of Locke's view of the role of culture in race uplift.

The endeavor of Harlem Renaissance artists, such as Sargent Johnson, to alter the visual aesthetic of black represention has a parallel in independent black cinema. Recent commentaries on black popular culture and mass media emphasize the importance of self-representation.[10] In "A No-theory Theory of Contemporary Black Cinema" and "Prime-time Blackness," I draw upon this literature to discuss the black image in film and television. I reject the pre-vailing concept of black cinema as inadequate. I offer a political rationale for eschewing accounts of black cinema that rely on bio-logically essentialized notions of black identity. The reservations I express regarding the standard critique of blaxploitation-era films emphasize the importance of political, as well as aesthetic, criteria of black cinema. This political notion of black cinema supports the movement for a nonessentialist Third Cinema.

I conclude with a discussion of the black image on prime-time television. Herman Gray's account of black television programming in the 1980s employs a more complex view of black identity. He draws attention to the constantly shifting cultural meanings asso-ciated with various signs of blackness. These meanings are perpetually under negotiation within the black community. Multicultural images of black people appeared on prime-time television when networks began to "narrowcast" to specific audiences in an effort to survive structural transformations in the television industry. Gray cites economic factors to explain the advent of black-oriented situation comedy. He interprets the social cleavages that were represented regularly in programs such as *The Cosby Show, A Different World*, and *In Living Color* as an indication of the reemergence of the race-class issue in black popular culture. In this instance mass media operated as a conduit for the expression of social difference and class antagon-isms in the black community. Gray's analysis of this more complex self-representation indicates how the meaning of blackness reflects an internal struggle within African-American culture. In addition to rejecting the claims of white conservatives, some black-oriented television programs in the mid-eighties also challenged monolithic constructions emanating from inside the black community.

Gray aims to incorporate multiple black perspectives into the pol-itics of race and representation by focusing on self-representation.

My aim throughout this book has been to treat the representation of black people as a dialectic of competing ideologies. But there is also an epistemological dimension. Social policy is often influenced by mainstream images that devalue black people and black culture. I rely on writings by nineteenth- and twentieth-century black intellectuals and artists to indicate the extent to which the dominant image of black people has been contested, through subversive and through oppositional practices. My reflections on arguments and ideas that challenge this image aim to sustain a tradition of resistance upheld by black social and political thinkers since slavery.

Chapter 1

Racist Discourse and the Negro-ape Metaphor

The use of ape images symbolically to represent black people is common in American culture. Public awareness of this xenophobic practice was heightened in the days following the infamous Rodney King beating, when national news programs repeatedly broadcast taped conversations from Los Angeles police radio in which arresting officers in the case referred to blacks as "gorillas in the mist."

When asked to respond to Ted Danson's blackface antics at a Whoopi Goldberg roast, Reverend Jesse Jackson chose to cite, as a more grievous offense, an AT&T internal newsletter that used the image of a monkey to represent African customers on a diagram of the company's global network. Reverend Jackson wanted to throw a spotlight onto the racism practiced by one of the most powerful and influential multinational corporations. What accounts for the persistence of this particular racist practice? Highlighting the political dimension of the Negro-ape metaphor allows for a better understanding of the strength of its underlying mythology. Ultimately this metaphor satisfies the need to provide a biological justification of antiblack racism, and supplies a convenient rationale for the ongoing subordination of black people.

The association of apes with black people in Western discourse was facilitated by the European discovery of apes and the continent of Africa at about the same time.[1] Since Aristotle's time and through the early Modern period, the representation of distant and alien people as monsters and inhuman variations of the species had flourished without explicitly making this association. Most of the conclusions drawn by Enlightenment thinkers, even by such a prominent naturalist as Linnaeus (1760), were based on second-hand sources, often travel accounts by traders. In the absence of scientific knowledge regarding the animal world, empirical investigations were framed by the more philosophical construct of a great chain of being, according to which the animal kingdom is hierarchically arranged with humans at the top.

The close resemblance between great apes and humans inspired Linnaeus and his contemporaries to search for a missing link. As scientific interest in primates and in black people as candidates for the missing link began to overlap, some investigators, such as Edward Tyson (1699), François Leguat (1708), and Buffon (1766), emphasized the similarity of certain apes to African Hottentots, while others, such as Sir John Ovington (1696) and Daniel Beeckman (1718), emphasized the purportedly simian characteristics of Hottentots. When viewing illustrations of chimpanzees by Prevost and by Buffon, Rousseau had trouble deciding whether these primates were animals or "primitive" humans who had been misidentified by careless observers. In the absence of scientific knowledge Rousseau relied on the chain-of-being idea to situate "natural man" as the missing link in the conceptual space between primates and "primitives."

The corollary to this classification was the belief that Hottentots were the hybrid offspring of ape-human matings. Although he had a scientific interest in the question of hybridity, Linnaeus rejected this widely held view. Jean Bodin (1566) had asserted earlier that certain alleged monsters in Africa were produced by sexual intercourse between humans and animals. Much later John Locke (1672) and Lord Monboddo (1774) continued to maintain that offspring could be produced by the copulation of apes and human females though, with no scientific basis to support this belief, the issue was relegated to folklore. The search by naturalists for the missing link culminated in the nineteenth century in Darwin's view of primates as the highest animals and black people as the lowest humans.[2] In keeping with this classification of black people as intermediary, Franz Boas, one of the early twentieth century's most progressive anthropologists, concluded from cranial measurements that the white race differs more from the higher apes than black people.[3] Such anthropological comparisons only reified the Negro-ape metaphor and lent scientific credence to mythology.

With Negro-ape mythology substituting for an official scientific account of the connecton between humans and primates, many early naturalists, such as Olfert Dapper (1688), supported the speculation of travelers that certain higher apes were the offspring of women and monkeys.[4] Although Sir Thomas Herbert's contention that physical and behavioral similarities between apes and Hottentots show the latter to be hybrids produced by unnatural interbreeding, the folklore regarding sexual contact between apes and humans rarely embraced the obvious implication that the black race is itself a byproduct of sexual intercourse between Europeans and apes. Travel accounts preferred instead to promulgate the idea of a sexual union of male apes and black females. Male apes were cast as extremely libidinous with a preference for human females that, in some reported cases, led them to coerce and enslave African children.[5] This aspect of Negro-ape mythology entailed a dangerous political ideology. If, as Monboddo and Buffon claimed, some Africans had already been enslaved by higher primates, the European enslavement of Africans could be rationalized by an appeal to the natural order.

Popular culture and the arts have been much more influential than science in contributing toward Negro-ape mythology. In Shakespeare's *The Tempest*, the slave Caliban is sometimes portrayed on stage as an ape. In addition to his subhuman appearance, crucial to Caliban's beastly character is an unbridled libido that leads him sexually to assault Prospero's daughter, Miranda. Prospero's desire to protect Miranda then justifies his subsequent enslavement of Caliban. Shakespeare's construction of Caliban as subhuman is ambiguous. The simian aspects are exemplified by his libidinous nature, along with his monstrous appearance; nonetheless, evidence of his humanity is established by the eloquence of his speech and his subsequent conspiracy to rebel. He is in certain respects both beast and human. However, Caliban's ambiguous species identity is also ambiguous with regard to race. His portrayal as a savage has been applied to nonAfrican colonial subjects as well. When English lords claimed sovereignty over Irish peasants in the twelfth century, according to Fredrickson, "The rationale for expropriating their land and removing them from it was that the Celtic Irish were savages, so wild and rebellious that they could only be controlled by a constant and ruthless exercise of brute force."[6] The radical Belgian political economist Gustave de Molinari observed in 1880 that England's largest newspapers "allow no occasion to escape them of treating the Irish as an inferior race – as a kind of white negroes."[7] Molinari's reference to the Irish as "white negroes" was informed by popular English caricatures of the time.

While Caliban's racial identity is not clearly specified by Shakespeare, his cinematic counterpart, the gorilla in *King Kong* (1933), is most certainly a black man.[8] Through the tale of a giant prehistoric gorilla which is brought to America in chains to be commercially exploited on Broadway, the 1933 film presents a colonial narrative imbued with Negro-ape mythology that alludes to the conquest and enslavement of Africans by Europeans. It is somewhat ironic that a non-fictional book by Paul Du Chaillu, *Exploration and Adventures in Equatorial Africa* (1861), was the inspiration for the fictionalized narrative in *King Kong*, while one of the film's numerous imitators, *Love Life of A Gorilla* (1937), proposed to be a documentary educational film of actual matings between gorillas and African women. *King Kong* trades on the sexual aspects of Negro-ape mythology to set up a symbolic lynching scenario as the dramatic climax. Racially motivated lynchings of black men have been rationalized in the social consciousness of whites as punishment for insolence, or violence toward whites, and gained a special justification as revenge for sexual transgressions against white women.[9] This pattern of representation has been adopted in Hollywood movies – quite blatantly at times. One reviewer of the film, *Patty Hearst*, for example, complained about the portrayal of the Symbionese Liberation Army revolutionary, Cinque, as "King Kong to Hearst's Fay Wray."[10]

The emotions incited by the horror genre permit spectators to avoid confronting the morality of the violence against a black man. The racial discourse in the film's subtext is tailored to leave unquestioned the social order that fostered, and culturally validated, racially motivated lynchings. The Arab aphorism quoted at the beginning of the film – that the beast is doomed by his affection for beauty – can be decoded in racial terms. The beast image represents the dominant culture's xenophobia about black people, while beauty is symbolized by white female purity. According to this interpretation of the beauty-and-the-beast leitmotiv, the tragedy of the beast's affection for beauty takes on a meaning quite different from the original fairy tale. The P. T. Barnum-like character, Carl Denham's, famous statement in the closing scene, that beauty killed the beast, would appear to apply to any black male lynch victim suspected of sexually assaulting a white woman.

In the two sequels to *King Kong*, this narrative was adjusted to accommodate audience sympathy for Kong's tragic fate. In *Son of Kong* (1933), a natural disaster provides the backdrop for the junior Kong's heroism. In the closing scene, amid the volcanic destruction of the island, the gorilla is shown holding Carl Denham above water while slowly sinking to his own death. The narrative underwent further modification in *Mighty Joe Young* (1948), again emphasizing the gorilla's altruism. The change from horror to melodrama reflects the fact that, by the late 1940s, American audiences were much better prepared to envision the end of the era of legal segregation and racially motivated lynchings. The gorilla in *Mighty Joe Young* is depicted as a nonlibidinous Caliban, a eunuch who faithfully obeys and protects Miranda. Unlike Kong's life-threatening violence, the havoc Mighty Joe Young wrecks on the dinner club is far outweighed by his risking his life to save a group of small children from a deadly fire. His close relationship with children is rewarded by a safe return to his master's plantation in Africa to live happily ever after.

Dino De Laurentiis's remake of *King Kong* (1976) went even further to tap the audience sympathy for the plight of the great ape. Aware of recent progress in civil rights, the narrative is updated to avoid the Miranda trap of pitting the character Ann Darrow's victimization against Kong's. Fay Wray's terrified screams are replaced by Jessica Lang's more consensual responses to Kong's sexual gestures, eliminating any justification for Kong's lynching. Instead, Ann Darrow, as well as her anthropologist lover (Jeff Bridges), are portrayed as environmentally conscious progressives with strong animal rights sentiments. Their abolitionist zeal indicates an ideological alliance with Kong against the capitalist excesses of his oppressor, a multinational oil company.

In the five decades since his cinematic debut, King Kong has become an icon of xenophobia frequently expressed as a metaphor in common parlance. His size and ferociousness are as important as his libido, for these contribute to the perception of his savagery, a perception that is used regularly to characterize black men. Rey Chow refers to this paranoid reaction to black men as the "King Kong syndrome."[11] The successful defense of the arresting officers in the Rodney King beating case relied heavily on the policemen's argument that, the infamous video notwithstanding, King continued to pose a violent threat. A journalist for *The Source* called this blatant appeal to the jury's latent xenophobia "the King Kong defense."[12]

Resistance to the xenophobia expressed in the Negro-ape metaphor in works by black artists and musicians frequently relied on deliberate appropriation of these highly charged images. In the field of music there has been a long tradition of minstrel songs that used ape images to represent black people. The themes of songs such as "Monkey's Wedding," "The Monkey Married The Baboon's Sister," "Monkey Land," and "Monkey Doodle Dandy" predate minstrelsy, but reemerged as popular college tunes.[13] (Throughout the 1930s and 40s blues and jazz also were referred to disparagingly in Hollywood films as "jungle" or "monkey" music.) This racist historical context is the vantage point from which to view the antiracist appropriations displayed in, for instance, Da Lench Mob's rap albums, *Guerrillas in the Mist* (1992) and *Planet of the Apes* (1995), the gorilla and monkey sequences in Grace Jones's performance video, *One Man Show* (1985), and in the work of visual artists such as Sonia Boyce and Carrie Mae Weems.

Although appropriations by black artists and musicians can be seen as healthy signs of overt contestation, they pale beside the advertising industry's shameless interpolation of black athletes. Patrick Ewing is presented towering above the New York skyline, Dee Brown attempts his King Kong dunk with the basket attached to the top of the Empire State Building, and Charles Berkeley engages in a showdown with Godzilla.

In the boxing world, the most recent incarnation of King Kong has been Mike Tyson. Tyson follows in the footsteps of South African heavyweight, Ezekiel Dhlamini, who chose the name "King Kong" to promote his career. Dhlamini's misfortunes were dramatized, after his death, in a successful jazz opera entitled *King Kong*. Similarly, a New York City television station used the closing scene from the 1933 film of Kong falling from the Empire State Building to introduce a special report on Tyson's troubled marriage to Robin Givens, a marriage that was referred to as a "beauty and the beast" relationship. Tyson's defense in his subsequent rape case undoubtedly was not aided by this construction. But when the role of the Negro-ape metaphor in Tyson's demise is considered aside Muhammed Ali's playful appropriation to promote his famous "Thrilla in Manila" bout with Joe Frazier ("I'm going to kill me a gorilla in Manila"), we can detect a subversive function even in the commercial realm. The lesson to be gleaned from such politically savvy appropriations is that the process of "demythification" involves a dialectic of recoded images. We continue to accept Du Chaillu's image of the gorilla as a social threat only by ignoring the counterimage of his oppression and resistance.

Chapter 2

Slavery, Modernity, and the Reclamation of Anterior Cultures

When Enlightenment philosophers, such as John Locke and Jean-Jacques Rousseau, employed the notion of slavery as a metaphor for tyranny, they were concerned with a fundamental tension in Western political theory between individual autonomy and political obligation. In large part they were reacting to an earlier proposal by Thomas Hobbes to resolve this tension on the side of absolute sovereignty. The emergence of modern consent theory occurred in the context of the European enslavement of Africans.[1] What are we to make of Hobbes and Locke championing a right of resistance to tyranny while directly involved in the slave trade? A major theme of Paul Gilroy's *The Black Atlantic* is that slavery, and the terror that maintained it, were complicit with the principles of reason espoused by modern philosophers.[2] Indeed, Locke's natural rights theory, along with his metaphorical notion of slavery as tyranny, provided the moral ground for Jefferson's argument for the right of resistance in the Declaration of Independence, an argument based on human rights that intentionally omitted any reference to the American system of chattel slavery.[3]

Although Gilroy criticizes several prevailing conceptions of modernity for not addressing racial issues, he points out Jurgen Habermas's account of Hegel on modernity as a paradigm of this shortcoming.[4] He is especially concerned with Habermas's references to the "progress" of modern society. Such statements have not sufficiently taken into account the slave's perspective, for any such view of Western civilization as progressing towards perfection by rational principles is called into question by the critical stance of the slave's vernacular cultural expression. From the slave's perspective, occidental rationality is comfortably situated within a system of racial terror. Walter Benjamin's notion of "the primal history of modernity" is reinterpreted by Gilroy to mean that "modern history could be seen as fractured along the axis that separates European masters and mistresses from their African slaves" (BA, 55). Although there are several steps taken by Gilroy to show this, the most crucial to his thesis regarding double consciousness is his appropriation of Hegel's parable concerning lordship and bondage. Gilroy proposes to reconstruct Habermas's "tidy holistic" conception of modernity with his own interpretation of the master-slave relation as a primary modernizing force.

Douglass's account of his fight with Covey is used by Gilroy to argue that Douglass presented a racialized version of Hegel's dialectic. Douglass's account raises a curious question of whether African slaves entered into the struggle with their European masters with resources drawn from African cultures. According to Gilroy, "it matters a great deal whether modern racial slavery is identified as a repository in which the consciousness of traditional culture could be secreted and condensed into ever more potent forms or seen alternatively as the site of premodern tradition's most comprehensive erasure" (BA, 197). Gilroy's position on the role of the slave's anterior culture in the master-slave dialectic is far from clear. He suggests that slavery radically transformed the black Atlantic anterior cultures. One might suppose that the extent to which African cultures survived slavery is a straightforward empirical question. Gilroy draws attention to some of the underlying conceptual issues. His concern, however, with showing the difficulties surrounding the Afrocentric view of tradition leads him to embrace a somewhat ambiguous view of the status of the "premodern images and symbols" that constituted the slave's "vernacular version of unhappy consciousness" (BA, 56). He needs a viable notion of African retentions to ground his claim that the slave's critical stance towards modernity "mobilises an idea of the ancient pre-slave past" (BA, 71). Moreover, his references to the Utopian aspirations of black Atlantic radicals seem consistent with the logic of the Afrocentric reconstruction of an African tradition disrupted by slavery. His critique of the Afrocentric notion of tradition leaves room to wonder why a return to the African idyll cannot supply the Utopia that is missing from the radical agenda of the Enlightenment project. In what follows I suggest a reply to these concerns by exploring some of Gilroy's remarks regarding the role of African retentions in the political struggles of the black Atlantic.

Hegel and Douglass

Hegel's master-slave parable contributes to a philosophical dialogue concerning slavery that can be traced in Western thought to Aristotle and the Greeks. Modern philosophy is characterized by a moral ambivalence towards slavery that ranges from patented endorsement to radical opposition. The various theoretical manifestations of this ambivalence were fostered by the fact that, under the rubric of natural rights, both conquest and resistance were justifiable. Shakespeare's portrayal of Caliban as a natural slave in *The Tempest* was dominated by his construction of a counterimage of Caliban's resistance. Hobbes presented an amoral justification of colonial conquest, but argued that slavery was an unjustifiable form of coerced servitude. Conversely, Locke developed a moralized account of colonial conquest that justified only a limited form of slavery. Although Hegel recognized slavery as a constituent of modernity, like Hobbes and Locke, his account was not directed in any historically specific way toward a resolution of the antinomies that arise from reflections on the enslavement of Africans by Europeans. His parable was largely a commentary on the Enlightenment, particularly, the state-of-nature idea employed by the social-contract theorists.[5]

Gilroy uses Douglass's account of his fight with Covey to discuss the difference between the male slave's and the master's view of civilization. In Hegel's parable the slave is motivated by a fear of death to submit to his conqueror. Douglass provides a quite different version of the struggle for recognition between master and slave. The slave, according to Douglass, prefers the possibility of death to continual enslavement. Gilroy claims that Douglass's everchanging position on violence moved him towards a view similar to Nietzsche's "transvaluation of post-sacral, modern values"

(BA, 64). With this existential dimension added to Douglass's version of the Hegelian dialectic, Gilroy argues that the slave conceived of death as a form of agency. The slave's view of death as a form of agency is further illustrated across gender lines by reference to Margaret Garner's tragic story in which she chooses to kill her children rather than return them to the slavecatchers. This case further illustrates Gilroy's general point that slaves actually practiced the opposite of what Hegel claimed.[6] Slave narratives such as Douglass's and Garner's indicate that the concept of freedom employed by slaves sometimes included the choice of death rather than bondage.

Gilroy cites Douglass's remarks regarding the magic root given to him by another slave, Sandy, as an indication of how certain aspects of a premodern culture were employed to engage in resistance. Although Douglass was skeptical of the root's power, he acknowledged that it nonetheless gave him the confidence to resist Covey. The root itself seems to stand between two different worldviews. Gilroy notes that Douglass considered Sandy's belief system regarding the magical powers of the root as mere superstition, but does not consider Sandy's opinion of its metaphysical status. Douglass represents an assimilated house slave who relied on a cultural retention maintained by a less-assimilated field slave. By juxtaposing the quite different cultural orientations of Douglass and Sandy to the root, the complexity of the relationship between slaves and their cultural retentions can be highlighted. Was Douglass unable to enter into Sandy's African worldview perhaps because he lacked the cultural sensibilities that were necessary to fully appreciate the field slave's African religious practices?[7] The predominantly Eurocentric worldview that governed Douglass's cultural sensibilities suggests an erasure that was not true of Sandy.

An important feature of Gilroy's view of the transformation of African retentions in the context of slavery can be gleaned from a consideration of Douglass's position on the relationship of African Americans to Africa. He maintained that the native land of African Americans is America. In his argument against colonization, he maintained that the African American owed no more to blacks in Africa than to blacks in America. He claimed that a blow struck for blacks in America was a blow struck for blacks in Africa, and cautioned that emigration to Africa would be detrimental to uplifting the race as a whole. "If we cannot make Virginia, with all her enlightenment and christianity, believe that there are better uses for her energies than employing them in breeding slaves for the market, we see not how we can expect to make Guinea, with its ignorance and savage selfishness, adopt our notions of political economy."[8] His concern with the future development of African Americans prompted him to respond to the advocates of emigration to Africa as enemies to "moral progress."

Certain aspects of Douglass's reasoning display a modernist tendency toward the double consciousness Gilroy attributes to black Atlantic political cultures. Douglass, for instance, raised the issue of racial hybridity as a ground for his stance against emigration. "It is pertinent, therefore, to ask . . . where the people of this mixed race are to go, for their ancestors are white and black, and it will be difficult to find their native land anywhere outside of the United States."[9] He also used a notion of racial hybridity to speak of the destiny of African Americans as a group. According to Douglass, the African American "will be absorbed, assimilated, and will only appear finally, as the Phoenicians now appear on the shores of the Shannon, in the features of a blended race."[10] His reference to the Phoenicians as a blended race echoes earlier remarks regarding the racial composition of the Egyptians that were presented in his public lecture, "The Claims of The Negro Ethnologically Considered."[11] In his dispute with the ethnologists, Douglass saw no need to insist upon viewing Egypt as a part of black Africa, although he argued quite forcefully that it was. He instead asserted the Enlightenment doctrine that "all mankind have the same wants, arising out of a common nature." Under the banner of human rights, Douglass proclaimed the equality of even the most "savage" African.

Nineteenth-century Nationalism: Delany and Blyden

Douglass's unfavorable view of Africa as a homeland for African Americans emanates from an assumption he shared with many of his adversaries. Although his stance against emigration was bitterly opposed, his low esteem for the role of traditional African culture in the modern world was widely shared. Douglass and many of his emigrationist detractors were in agreement regarding the need to modernize Africa. For this reason the political agendas of nineteenth-century nationalists such as Martin Delany and Edward Blyden displayed little concern with reclaiming an anterior African culture. Their political-economic concerns were focused on securing a modern nation state that would ensure the social elevation of black people. As Gilroy notes, they were quite skeptical of "Africa's capacity for civilization" (BA, 192). Blyden, for instance, saw colonialization as a means to civilize Africa, whereas Delany considered Texas, Haiti, and Central America as alternative sites for emigration. Douglass's exchange with Garnet is a good illustration of how his disagreement with the emigrationists reflected this concern. Garnet wrote to Douglass asking him to reply to the question, "What objection have you to colored men in this country engaging in agriculture, lawful trade, and commerce in the land of my forefathers?"[12] Garnet's question, as well as Douglass's reply, expressed a desire to modernize Africa, a desire that was quite prevalent among nineteenth-century black intellectuals.

Blyden cast his argument for the modernization of Africa in religious terms. He invoked the notion of God's Providence to ground his claim that African Americans have a duty to return to their "fatherland."[13] He argued, by analogy with the ancient Hebrews, that slavery was God's way of preparing African Americans for their civilizing mission – a kind of "purifying by fire."[14] Gilroy points out that Blyden's black Zionism was based on a notion of racial purity. He spoke of African Americans as "exiled Africans" in an alien land. He even questioned whether mulatto spokespersons, such as Douglass, should be included in the black race. Underneath the political disagreement between Blyden and Douglass lay a more fundamental issue concerning biology and racial identity. Blyden's advocacy of black racial purity as a criterion for racial classification reflects the influence of scientific racism on nineteenth-century black intellectuals.

Delany's class analysis of the plight of African Americans contrasted quite sharply with Blyden's religious-based argument for emigration. According to Delany, any such appeal to spirituality as a means of social elevation is fundamentally misguided, for religion cannot provide the means for achieving an economic goal. He maintained only a tenuous commitment to Africa as the site of emigration. This was due in part to his belief that African Americans had been reduced by slavery to a class of servants based on racial heritage. Although he had great pride in his African heritage, unlike Blyden, the African origin of black people held little significance for his view of emigration and was not the basis for his argument. He argued that African Americans should emigrate to any country that would allow them to flourish.

Various notions of "progress" and "civilization" were central to the social-elevation theories of nineteenth-century black nationalists. I have already indicated how the civilizing mission of their political agendas speaks to their recognition of the importance of modernization. In many cases their vision of the role of the black Atlantic in the modern world generated a quest for a black nation-state that would be economically competitive with Europe. To a large extent, then, their view of modernization was based on the Eurocentric model of the Enlightenment. In many cases, the Utopia sought was a black version of Western society. Given the resolve of many nineteenth-century black nationalists to stake a claim for African people in a global economy dominated by Europe, it seems that, rather than reject the political agenda of the Enlightenment, they aimed to carry it through in a manner that served the interests of black people.

Gilroy's Critique of Afrocentricism

The idea that the experience of enslavement had a detrimental impact on preslave traditions is not peculiar to Afrocentricism. Gilroy's observation, that a preoccupation with the discourse of tradition is a crucial part of the black Atlantic critique of modernity, seems to be the basis for his somewhat rhetorical question, "what elements of invariant tradition heroically survive slavery" (BA, 189). He resists treating this as a straightforward empirical question, for one consequence of the Afrocentric emphasis on African antiquity is that the memory of slavery becomes something that interferes with the discernment of the elements that survived. To show that this orientation to tradition is misguided Gilroy quotes Molefi Asante's claim that the slave experience produced only "made-in-America Negroes" (BA, 189). Asante insists that the focus on slavery, an aberration, as the womb of African-American culture must be rejected as perpetuating a dangerously negative image of

African Americans as disconnected from their African origin. Gilroy criticizes this Afrocentric doctrine for its commitment to a narrative of Western civilization that only couches a different set of political interests in the same terms. He takes to task the Afrocentric notion of tradition as a means of establishing a contiguous relationship between contemporary black life and its African past. In some cases, advocates of Afrocentricism view themselves as attempting to "rescue and reconstruct" this African tradition.[15]

Gilroy argues for a redefinition of tradition that requires a different understanding of modernity. The existential "rapport with death" in black Atlantic popular cultures, according to Gilroy, "has generated some vernacular philosophical preoccupations that are absolutely antagonistic to the enlightenment assumptions of Afrocentricism" (BA, 198). He contends that slavery constituted "an intervening history in which tradition and modernity come together, interact, and conflict" (BA, 191). Here Gilroy's claim that tradition and modernity are in conflict does not match his claim elsewhere that his revision of this concept banishes its use "as modernity's polar opposite" (BA, 188). This apparent inconsistency arises in part from his lack of clarity regarding an important difference between the, perhaps *unconscious, persistence* of an African retention in black cultural practices and the more *self-conscious reclamation*, or reconstruction, of some past African tradition. It may also be due in part to the fact that his own notion of tradition seems to reflect an ironic skepticism towards the value of the premodern. In some passages his remarks seem to celebrate premodern African retentions as emancipatory and, in others, his remarks seem to dovetail with Richard Wright's view of African life as "the mumbo jumbo of traditional societies" (BA, 192).

To get at the "vernacular philosophical preoccupations" that constitute a critique of Asante's Enlightenment assumptions, Gilroy analyzes black music to uncover another version of the "turn towards death." He pits the political ideology of black intellectuals such as Asante against this critical stance embedded in the expressive cultures of the black Atlantic to show that the latter are antagonistic to some of the former's assumptions regarding civilization and progress. Stories about death that are repeatedly told in black vernacular culture, with or without music, according to Gilroy "constitute the black Atlantic as a non-traditional tradition" (BA, 186).

This tradition can be defined as an "asymmetrical cultural ensemble" that cannot be understood in terms of the binary codes of African authenticity-purity-origin versus New World hybridity-creolization-rootlessness; it evades the contrast between a positive image of ancient Africa and a negative image of contemporary America (BA, 198). Tradition, in Gilroy's sense of the term, refers to "the living memory of the changing same" (BA, 198).

Gilroy's revisionist notion does not place tradition in opposition to modernity but instead establishes a two-way connection between them. By recognizing that Africa has also been transformed by cultural influences from the diaspora, he argues for a "crossroads" view of the relationship between tradition and modernity that captures the suggestion of "intermixture and cross-fertilization" (BA, 199). Surprisingly, rather than deny a role for African retentions in contemporary black Atlantic cultures, Gilroy's reflections on black vernacular culture are grounded on his acknowledgment of what he calls "the most enduring Africansim of all" (BA, 200).

Everyone knows that black music has an African origin. Gilroy points out, however, that "there is a direct relationship between the community of listeners constructed in the course of using that musical culture and the constitution of a tradition" (BA, 198). He focuses on the active dynamic process of black Atlantic music-making to show the political significance of the deceptive content of the love stories. Recognizing the priority of form over content is a necessary move because it accords with the changing role of the storyteller in a modern world. Gilroy presents a conception of the history of black Atlantic music as an illustration of Walter Benjamin's dictum that, in modern society, the practice of remembrance is organized in novel ways owing to the fact that "the gift for listening is lost and the community of listeners has disappeared" (BA, 200).

This shift in the role of the storyteller is matched by another shift in content away from the nineteenth-century stories about the ordeal of slavery toward love and loss stories in the twentieth century. Gilroy tells us that this new genre accords with a group desire, tantamount to a "cultural decision," not to communicate about the experience of slavery openly in story and song. These love and loss stories nonetheless express displaced feelings of mourning and yearning caused by the "unspeakable terror" of slavery. Gilroy refers to Percy Mayfield's song "The River's Invitation" as an African retention. The lyrics express a consciousness of African ecology and cosmology that illustrates the persistence of a theme of death as freedom from suffering.[16] This example shows how vernacular expressions of African retentions in black popular culture have been transformed by the experience of enslavement. Tradition in this sense is a derivative of cultural activity that has been shaped by social memory.

Retentions and Reconstructions

Gilroy recognizes the slave's music, in some sense, to be premodern, modern, and antimodern all at once. Indeed, for the artistic practices of the slaves to have been both inside and outside of modernity, one would think that there had to be some residue of their anterior African culture. But Gilroy holds that their artistic practices contained "a critique forged out of the particular experiences involved in being a racial slave in a legitimate and avowedly rational system of unfree labor" (BA, 57). This statement seems to disavow his acknowledgment of the vernacular expression of African retentions. In speaking of the "independent vitality" of the slave's critical cultural stance towards modernity, however, he suggested that the slave embodied a European and a non-European worldview. It is not entirely clear whether the slave's critical stance is at least partly grounded on his decidedly non-European philosophical-cum-aesthetic disposition.

Music is Gilroy's paradigm of a transformed cultural retention. Love and loss songs in twentieth-century black music constitute a disguised expression of the suffering caused by slavery. These songs are a transcoded expression of slavery's unspeakable horror. Gilroy deliberately positions black music at par with more cognitive, conceptual, representational art forms in order to challenge Hegel's privileging of written language as the highest expression of human consciousness. He selected music from the various cultural forms that survived slavery because it best fits his model of tradition as the enduring "changing same." For Gilroy, African musical practices need not have survived relatively unaltered to count as retentions.

Gilroy's emphasis on the survival of form rather than content is a key to understanding his account of black Atlantic music as a transformed retention. References to the premodern usually suggest vestiges of a traditional African culture. Similarly, the idea of modernity is usually associated with European cultural influences. Because, according to Gilroy, modern black cultural forms originated in the West as hybrid creations, he views African-American music as a "cultural mutation" produced by the "creolisation" of premodern African and modern European elements (BA, 199). The status of African-American music as a transformed retention involves the inescapable "doubleness" that derives from its hybrid form, a feature that accounts for its being inside and outside of modernity's aesthetic conventions (BA, 73).

Gilroy refers to the black Atlantic critique of modernity as something that was forged out of slavery and thereby places that critique inside modernity's aesthetic conventions, but which also has "a principle of negativity" that places it outside (BA, 68). He tells us that in the period after slavery the memory of slavery itself was used to supplement the retention of some aspect of anterior culture. This does not mean that some aspect of a static African tradition frozen in time has been retained. In his discussion of the debate about jazz tradition between Wynton Marsalis and Miles Davis he argues that black music traditions are part of a process of ongoing "displacements and transformations" (BA, 97).

Gilroy is committed to saying that the critique of modernity embedded in black music practices articulates a memory of a preslave past as well as a memory of slavery itself. To the extent that the critical stance in black music opposes the rationality of modernity, it is a premodern variety of antimodernity. This is suggested, for instance, by Gilroy's claim that Utopia enters the consciousness of the black Atlantic as a form of "jubilee" (BA, 212). Gilroy uses the concept of jubilee to mark a break with the Western concept of time. He tells us that it is "a liberatory, aesthetic moment which is emphatically anti- or even prediscursive," a moment that "has the upper hand over the pursuit of utopia by rational means" (BA, 68 and 71). There is no static African tradition frozen in time because remembrance of a preslave past is *actively* practiced in black music as recurring acts of identity operating through the call and response mechanisms produced in the interaction of performer and audience.

The memory of slavery itself provides the basis for what Gilroy refers to as "rescuing" or "redemptive" critiques. Toni Morrison's *Beloved* is a retelling of the Margaret Garner story that involves the construction of a social memory. Gilroy's endorsement of these reconstructions of the memory of slavery seems inconsistent with his criticism of the Afrocentric reconstruction of the memory of a preslave past. He rightfully criticizes the Afrocentric focus on the preslave past for, in the history of African Americans, that memory of the past has been occluded by the memory of slavery. But is this true of the entire black Atlantic? It seems that New World slaves had a right to overthrow their masters, burn the plantations, and return to a traditional village life in the forest. In the documentary film, *I Shall Moulder before I Be Taken*, the African rituals practiced by the Saramaccas indicate how this sort of reconstruction of a preslave past was carried out by a group of Maroons in Suriname.[17] The film depicts cultural retentions in the form of practices that express a social memory maintained by the descendants of a group of slaves who rebelled and gained their freedom. In this case, although the African retentions have been transformed, they nonetheless involve much more than a momentary "jubilee." Rather, the Saramaccas have reconstructed a premodern village life that has endured well into the twentieth century.

Gilroy's account of the transformation of African retentions does not apply equally to black Atlantic cultures in all parts of the New World where slavery was less disruptive and where there was less contact with European influences. The cultural transformations experienced by slaves in the United States cannot serve as a paradigm of the retention of black religious practices in Brazil, Cuba, and other paces in Latin America where erasure was far less than in the United States. The rescuing and redemptive critiques Gilroy approves of are reconstructions that ritualize the practice of remembrance. When consideration is given, in this isolated fashion, to the relationship between the transformed retentions in various black Atlantic African religious music and some of the various attempts by religiously minded musicians to reclaim and reconstruct an anterior African religious music tradition, the idea of reclaiming an anterior culture appears less problematic. But in the American context this appearance is misleading, for Gilroy rightfully insists that there is no anteriority for African-American culture that can override the profound influence of slavery. It would be an error, however, to suppose that this insight regarding African-American culture uniformly applies throughout the black Atlantic. Perhaps most of the black Atlantic is closer to Douglass's modernist orientation to the magical root. There has to be some allowance made for Sandy's premodernist orientation as well.

Chapter 3

Frederick Douglass on the Myth of the Black Rapist

At a news conference following the O. J. Simpson trial, prosecution attorney Chris Darden predicted that affirmative action would suffer because of the "not guilty" verdict from the mostly black jury. Prior to the verdict, on CNN's *Capitol Gang*, a similar assessment had been voiced by a group of white male news commentators, all of whom agreed that Democrats would be hurt more than Republicans by a "not guilty" verdict. Why was there this expectation (expressed through mass media) that the crime of an individual black man would have such deleterious political consequences for African Americans as a group? Although revenge by white voters for the "not guilty" verdict is ostensibly the reason for this white backlash, the ever-present social taboo regarding interracial sexual relations cannot be ruled out as a factor.[1] We need only to recall George Bush's effective use of the image of convicted rapist Willie Horton to win his bid for president to see that the idea that all African Americans must pay a political price for the offense of a single black rapist continues to structure race relations in America.

Commentators have offered various interpretations of the social and political function of the historical practice of lynching black men for alleged sexual offense against white women, yet they have not sufficiently considered the social and political significance of the figure of the black rapist in relation to the time-honored cultural norm proscribing interracial sexual contact between black men and white women.[2] One means of discerning the social and political significance of this proscription is by considering the manner in which the question of social equality for African Americans has been influenced by a racist myth.[3] Following the suggestion of several commentators, I will be particularly interested in determining whether there is an economic basis for this proscription.

The idea that African Americans, as a group, are not entitled to full citizenship because of white fear that black men will ravish white women was called into question by Frederick Douglass. In 1894, a year before his death, he published as a pamphlet his lecture on lynching.[4] He argued that the basic aim of lynching was disfranchisement, and attempted to expose the political motive underlying this practice by deconstructing the claim made by apologists that lynchings were necessary because *white women in the south were menaced by black rapists*. I shall refer to the view of black people on which the apologists' claim is grounded as the myth of the black rapist. According to this view, black men are prone to rape because black people *as a racial group* are bestial.[5]

Even with his added rhetorical flourish, Douglass's attempt to counter this claim, and the underlying myth that supplied its force, was deeply indebted to the view presented by Ida B. Wells-Barnett in 1892. I want to examine Douglass's account of the social and political function of the rape accusation to show its connection with Wells-Barnett's proposal to understand lynching in terms of the political economy of patriarchy and racism. I highlight certain elements of a very rudimentary political economic analysis that are present in their writings. Douglass misconstrued the origin and nature of the myth of the black rapist. Perhaps this was due to his tendency to conflate notions of race and class in his argument against lynching. Nevertheless, I indicate how this conflation reveals an important insight, available to Douglass, regarding the viability of an economic account of racism and patriarchy. The insight I attribute to Douglass, along with the political economic view suggested by Wells-Barnett, still applies to race and gender relations in America, if not more so. In highly publicized cases involving the alleged sexual violation of a white woman by a black male suspect, there is a noticeable inclination by various representatives of the criminal justice system to circumvent due process.[6] This legal practice is historically tied to racially motivated lynchings. Often rationalized by moral outrage, legal lynchings continue to be justified by a tacit appeal to a racial myth about black people – a myth Wells-Barnett confronted and Douglass evaded.[7]

Douglass's Elenchus

When Douglass published *Lessons of the Hour* as a pamphlet in 1894, he had already revised several earlier versions.[8] His lectures on this subject incorporated some of the white southern criticisms of his article "Lynch Law in the South," which had appeared in the *North American Review* in July 1892. Most of his revisions, however, were influenced by Wells-Barnett, including many of his embellishments of her basic strategy of presenting the political motivations of the white southern apologists. He aimed to expose the rape accusation as a recent "invention."[9] The lynching of black men accused of sexually assaulting white women had become such a common practice by 1892 that it was often referred to simply as the "Negro problem." When addressing this subject, Douglass was well aware of the widespread acceptance of the white southerner's justification of lynching. The majority of his discussion was a critical examination of their arguments that aimed to dispel the myth southerners had used to win the support of progressive whites in the north. Although his counterarguments were forcefully delivered, he showed signs of an awareness that, despite his sound reasoning, the myth that ultimately supplied the justification of lynching continued to operate subconsciously in the minds of many white Americans.

In his earlier writings on lynching Douglass placed a greater emphasis on the economic function of racial antagonism. He pointed out in "Lynch Law" that "the horror now excited is not for the crime itself," but rather is due to racial prejudice.[10] Nevertheless, he speaks of this "racial prejudice" in terms of an appeal "to the well-known hatred of one class towards another." These remarks set up two views of the cause of lynching. The analogy he drew between the persecution of Jews in Russia and of Chinese Americans in California and the lynching of African Americans suggests an analysis based on class. But, given that he also wanted to say that "race and color," and not the crime itself, is what arouses popular wrath, it is not clear how the class analysis he proposed can be sustained. He appealed to what he considered to be a socio-logical law to offer an explanation of the lynching of black people in the south – an explanation that combined overlapping notions of race and class. With explicit reference to the Memphis case that initiated Wells-Barnett's career as an antilynching activist, he stated "The negro meets no resistance when on a downward course. It is only when he rises in wealth, intelligence, and manly character that he brings upon himself the heavy hand of persecution."[11] The point of Douglass's analogy between African Americans and other ethnic groups was to indicate an economic basis for the racial antag-onism that frequently resulted in lynching.

The legacy of slavery was a central feature of many of the argu-ments Douglass marshaled to refute the apologists for lynching. He traced the continuity of the white southerner's lynching of black people with their treatment of slaves, noting that only a concern with loss of property had prevented the wholesale killing of slaves. In this regard emancipation had been an important factor contri-buting to an increase in lynching during and after reconstruction. A similar theme, related to slavery and the Civil War, is reviewed in his introduction to Wells-Barnett's pamphlet, *The Reason Why*.[12] After insisting that lynching, as a ritualized social practice, was logically consistent with the white southerner's former treatment of slaves, he again invoked, as a sociological law, the idea of the lowly class suffering the resentment of society for aspiring to rise. He wanted to present an account of lynching "on the same prin-ciple by which resistance to the course of a ship is created and increased in proportion to her speed" and cited class, not race, as the crucial factor.[13] "The Negro is just now under the operation of this law of society. If he were white as the driven snow, and had been enslaved as we had been, he would have to submit to this same law in his progress upward."[14] Here Douglass seems to view lynching as "simply an incident of a transitional condition" due to "the depravity, of human nature."[15] By deracinating slavery and employing it as a paradigm of economic exploitation, he wanted to account for lynching, even as a racist practice directed toward black people, in terms of political economy.

In a manner similar to the famous address Booker T. Washington would give a year later in Atlanta, Douglass presented the case for understanding the so-called Negro problem as a national problem, and appealed to the self-interest of the nation as a whole to solve it. Washington, however, would have been reluctant to openly agree with Douglass's assertion that the reference to lynching as a "Negro problem" was a misnomer.[16] Washington's solution to lynching was essentially to accommodate the *de facto* repeal of the Fifteenth Amendment and to support miscegenation legislation. By contrast, Douglass criticized the racial views held by white southerners and appealed to whites in the north not to trust the southerner's claims regarding black people. As part of the solution to lynching, he insisted upon the legal enforcement of the human rights guaranteed by the Constitution, especially the hard-fought right to vote.

For Douglass, the central issue was the accused black rapist's constitutional right to a fair trial. He highlighted the need of the southern mob to feed its vengeance by shooting, stabbing, and burning victims after they were already dead. "[W]hat is the special charge by which this ferocity is justified, and by which mob law is excused and defended even by good men North and South?"[17] Douglass's reference here to "the special charge" is important to consider in connection with the black rapist myth. He was concerned about the fact that a mere charge could justify such ferocious acts of vengeance. Showing no awareness of white mob reaction to a black man accused of raping a white woman as a ritualized cultural practice influenced by racial mythology, he attempted to push through his constitutional rights argument for due process.[18]

Douglass's main line of attack in his defense of the reputation of black people against the "special" charge was to demonstrate, by counterargument, that the motive behind it was "nothing less than the Negro's entire disenfranchisement as an American citizen."[19] After noting the fact that this charge was not brought up in any prior period, he suggested two possible reasons: first, there was no foundation for such a charge and, secondly, it was not necessary under slavery to justify lawless violence against black people. During slavery and the Civil War the old charges of insurrection, or insolence, were considered sufficient, but in the present period the new charge of assaulting white women "has now swallowed up all the other ones."[20] The aim of the new charge was "to blast and ruin the negro's character as a man and a citizen."[21]

Douglass believed that low esteem for the moral character of black people was a crucial factor inhibiting the social elevation of

African Americans.[22] For this reason he proposed to meet the charge in the form in which it was presented. "I know that I cannot prove a negative; there is one thing that I can and will do. I will call in question the affirmative. I can and will show that there are sound reasons for doubting and denying this horrible charge of rape as the special and peculiar crime of the coloured people of the South."[23] Rather than deal with the "special and peculiar" nature of the rape charge, he instead interpreted the question of "negro character" and "manhood" more broadly – not once mentioning anything sexual.[24] His refutation, though well argued and quite logical, nonetheless was unconvincing precisely because he did not deal with the main thrust of the charge. He simply ignored a widely shared concern regarding interracial sexual relations and, consequently, he failed to appreciate that his exposing the political objectives of the white southerner was consistent with the white southerner's claim that the charge was well grounded.

A rejoinder to this effect by a white southerner was cited by Wells-Barnett. In defense of lynching, he presented a quite different account of Douglass's claim regarding the relative absence of the charge under slavery and during the Civil War.

The commission of this crime grows more frequent every year. The generation of Negroes which have grown up since the war have lost in large measure the traditional and wholesome awe of the white race which kept the Negroes in subjection, even when their masters were in the army, and their families left unprotected except by the slaves themselves. There is no longer a restraint upon the brute passion of the Negro. . . . The Negro as a political factor can be controlled. But neither laws nor lynchings can subdue his lusts. Sooner or later it will force a crisis. We do not know in what form it will come.[25]

The point Douglass sought to establish regarding the white southerner's political motives, namely his desire to disfranchise African Americans, is well represented by these remarks. But they also contain elements of the black rapist myth that Douglass failed to address adequately. Douglass cited the plantation rape of slave women by white masters to indicate that the white southerner's moral outrage was not a reaction to the crime of rape, but to the reversal of racial roles. As a counterargument this criticism was very lame, for it was only a further indication that Douglass failed to fully appreciate the power of the antiblack racism conveyed by the myth. He displayed a limited comprehension of the reason why sexual assaults by white men on black women were not viewed as rape by white southerners. He seemed completely unaware that the racist discourse that fostered the black rapist myth also subsumed black women, as members of the bestial race, under a twin myth as "sexual savages" incapable of being raped.[26]

One of the strongest objections to Douglass's argument along these lines came from a black southerner. Reverend E. K. Love, a Baptist pastor in Savannah, Georgia, delivered an impassioned sermon titled "Lynch-Law and Raping" that in effect condoned lynching.[27] He even proposed a modification of the criminal justice system to facilitate this. In what could have been a blueprint for the "justice" sought in the Central Park rape trial, Reverend Love asserted:

The ravishers can be punished far more effectually by law and be killed just as dead by an officer of the law as by 500 masked outlaws. If shooting and hanging are not bad enough, then let the terrible penalty of Duillius be added to our statute books, that whosoever commits rape, "shall be burned alive" or any other barbarous or inhuman death. Only let our law say so. If there is a fear that the courts may be too slow in bringing the criminals to justice, let the law remedy that.[28]

The "law and order" Reverend Love contends for here is a far cry from that which Douglass wanted to uphold. Although Douglass also was not entirely opposed to lynching under special circumstances where there is no law enforcement, he argued that, given the white southerner's motives, there is sufficient reason to be skeptical of this practice in cases where black men are accused of raping white women.[29]

In what appears to be an endorsement of lynching, Reverend Love staked out a position that resonated more with the views of the white southerners Douglass had contested. Unlike Douglass, he recognized a commendable social and political purpose of lynching.

There is such a healthy sentiment among the white people, that if the Negroes cross the line they must do so by force and this is rape, and for this they must die and this we must approve. It would be the same with white men forcing themselves on our side if we had the sentiment worked up among our women that it is death to cross the line. Be it said to our shame, that some of our girls and women can engage in this business and can even marry our best and hardest working young men. This is sometimes done even after they have become mothers. As long as this is the case, we cannot work up a healthy sentiment among us along this line. If for this state of things, the vile class of Negroes mean to get even with whites by raping their women, they should and must die, every guilty man of them. Not in one case out of a thousand is a colored woman raped by a white man and hence the raping of white women cannot be in retaliation.[30]

Reverend Love's refusal to admit that black women were often raped by white men is an indication that, like his white southern counterpart, he was more concerned with preventing consensual interracial sexual relations than with rape as such.[31] He aimed to invalidate the revenge motive often attributed to black men accused of raping white women by guilt-ridden white southerners.[32] His endorsement of lynching, as well as his acceptance of certain aspects of the black rapist myth, is accompanied by a strong commitment to the social norm prohibiting interracial sexual relations. His argument for law and order parallels the argument Douglass presented but, contrary to Douglass, he shared the white southerner's fear of miscegenation as a threat to the social order. Rather than advocate the right of an accused black rapist to a fair trial, the main point of his sermon was to stipulate that the lynching in such cases be carried out legally.[33]

Wells-Barnett on Lynching and Miscegenation Laws

Wells-Barnett understood the need, to which Douglass referred in his lecture, to present a black perspective to correct the views of whites, in the north and in the south, who had spoken on the topic. Having brought to Douglass's attention the political consequences of black leaders not speaking out against lynching, she persuaded him that a black voice was required to bring out the whole truth. The fact that Douglass was prompted by Wells-Barnett to lecture on the subject of lynching has been taken by some commentators as grounds for a more skeptical interpretation of his view. William

McFeely takes Douglass to task for not including a discussion of the "scourge" of lynching in the last version of his autobiography.[34] With regard to Douglass's article for the *North American Review*, McFeely claims that Douglass "did not fully disavow the widely accepted assumption that the victims of the horrible executions were to blame for their fate, that black men were indeed a sexual threat to Southern white women." He cites Wells-Barnett's remarks that Douglass "had begun to believe it true that there was increased lasciviousness on the part of Negroes."[35] Wells-Barnett's claim, however, is not warranted by anything Douglass states in his writings on this subject.[36] Indeed, the view McFeely wants to attribute to Douglass flies in the face of Douglass's attempt to show, in the light of the facts adduced by Wells-Barnett, that the black rapist myth was a politically motivated "invention."

When Douglass lectured on the subject of lynching he always made a point of distinguishing between his denial of the myth and a blanket denial of the offense. In *Lessons of the Hour*, for instance, he claimed, "I do not pretend that Negroes are saints and angels. I do not deny that they are capable of committing the crime imputed to them, but I utterly deny that they are any more addicted to the commission of that crime than is true of any other variety of the human family."[37] According to Douglass, the charge falsely attributes to black men an "addiction" to ravish white women – a term that suggests an uncontrollable desire. It is worth noting that, as part of his denial of this charge, he invokes the membership of black people in the "human family." As I have already noted, the myth's attribution of a bestial nature to black men entails a parallel view of black women. Douglass recognized that the most important aspect of the sexual charge against black men was the social implication it carried for the race as a whole, yet it seems he did not recognize that the lynching of black men, as well as the rape of black women, were rationalized and justified on the ground that the black race is not fully human.[38]

There is an important reason why Douglass's failure to address this implication adequately should not be taken as his capitulation to the myth. He was sharply focused on showing the political motives behind the white southerners' "invention" of the rape accusation without displaying any awareness of the issue of paramount concern to them, namely, the prevention of miscegenation. But the fear of miscegenation, shared by whites in the north as well as in the south, is what allowed the myth to operate so effectively as a justification in lynching cases, nearly two-thirds of which involved no accusation of rape. Although I will suggest the opposite, Douglass's interracial marriage to Helen Pitts might be thought to have inhibited him from raising this issue.[39] There is sufficient reason to think that, even if this were true, his shortcomings in this regard need not be construed as due to his acceptance of the black rapist myth.

Support for the skeptical interpretation of Douglass nevertheless can be found in a letter he wrote to Wells-Barnett thanking her for her paper on lynching.[40] Douglass stated "There has been no word equal to it in convincing power. I have spoken, but my word is feeble in comparison." He seems to admit here that his attempt to refute the apologists for lynching had not been very effective. A similar tone of skepticism can be detected in some of his remarks in *Lessons of the Hour*. For example, with regard to the charge against black people, he asserted "Now it is in this form that you and I, and all of us, are required to meet it and refute it, *if that can be done*."[41] The reason he gave for thinking his attempt to counter the arguments of the supporters of lynching was 'feeble' by comparison with Wells-Barnett's was that she spoke from a knowledge of the facts regarding lynching. But there were other reasons. Chief among them was the fact that Douglass could not speak as forcefully as Wells-Barnett on the subject of lynching because his interracial marriage was viewed by blacks and by whites as a violation of the social taboo that the practice of lynching aimed to enforce.[42]

When compared with Douglass's advocacy of law and order as a solution to lynching, some of the remedies proposed by Wells-Barnett rendered his view "feeble" in another important sense. His strong commitment to the enforcement of constitutional law made him reluctant to advocate violence, although he suggested that the mob rule of lynch law would eventually provoke retaliation.[43] He spoke of vengeance and anarchy as natural outcomes of lynching, but he never went as far as Wells-Barnett to advocate the use of armed self-defense against lynching. Conversely, on grounds of human rights and self-respect, Wells-Barnett presented a strong case for the use of violence by African Americans as a countermeasure.

[T]he only case where the proposed lynching did not occur, was where men armed themselves in Jacksonville, Fla. and Paducah, Ky., and prevented it. . . . The lesson this teaches and which every Afro-American should ponder well, is that a Winchester rifle should have a place of honor in every black home, and it should be used for that protection which the law refuses to give. When the white man knows he runs as great risk of biting the dust every time his Afro-American victim does, he will have greater respect for Afro-American life.[44]

The importance of armed self-defense was again championed by Wells-Barnett in her report of the killing of Robert Charles by a New Orleans mob.[45] Charles had become the target of an intense manhunt for killing a policeman in self-defense. Rather than allow himself to be captured and lynched Charles decided to fight to his death. Relying on details provided by several white New Orleans newspapers, Wells-Barnett tells this story with a deep sense of pride in the fact that Charles not only fought back, but earned the respect of the white press for his excellent marksmanship. She was especially keen on reporting numerous acts of cowardice by the white men who pursued Charles.[46]

By comparison with Wells-Barnett, who always spoke with facts gleaned from white newspapers, Douglass stated his position on armed resistance to lynching only hypothetically. In a very important passage that criticizes the mortgage system in the south as a new form of slavery Douglass, somewhat facetiously, painted a pacifistic image of African Americans.

Had he been a turbulent anarchist he might indeed have been a troublesome problem, but he is not. To his reproach, it is sometimes said that other people in the world would have invented some violent way in which to resent their wrongs. If this problem depended upon the character and conduct of the Negro there would be no problem to solve; there would be no menace to the peace and good order of Southern Society. He makes no unlawful fight between labor and capital. That problem, which often makes the American people thoughtful, is not of his bringing, though he may some day be compelled to talk of this tremendous problem in common with other laborers.[47]

Notice that Douglass's reference to an "unlawful fight between labor and capital" was in the context of a discussion of the so-called Negro problem. He, of course, wanted to establish that the real problem was not the moral character of the Negro, but the reconstitution of slavery in a new form. Lynchings were the political counterpart to the economic exploitation of black labor in the south.[48] Sometimes he spoke of anarchy in connection with retaliation by African Americans for lynching, but he seems to have considered the dispute between labor and capital, if left unresolved, as having an even greater potential to produce this outcome.

In certain respects Douglass's remarks regarding economic matters were also feeble by comparison with Wells-Barnett's. His concern regarding the exploitation of black labor in the south was reformulated by Wells-Barnett as a remedy to lynching.

To Northern capital and Afro-American labor the South owes its rehabilitation. If labor is withdrawn capital will not remain. The Afro-American is thus the backbone of the South. A thorough knowledge and judicious exercise of this power in lynching localities could many times effect a bloodless revolution. The white man's dollar is his god, and to stop this will be to stop outrages in many localities.[49]

What Douglass saw as the real cause of 'the Southern trouble', namely, a host of economic issues pertaining to labor and capital, Wells-Barnett saw as a potential solution and advocated using as a mode of resistance.

For Douglass, the root cause of the so-called Negro problem was really economic and not social. Wells-Barnett's thorough investigation of reports on lynching had convinced him that lynching was a form of economic scapegoating.[50] Averring to Lincoln's blaming slavery for the Civil War as a cause of earlier riots in which large numbers of African Americans were killed, he maintained that once again African Americans were being blamed because of the present economic crisis facing the south. He compared the practice of calling this economic crisis a "Negro" or "race" problem with the former practice of blaming slaves. "In old slave times, when a little white child lost his temper, he was given a little whip and told to go and whip 'Jim' or 'Sal,' and he thus regained his temper. The same is true to-day on a large scale." The point Douglass sought to illustrate with this example was that "He [the black man] has as little to do with the cause of the Southern trouble as he has with its cure."[51] The black rapist myth, according to Douglass, was invented after emancipation as a means of scapegoating African Americans for all of the south's troubles. It was created specifically to justify withholding citizenship from African Americans by representing black men as "moral monsters."

One rather puzzling aspect of Douglass's account of the origin of the black rapist myth is his convenient neglect of the history of a racist discourse used to justify colonial conquest and slavery. His contention that the *charge* did not exist prior to its post-Civil War invocation by white southerners implies, wrongly, that the myth was merely a creation by white southerners. He was right to the extent that the charge *per se* was a recent normative construction not required before emancipation. The white southerner's use of the legalistic lexicon of crime and punishment to legitimate lynching, however, was an expression of a long-standing racist ideology. In Western literature the idea of a dark villain threatening a white goddess can be traced to Greek mythology regarding the conquest of fair Persephone by Hades.[52] Similarly, in the modern era we can see the emergence of this figure in Shakespeare's plays *Titus Andronicus*, *Othello*, and *The Tempest*. And, as Douglass well knew, long before the end of the nineteenth century, the idea that black people were more closely related to the lower primates had gained scientific support.[53] As I shall indicate shortly, this quite important lapse is consistent with Douglass's evasive treatment of miscegenation as an issue in his debate with the apologist for lynching.

Wells-Barnett directly addressed the white southerner's worry about miscegenation as the source of the black rapist myth. Like Douglass, she wanted to show that "The Afro-American is not a bestial race" by exposing the political motives of the supporters of lynching.[54] Douglass related the question of the African American's moral character to earlier struggles, under slavery, to gain the right to such matters as baptism, marriage, and education. Both he and Wells-Barnett understood the debate about lynching to raise the question of justice in a manner that *presupposed* black people were not entitled to it. As in the case of animals that attack humans, lynch law applies to people who are considered beyond the pale of human sympathy.

In addition to identifying the white southerner's political motive of disfranchisement, Wells-Barnett went a step further than

Douglass and identified a social function of the black rapist myth. She maintained that the lynching of black men accused of raping white women also functioned as a means of enforcing miscegenation laws that prohibited interracial sexual contact.

The miscegenation laws of the South only operate against the legitimate union of the races; they leave the white man free to seduce all the colored girls he can, but it is death to the colored man who yields to the force and advances of a similar attraction in white women. White men lynch the offending Afro-American, not because he is a despoiler of virtue, but because he succumbs to the smiles of white women.[55]

If, as Wells-Barnett maintains here, one purpose of lynching was to prevent miscegenation, then Douglass's voice as spokesperson for the race was indeed compromised by his interracial marriage. Unbridled with the innuendo of social transgression that surrounded Douglass's interracial marriage, Wells-Barnett was free to attack the white southerner's view of lynching as a legitimate deterrent to consensual sexual relations between black men and white women. She endeavored to expose the black rapist myth by showing, with empirical evidence, that rape accusations were employed to enforce miscegenation laws that white women had violated. Citing the details of case after case of southern white women who had consensual sexual relations with black men, she argued that miscegenation laws were designed to enforce a social taboo that restricts the *desires* of white women. Needless to say, this claim infuriated southern white men (who publicly threatened to lynch her), as well as her white women detractors in the north.[56]

The Politics of Rape and the Miranda Trap

Some commentators have interpreted Wells-Barnett's focus on revealing the truth about the willingness of white women to enter into consensual sexual relations with black men as counterfeminist. Alice Walker and Valerie Smith understood her to be defending the black male rapist at the expense of the white female victim, because of her emphasis on documenting admissions by white women that they were involved in consensual relationships with black men lynched for rape.[57] Smith questions Wells-Barnett's reference to the "willing victims" of an alleged black rapist.[58] She points out that this expression is the opposite of an implied "unwilling victim." Taking this a step further, Walker understood Wells-Barnett to advocate silence in the latter case. This interpretation of Wells-Barnett seems to ignore her remarks regarding the guilty black rapist. In the preface to *Southern Horrors* she stated very clearly that "This statement is not a shield for the despoiler of virtue, nor altogether a defense for the poor blind Afro-American Sampsons who suffer themselves to be betrayed by white Delilahs."[59] Wells-Barnett saw a clear difference between "willing" (white Delilahs) and "unwilling" victims. The point she insisted upon was that white southerners pretended to see no difference between them. Because miscegenation was the issue – not rape – she considered the white lynch mob's failure to respect this distinction to be an important factor that must be addressed by a consistent social policy.[60] Walker and Smith mistake Wells-Barnett's demand for justice for an accused black rapist with a commitment to remain silent when he is guilty.

Smith also seems worried that Wells-Barnett's apparent lack of concern for the "unwilling" white women victims indicates an unacceptable prioritizing of race over gender. Wells-Barnett's stated aim was to prove that black people and not a bestial race – an objective that included a concern with the reputation of black women as mythical whores incapable of being raped.[61] Smith and Walker overlook Wells-Barnett's black feminist challenge to white feminists, many of whom she openly criticized for granting race greater priority over gender. She urged white women to speak out when black women were raped by white men, as well as when black men were falsely accused of rape, because the word of a white woman carried greater weight in a court of law. Motivated by the general lack of response from white women, she acted in the interest of black women which, in this case, intersected with the interests of African Americans as a group.[62]

The question of whether to give race priority over gender was also faced by Douglass in his clash with white feminists over their stance against the ratification of the Fifteenth Amendment.[63] Some of the feminists in the Equal Rights Association, including Susan B. Anthony and Elizabeth Cady Stanton, were against extending suffrage to black men if women were not included. With an eye

to solving the problems posed by reconstruction, Douglass advocated support for the Fifteenth Amendment as a means of paving
the way for extending the vote to women. This was opposed by
some women who appealed to the white southerner's "ignorant
Negro voter" argument, protesting that, before black men are given
the ballot, intelligent and cultured white women should be enfranchised. The pernicious political consequence of this split in the Equal
Rights Association surfaced when the argument was advanced that
the enfranchisement of women would provide a bulwark in the
south against "Negro rule."[64]

To garner support for the ratification of the Fifteenth Amendment,
Douglass attempted to distinguish the "Negro question" from the
"women question" and cited the practice of lynching as sufficient
warrant for granting race priority over gender.

When women, because they are women, are dragged from their homes and
hung upon lamp-posts; when their children are torn from their arms and
their brains dashed upon the pavement; when they are objects of insult
and outrage at every turn; when they are in danger of having their homes
burnt down over their heads; when their children are not allowed to enter
schools; then they will have an urgency to obtain the ballot.[65]

Douglass's eloquent oratory carried the measure, but some of the
feminists at this meeting preferred to see it defeated. Soon after
this convention the Equal Rights Association dissolved and was
replaced by the National Woman's Suffrage Association, which
divorced itself from the question of Negro suffrage.[66] Douglass,
of course, had no reason to think at that time that his linking of
lynching with black male suffrage later would be a stimulus for
latent racism in the women's movement. But, once the association
of rape with lynching was established, the strained alliance between the women's movement and the antilynching movement
was severely damaged.[67] The rise in support for the repeal of the
Fifteenth Amendment among progressive white women lent credence to Douglass's assessment of the myth's political function.
He interpreted their break with the antilynching movement as a
clear sign of the success of the white southerner's campaign "to
disfranchise the colored voter of the South in order to solve the
race problem."[68]

Miscegenation and Citizenship

From a political realist standpoint, white feminist opposition to the ratification of the Fifteenth Amendment was not entirely unwarranted given their concern that the enfranchisement of black men could shift the existing balance of power in some way unfavorable to their interests.[69] Bettina Aptheker supports the opposite position, taken by Douglass, on the ground of long-term gain for white women.

> Posed in terms of the priority of rights the debate over the Fifteenth Amendment was indeed insoluble. . . . Black suffrage was a strategic question forced by the particularity of historical circumstances in the United States. . . . Precisely because passage of the Fifteenth Amendment was intended to advance the cause of Afro-American freedom, it inevitably would have rebounded to the benefit of women, but only a class-conscious element could have seen that point in 1869.[70]

Aptheker underscores the historical circumstances that prevented white feminists from seeing this point regarding class. Both Douglass and Wells-Barnett cited economic competition between the races as an underlying cause of lynching but, given the legacy of slavery and Reconstruction, they were equally compelled to grant priority to the "Negro question."

To overcome the limitations of prioritizing gender and race Wells-Barnett and Douglass needed a more fully developed economic account of patriarchy and racism. Although she was critical of the complicity of white women, to her credit Wells-Barnett held white men responsible for lynching. She publicized the hypocrisy of miscegenation laws to bring to light the manner in which white women were being used by white men to oppress African Americans as a group. Her objective was to draw attention to the injustice of miscegenation laws by challenging the prerogative of white men to violate them with impunity. With full recognition that the myth of the sexual purity of white women was a correlate of the twin myths regarding the sexual savagery of African-American men and women, she wanted to reveal the manner in which this hypocritical sexual mythology served the interests of white men. Her indictment of white southern patriarchy was presented as a fundamental question regarding social policy: if such relations are illegal why are only black men punished for this violation?

Had Douglass chosen to address the political aim of using lynching as a means of enforcing the social taboo against interracial sexual relations perhaps he would have presented a more explicit economic account of miscegenation laws. Instead, he expressed a concern regarding the moral consequences.

Depriving the Negro of his vote leaves the entire political, legislative, executive and judicial machinery of the country in the hands of the white people. The religious, moral and financial forces of the country are also theirs. This power has been used to pass laws forbidding intermarriage between the races, thus fostering immorality. The union, which the law forbids, goes on without its sanction in dishonorable alliances.[71]

These remarks may seem naïve in a social context heavily infused with anxiety regarding miscegenation. Nevertheless, they were consistent with Douglass's political economic view of racism. His assertion that the "financial forces of the country" are in the hands of white people is particularly instructive.

Commentators have noted that since the early days of slavery miscegenation laws had been instituted to protect the property of white males.[72] Prior to the institution of these restrictive codes the offspring of interracial couples, being an intermediate caste, were deemed free citizens. In some of his earlier writings on emigration and colonization Douglass appealed to an American birthright and lineage as part of the African-American heritage, but without any reference to European ancestry. In his pamphlet on lynching, however, he claimed a right to American citizenship *by blood*, as well as by soil.[73] He advanced a mixed-race view of African Americans to argue against emigration as a solution to the race problem.

The native land of the American Negro is America. His bones, his muscles, his sinews, are all American. His ancestors for two hundred and seventy years have lived and labored and died, on American soil, and millions of his posterity have inherited Caucasian blood.

It is pertinent, therefore, to ask, in view of this admixture, as well as in view of other facts, where the people of this mixed race are to go, for their ancestors are white and black, and it will be difficult to find their native land anywhere outside of the United States.[74]

What appears to be an evasion of the miscegenation issue in Douglass's argument against the apologists for lynching turns out to have a profound political thrust. He cited the fact of miscegenation (albeit illegal) to set up his contention that European ancestry entitled African Americans to all the rights guaranteed by the Constitution. The so-called Negro problem is really a national problem in the sense that to disfranchise African Americans in the south was "to surrender the constitution to the late rebels for the lack of moral courage to execute its provisions."[75]

One troublesome implication of Douglass's argument regarding the constitutional rights of African Americans is that the guarantee of due process allows the possibility, even if unlikely, that a guilty black rapist will escape punishment. In America, this guarantee of due process includes, among other things, an opportunity, as it were, for a guilty defendant in such cases to win acquittal. Given his somewhat agnostic remarks regarding the justification of lynching, Douglass leaves open the question of whether the lynching of a guilty black rapist would be justified in cases where this is likely to occur. He cites the fact that black voters had never exercised their political power in such a disloyal fashion, but what if they were to do so in judicial cases where racism is perceived to be a factor?[76]

The only excuse for lynch law, which has a shadow of support in it, is that the criminal would probably otherwise be allowed to escape the punishment due to his crime. . . . But for it there is no foundation whatever, in a country like the South, where public opinion, the laws, the courts, the juries, the advocates, are all against the Negro, especially one alleged to be guilty of the crime now charged. That such an one would be permitted to escape condign punishment, is not only untenable but an insult to common sense. The chances are that not even an innocent Negro so charged would be allowed to escape.[77]

He clearly did not assume that due process would lead to justice, but rather expressed concern that the racism which justified physical lynching would continue to justify legal ones as well.[78] The apologists maneuvered Douglass into accepting a view that excuses lynching when deemed necessary to prevent a guilty black rapist being set free. But there was no reason for Douglass to view the fact that a guilty black rapist may avail himself of the same legal means of avoiding punishment as a guilty white rapist as a justification of lynching. By not condemning lynching in principle he allowed the empirical possibility of cases in which mob action would be excused when such action expressed a legitimate public moral outrage. Although he realized that to suppose a need to deny that black men are ever guilty of raping white women would only reiterate the myth, he also understood that it was in the interest of African Americans for black leaders to condemn publicly both rape and lynching. When he proposed due process as a remedy, he never countenanced the thought that a guilty black rapist might escape punishment.

Chapter 4

Du Bois on the
Invention of Race

In his well-known address to the newly founded American Negro Academy, Du Bois entertained the question of the fate and destiny of African Americans as a group, asking somewhat rhetorically, "Does my black blood place upon me any more obligation to assert my nationality than German, or Irish or Italian blood would?"[1] His answer was that it is "the duty of the Americans of Negro descent, as a body, to maintain their race identity."[2] The argument he advanced to support this claim has been sometimes understood to suggest that African Americans as a group are obligated to maintain and to perpetuate their culture in order to retain their authenticity.[3] We should resist, however, becoming overly focused on this aspect of Du Bois's view, for it is fairly clear, on even the most cursory reading of his essay, that he was not particularly concerned with the African past as a standard for measuring the authenticity of African-American culture. Indeed, he proposed to resolve the dilemma of African-American double consciousness by appealing to a revisionist analysis of the concept of race that eschews a biological essentialist account of racial identity.

One very good reason for supposing that Du Bois was primarily concerned with the question of authenticity is his repeated criticism of African Americans striving for "self-obliteration," seeking "absorption by the white Americans," or pursuing "a servile imitation of Anglo-Saxon culture."[4] Although there certainly was a concern with authenticity expressed in these remarks, I believe that it is

somewhat misleading to take this to have been his primary motivation for raising these issues, for there is a very important reason
why such issues were not in the foreground of his discussion of
race, and why they do not figure into his argument regarding the
obligation of African Americans to maintain their race identity.
Hence, I shall present a reading of Du Bois's essay that, with regard
to the question of racial identity, deviates from several recent
interpretations.[5]

Du Bois's argument for the claim that African Americans are
obligated to retain their race identity is connected with his early
view of the role of culture in the African-American quest for social
equality.[6] In particular, he maintained that the cultural integrity
of African Americans is crucial for their gaining acceptance as social
equals. The view Du Bois articulated in 1897 displays the late
nineteenth-century historical context of African-American social
thought; consequently, many features of the argument he presented
can be found in the writings of his contemporaries. By contextual-
izing his argument I aim to show that he presented a notion of race
that was in keeping with his own version of a race-uplift theory
of social change. According to my interpretation, his revisionist
account represents a view of race identity that accorded with the
prevailing African-American social philosophy at the turn of the
century. I will begin with a brief discussion of his definition of race,
followed by a sketch of some of the historical sources from which
he may have drawn certain ideas to develop his argument for the
duty of African Americans to retain their race identity. I want to
defend the plausibility of Du Bois's sociohistorical view of racial
identity against several, quite damaging, criticisms, and thereby salvage the major thrust of his argument.

A Revisionist Concept of Race

With the aim of presenting an account tailored to fit his theory of
social change, Du Bois proposed the following definition of race:

It is a vast family of human beings, generally of common blood and language, always of common history, traditions and impulses, who are both
voluntarily and involuntarily striving together for the accomplishment of
certain more or less vividly conceived ideals of life.[7]

Unless we bear in mind why Du Bois was motivated to write about African-American identity, his definition of race will seem quite implausible, especially his stipulation that a racial group must *always* share a common history, traditions, and impulses, but need not always share a common blood or language. The reason Du Bois's proposal seems implausible is because he meant to implicitly contest the way the received view, which places a greater emphasis on common blood, has been socially constructed. Unfortunately, the insight that underlies his definition is diminished by the twofold nature of his account, an account that involves a deconstruction of the received view as well as a reconstruction of his alternative conception.

Du Bois opened his essay with the statement that African Americans are always interested in discussions regarding the origins and destinies of races because such discussions usually presuppose assumptions about the natural abilities, and the social and political status, of African Americans, assumptions that impede African-American social progress. He noted that the undesirable implications of some of these assumptions have fostered a tendency for African Americans "to deprecate and minimize race distinctions."[8] He took himself to be giving voice to their aspiration for social equality by advancing a conception of African Americans that would allow a discussion of racial distinctions while accommodating the tendency of African Americans, under the dominating influence of racism, to want to minimize references to physical differences in such discussions.

Du Bois was interested in formulating non-biological criteria for a definition of race mainly because he wanted to provide a more adequate ground for the group identity he considered a crucial component in the African American's social agenda. He made this clear when, with reference to the idea of race in general, he spoke of "its efficiency as the vastest and most ingenious invention for human progress."[9] He suggested that, following the success model of other groups, African Americans must *invent* a conception of themselves that will contribute to their social elevation as a group. His revisionist notion of race was therefore proposed at the outset as something African Americans must self-consciously adopt for political purposes. We can notice that he did not fail to acknowledge the social construction of the concept of race when, in his citation of the eight distinct racial groups, he qualified his reference to them with the phrase "in the sense in which history tells us the word must be used."[10] What shows us that he aimed to deconstruct the received view, however, is the way he juxtaposed his sociohistorical concept of race with what he referred to as "the present division of races," namely, the scientific conception of the three main biological groups, for he goes on to point out that biology cannot provide the criteria for racial identity because, historically, there has been an "integration of physical differences."[11] This fact leads him to conclude that what really distinguishes groups of people into races are their "spiritual and mental differences."[12]

Some of Du Bois's readers have rejected his sociohistorical definition of race in favor of a definition based on physical differences.[13] What Du Bois's detractors tend to overlook, however, is the fact that his definition does not deny the obvious physical differences that constitute race, nor does his discussion of race display any special commitment to the sociohistorical view he sets forth. A close reading will reveal that he meant only to deny the *viability* of a strictly biological account of race, and, furthermore, to assert that an empirical study of history will show this to be the case. Based on his own survey of anthropological findings, he tells us that, when different groups of people came together to form cities, "The larger and broader differences of color, hair and physical proportions were not by any means ignored, but myriads of minor differences disappeared, and the sociological and historical races of men began to approximate the present division of races as indicated by physical researches."[14]

The aim of Du Bois's deconstruction of the concept of race was to create a means of employing the prevailing definition of race based on genetics, that is, to allow him to continue speaking of "the black-blooded people of America," or the "people of Negro blood in the United States," while at the same time leaving room for him to question any undesirable implications of such definitions, that is, to override definitions that imply that the physical differences which typically characterize the various races somehow justify social inequality.

The African-American Cultural Imperative

But what bearing does Du Bois's revised notion of race have on his argument for the claim that African Americans have a duty to retain their race identity? As Boxill has noted, one important reason Du Bois cites to support this imperative is that African Americans have a distinct cultural mission as a racial group.[15] On behalf of the Negro Academy, Du Bois asserted that "We believe that the Negro people, as a race, have a contribution to make to civilization and humanity, which no other race can make."[16] But what exactly is this unique contribution? I am not sure whether Du Bois had an answer to this question. He weakly stated that African Americans are "a nation stored with wonderful possibilities of culture," which suggests that they do not yet have any such cultural contribution to make. He then goes on to speak of "a stalwart originality which shall unswervingly follow Negro ideals."[17] And, though he makes passing references to "Pan-Negroism" and the "African fatherland," at no point does he advocate reclaiming any African cultural retentions.[18] Instead, he prefers to tell us that "it is our duty to conserve our physical powers, our intellectual endowments, our spiritual ideals."[19]

What then did Du Bois mean when he spoke of the duty of African Americans to conserve their race identity in order to make a cultural contribution? His view of what constitutes African-American culture seems especially problematic when we consider some of his remarks regarding African American identity. He states that:

We are Americans, not only by birth and by citizenship, but by our political ideals, our language, our religion. Farther than that, our Americanism does not go. At that point, we are Negroes, members of a vast historic race that from the very dawn of creation has slept, but half awakening in the dark forests of its African fatherland.[20]

If African Americans share the same language, religion, and political ideals with other Americans, there does not seem to be much left for them to uniquely contribute to American culture.[21] Although, in some places, Du Bois spoke of the African American's special mission in terms of a distinct cultural contribution, he seems to have had more than simply culture in mind. I suspect that he really meant to speak of a *political* mission that culture in some way enables African Americans to carry out. This is suggested, for instance, by his remarks regarding "that black to-morrow which is yet destined to soften the whiteness of the Teutonic to-day."[22] What Du Bois may have meant here is simply that, through the establishment of a culturally pluralistic society, white cultures will no longer dominate. Instead, social equality will be fostered through a cultural exchange between the various races.

If we consider Du Bois's sociohistorical definition of race, along with his belief that African Americans have a special mission, his rejection of biological essentialism and his failure to make use of the idea of African cultural retentions, begin to appear quite troublesome.[23] For, as Appiah has keenly observed, his talk of Pan-Negroism requires that African Americans and Africans share something in common other than oppression by whites.[24] This lacuna in Du Bois's argument can be explained to some extent by considering the *tentative* nature of the duty of African Americans to conserve their race identity. According to Du Bois, this duty lasts only "until this mission of the Negro people is accomplished."[25] These remarks imply that the special mission of African Americans has more to do with their struggle for social equality than with their making a cultural contribution. Once social equality has been achieved, this duty no longer exists. We can see the explicitly *political* nature of this mission clearly expressed in the following remarks: "[African Americans] must be inspired with the Divine faith of our black mothers, that out of the blood and dust of battle will march a victorious host, a mighty nation, a peculiar people, to speak to the nations of earth a Divine truth that shall make them free."[26]

Although the imperative to make a cultural contribution has more to do with politics than with culture, there is nonetheless a link between them, for African Americans must be inspired "out of the blood and dust of battle" to produce a unique culture that will contribute to world civilization. What makes African-American culture unique is its hybrid genesis within the context of racial oppression in America. The need for African cultural retentions is diminished given that the culture forged out of this experience will enable African Americans to assume a role of political leadership among other black people. Du Bois's argument for the claim that African Americans have a duty to conserve their race identity is backward-looking in the sense that it makes reference to the historical oppression of African Americans, as a diaspora group, as a ground for this duty. His argument is forward-looking in the sense that it foresees an end to the continuance of this oppression and, hence, an eventual release from the imperative.

Nineteenth-century African-American Social Thought

Some commentators have invoked biographical facts about Du Bois's own racial background to explain why he wanted to advance a sociohistorical account of race.[27] While it is not unfair to see this as an important factor influencing his thinking about race, it is a plain misunderstanding to suppose that the reconstruction Du Bois proposed was wholly original. When we consider his argument within the context of African-American social thought at the turn of the century, certain, quite noticeable, details indicate the influence of his contemporaries. He alludes to many concerns that had been expressed on both sides of the perennial separatist-integrationist debate by combining, under his own concept of cultural pluralism, certain tenets drawn from various doctrines that appear in the writings of earlier emigrationist-assimilationist thinkers such as Edward Blyden and Frederick Douglass, although one of the most abiding and dominant influences on his thinking was clearly Booker T. Washington. We can notice the traces of Du Bois's nineteenth-century influences by paying careful attention to the way certain ideas crop up in his essay.

According to Wilson J. Moses, Du Bois's argument in "The Conservation of Races" was directly influenced by Alexander Crummell, whose inaugural address to the Negro Academy expressed a similar preoccupation with the idea of "civilization" as a means of social elevation.[28] Crummell, along with other nineteenth-century activists such as Henry Highland Garnet and Martin Delany, was prominent among the supporters of the African Civilization Society. The goals and values represented in nineteenth-century African-American nationalism were often situated in arguments regarding the development of "civilization" as a means of group elevation. With an eye to the place of African Americans in a world civilization, Du Bois seems to reflect Blyden's earlier call of Providence in his talk of an "advance guard" of African Americans who must "take their just place in the van of Pan-Negroism."[29] Appiah has suggested this reading, perhaps inadvertently, when he characterizes Du Bois's remarks regarding the African-American message for humanity as deriving from God's purpose in creating races.[30] The claim Du Bois makes here, regarding the leadership role of African Americans vis-à-vis other black people in Africa and the diaspora, seems to capture the gist of Blyden's argument for emigration, though emigration was a view that Du Bois never embraced.

Despite the fact that his mention of "Pan-Negroism" presages the Pan-Africanism he would later adopt, in 1897 Du Bois seems to have believed that the uplift of Africa, and black people everywhere, could best be brought about by African Americans pursuing cultural self-determination in America. Of course, the problem this poses for his sociohistorical account of race is that African-American and African cultures are significantly different. The idea of "Pan-Negroism" he derived from that account, that is, "Negroes bound and welded together," failed to recognize the important cultural differences among the various groups of African and African diaspora people.[31]

By contrast with Blyden's black nationalism, Frederick Douglass saw ex-slaves as Americans. He believed that, once African Americans were educated and allowed to demonstrate their equality with whites, assimilation into the American mainstream would someday be possible. In some of his remarks, Du Bois avers to Douglass's view that slavery had severely damaged the dignity and sense of self-worth of African Americans. He maintained that the first step toward social equality will be "the correction of the immorality, crime and laziness among the Negroes themselves, which still remain as a heritage from slavery."[32]

Under the legal segregation that followed slavery, Douglass's assimilationist view found a new expression in the philosophy of Booker T. Washington. Washington's strategy for changing the socioeconomic conditions of African Americans was to appeal to the self-interest of whites. He gave priority to economic development as a key to the elevation of African Americans as a group. Rather than demand social equality, Washington believed it would gradually come with the economic progress of the group. Notwithstanding their much-heralded disagreement over the role of political agitation, Du Bois seems to have accepted certain aspects of Washington's strategy. Along with Washington, for instance, Du Bois advocated social separation from whites "to avoid the friction of races."[33] And Du Bois's assertion that, "No people that laughs at itself, and ridicules itself, and wishes to God it was anything but itself ever wrote its name in history" seems to be a rewording of Washington's famous statement at the Atlanta Exposition that "No race that has anything to contribute to the markets of the world is long, in any degree, ostracized."[34] Both claims are reminiscent of Douglass's earlier concern with the self-esteem of African Americans as a group. Unlike Washington, however, Du Bois placed a greater emphasis on the cultural status of African Americans. He argued against "a servile imitation of Anglo-Saxon culture" on the ground that African Americans have a unique cultural contribution to make and that to accomplish this they must not assimilate.[35] For Du Bois, social equality would be attained through the distinctive cultural achievements of African Americans, who must retain their race identity to accomplish this.

When we consider Du Bois's idea of African Americans gaining social equality through their cultural achievements, we must not overlook some of the earlier proponents of this suggestion, namely, members of the various literary societies in the early part of the nineteenth century and the New Negro literary movement at the beginning of the 1890s.[36] Maria W. Stewart followed David Walker in the tradition of advocating moral uprightness as the basis for elevating the race, a tradition that was perpetuated throughout the nineteenth century by various African-American voluntary associations.[37] We can notice the sense of a mission, for instance, in Anna Julia Cooper's advocacy of an African-American literature "to give the character of beauty and power to the literary utterance of the race."[38] In this vein, then, we should understand Du Bois's statement that "it is our duty to conserve our physical powers, our intellectual endowments, our spiritual ideals." His somewhat vague proposition here emanated from a history of ideas that assigned a specific role to culture in the elevation of African Americans as a group.

Indeed, as a cornerstone of many turn-of-the-century theories of social change, the African-American cultural imperative created a strong expectation that educated African Americans would employ their intellectual resources in the service of race uplift. On the assumption that culture and politics must coincide, Frances E. W. Harper and Pauline E. Hopkins presented arguments in their novels for the obligation of the elite group of black people, namely mulattoes, to refrain from marrying whites, or passing, and instead devote themselves to the betterment of African Americans as a group.[39] They aimed to influence some members of the group to remain loyal and to assume responsibility for elevating other members by arguing that there is a special duty requiring a sacrifice of social privelege. Du Bois seems to have heeded their teachings when he spoke against the loss of race identity in "the commingled blood of the nation," and when he raised the question "is self-obliteration the highest end to which Negro blood dare aspire?"[40]

The duty to conserve African-American racial identity so as to develop a distinct culture derives from an historical context in which the oppression of African Americans as a group obtains. Under such conditions the function of culture is to resist oppression. Even if we accept the idea that African Americans are, in some sense, collectively obligated to resist oppression, we might still wonder whether they are, for this reason, obligated to conserve their racial identity so as to develop a distinctive culture. With regard to the oppression experienced by African Americans it seems that, for Du Bois, the right of resistance is tantamount to the right of cultural self-determination. Although African Americans are, perhaps collectively, obligated to resist oppression in the sense that every African American has a *right* not to acculturate into the American mainstream, this does not establish that African Americans have a *duty* to conserve a distinctive culture.[41]

Race, Ethnicity, and Biology

When Du Bois defines race in terms of sociohistorical, rather than biological, or physical, criteria, he seems to have blurred an important distinction between race and ethnicity, where the former is understood to refer to biological characteristics and the latter refers chiefly to cultural characteristics.[42] Several commentators have taken him to task for lapsing into this confusion. Their criticisms, however, seem to presuppose that people can be divided into biologically distinct racial groups that develop in relative isolation. Du Bois's contention was that this ideal type model of racial and ethnic groups lacks empirical validity, for sociohistorical factors have a greater significance for understanding the essentially *political* genesis, structure, and function of such groups.

Appiah, for instance, objects to Du Bois's sociohistorical definition on the ground that a group's history, or culture, *presupposes* a group identity and, therefore, cannot be a criterion of that group's identity.[43] He attempts to refurbish Du Bois's talk of a common history by adding a geographical criterion such that a group's history is to be understood as (in part) the history of people from the same place. This move, however, seems needless on two counts. First, Du Bois makes clear that an important part of the history of African Americans is their African past, and, because he had little concern with cultural retentions, his point was largely a matter of geography. Secondly, as a criterion of group identity, geography does not add much, given that there are racially and culturally diverse peoples in various locations.

A similar objection has been raised by Boxill who points out that it is simply false to maintain that every black American shares a common culture. Instead, Boxill proposes a physical definition of race that is reflected in the way the racist classifies people into races, whether they share a common culture or not: "I propose that, insofar as black people are a race, they are people who either themselves look black – that is, have a certain kind of physical appearance – or are, at least in part, descended from such a group of people."[44] Boxill, however, is a bit too hasty in his dismissal of the obvious fact that the American system of classification, constructed on the basis of a racist ideology, breaks down when people of mixed blood do not neatly fit into the prescribed racial categories. He makes reference to the notion of "passing" to show that, with regard to people of mixed blood, a physical definition of race still offers the best account. But he overlooks the fact that this notion is fairly limited to the United States and perhaps to similar societies with a majority white population.[45] Moreover, as I shall indicate shortly, many times the practice of racism, which informs Boxill's definition, seems to conveniently disregard the biological criteria he takes to be essential.

The best way to meet the objection, that a definition of race based primarily on sociohistorical criteria confuses race with ethnicity, is to accept it. In the United States the alleged confusion seems to have become a matter of institutionalized practice. College application forms, for instance, frequently display some such confusion when under the ethnic identity category they list *racial* designations such as "black" and "white" along with *ethnic* designations such as "Japanese" and 'Hispanic." It becomes clear that such a system of racial and ethnic classification is constructed for political purposes when we take note of certain combined categories such as "Hispanic, not white" or "Hispanic, not black."[46] As primarily a linguistic designation, the term "Hispanic" can apply to groups of people who consider themselves white, black, or mixed blood. Why then is there a need for a special category that designates a racial distinction between blacks and whites?

The idea that various notions of race have been constructed by racists for political purposes was well recognized in nineteenth-century African-American social thought. In his 1854 essay "The Claims of the Negro Ethnologically Considered," Douglass accused the slaveholders of seeking a justification in science for the oppression of slaves. He pointed out that, by engaging arguments that amount to "scientific moonshine that would connect men with monkeys," they wanted "to separate the Negro race from every intelligent nation and tribe in Africa." Douglass surmised that "they aimed to construct a theory in support of a foregone conclusion."[47]

A similar accusation was published anonymously in 1859 in an article in the *Anglo-African Magazine*. The author begins with the claim that there is no pure, unmixed Anglo-Saxon race, arguing that all whites with various ethnic backgrounds (even with Egyptian blood) still claim to be Anglo-Saxon. The author then refers to the construction of the Anglo-Saxon race as "a legendary theory."[48] The underlying racism of this theory, which relies on the Bible, is exposed by raising the question: if the curse of Canaan is used to prove that black blood is contaminated, what about the curse that marked out Anglo-Saxons for slavery? According to the author, Noah's curse did not point specifically to black people because Cush and Canaan were both sons of Ham. Ethnologists who use Biblical references to establish racial distinctions that imply black inferiority employ "a curious chain of evidence," for there is no African race, that is, no group with pure African blood. The author reduces to absurdity the Biblical evidence for this belief, according to which:

First, – Abyssinians belong to a white race.
Secondly, – Ethiopians were the same as the Abyssinians.
Lastly, – the Negroes were Ethiopians.[49]

The conclusion drawn from this *reductio* argument was that Negroes (Ethiopians) belong to the white race. The author's purpose in presenting this argument seems to have been to urge that all racial terms be treated as misnomers.

These nineteenth-century discussions of race indicate two of the most important factors underlying Du Bois's deconstruction of the biological concept of race, namely, racism and intermingling. Although the identity of every racial, or ethnic, group will involve (a) physical, or biological, criteria and (b) cultural, or sociohistorical, criteria, it seems to be the case that in any given society whether (a) gains precedence over (b) seems to be a matter of politics, that is, racism. But, even in societies such as the United States where biological criteria have gained precedence, the fact of intermingling has rendered any attempt to establish rigid biological racial classifications problematic. When we consider groups such as Chicanos, Amerasians, or Cape Verdians it becomes clear that ethnic designations are needed to accommodate interminglings that have resulted in the creation of group identities that are based almost entirely on sociohistorical criteria.[50]

The Dilemma of Biological Essentialism

One major shortcoming of Du Bois's sociohistorical concept of race is that it fails to make clear how, in the face of racism, African Americans are supposed to invent, or reconstruct, a concept of black identity that will contribute to the progress of the group. Racism is firmly grounded in scientific thinking regarding biologically determined racial types such that, for conceptual reasons, it seems undeniable that there are fundamentally white, black, and yellow people, despite any other ethnic, or cultural, designation that applies to them.[51] As Appiah has noted, Du Bois's proposal to replace the biological concept of race with a sociohistorical one "is simply to bury the biological conception below the surface, not to transcend it."[52] What is at issue, however, is whether the rigid dichotomy between race and ethnicity is tenable. Du Bois introduced sociohistorical criteria as a way to give an account of African-American group identity without presupposing this dichotomy. His insight was to draw from the history of racial intermingling in the United States an objection to the biological essentialism of scientific classifications, as well as a ground on which to reconstruct African-American group identity in a social context dominated by a racist ideology.

With regard to the political aspect of Du Bois's reconstruction-ist project there is an interesting dilemma posed by the ideo-logical competition between Pan-African nationalists and Pan-Indian nationalists, both of whom have made appeals for unity to the same mixed-blood populations.[53] Each nationalist group wants to lay claim to much of that same constituency as rightfully belonging to it, and each would justify this claim by reference to the relevant bio-logical ancestry. Their respective injunctions regarding group loyalty make use of an essentialized conception of group membership for political purposes. In keeping with the biology inherent in their respective appeals for group loyalty, persons mixed with both African and Indian ancestry are asked to identify with the group that best represents their physical appearance.[54]

It is worth noting that the nationalist's motivation for establish-ing such rigid biological criteria for group membership is strictly political. Because black people and Indians are oppressed on the basis of race, rather than culture, the nationalists are rightfully inclined to seek to reconstruct the group identity of black people, or Indians, on strictly racial grounds. Du Bois, of course, recognized this and sought to achieve the same political ends as the nationalists but without invoking the categories of race handed down from scientific racism. He wanted to accommodate the fact that intermingling had become an important feature of the history of African Americans as a group. For Du Bois, then, group loyalty need not rely on a biological essentialism, given that most African Americans are of mixed blood. As a criterion of group identity, he proposed to give culture a greater weight than physical characteristics.

The way biology is used to rationalize the American system of racial classification gives rise to an interesting puzzle regarding the dichotomy between race and ethnicity. Consider, for instance, the case in which two siblings are racially distinct, in some genetic sense, but have the same physical characteristics, as when a white male has offspring by both a black and a white female.[55] We can speak of the offspring as being racially distinct on wholly genetic grounds, given that one child has two white parents and the other is of mixed parentage. The fact that this particular genetic difference should matter with regard to racial classification suggests a reason why race and ethnicity are not interchangeable concepts, namely, only the offspring of two white parents can be considered white.[56]

This particular application of biological criteria becomes much more problematic, however, when the practice of tracing genetic background fails to correlate neatly with the practice of using physical characteristics as a basis for racial classification. We can see this problem by considering an example that involves a multiracial ethnic group that overlaps both black and white racial categories. Suppose that the female offspring of black/white mixed-blood parents has the same physical characteristics as the male offspring of non-black Hispanic parents, and further that they marry and have two children (a boy and a girl) both of whom, in turn, marry whites. Both are genetically black because of their mother's mixed blood but, because the girl no longer has a Spanish surname, her children will be classified as white, while her brother's children will be classified as Hispanic. What this shows, I think, is not only that concepts of race and ethnicity are sometimes interchangeable but also that, for sociological reasons, at some point genetics frequently drops out of consideration as a basis for racial classification.[57]

We might wonder whether the emphasis Du Bois placed on sociohistorical criteria avoids the nationalist dilemma that arises on the biological essentialist account. Suppose that there are two persons with the same racial and cultural profile, that is, each is of mixed heritage (with one black parent), each has the physical characteristics of a white person, and each has been acculturated into a white community. What if one decides to choose a black identity despite her white cultural background? Can her newly acquired consciousness allow her to transcend her cultural background? Given the American system of racial classification, based on genetics, she is entitled to claim a black identity, something which seems to be ruled out on strictly sociohistorical grounds.[58]

In many cases, where members of multiracial ethnic groups seem to have pretty much adopted some version of Du Bois's sociohistorical criteria for their own group identity, we can notice that the race-culture ambivalence engendered by the American system of racial classification is frequently resolved along cultural lines. For black Latinos, such as Puerto Ricans, Cubans, or Dominicans, language exerts an overriding influence on their group identity. Latinos with black ancestry would, in many instances, be more inclined to identify with people who share their cultural orientation than with people who share their physical characteristics, despite a great deal of pressure from the dominant society to abide by the prescribed racial classifications.[59]

Du Bois has been taken to task for giving insufficient attention to the cultural differences among different groups of black people in various parts of the world. Indeed, his sociohistorical notion seems to break down when applied to culturally distinct groups of black people. But, if in many cases culture gains precedence over race as a basis for group identity, he must have thought that there is something universal, or essential, in the cultures of all the various black ethnic groups, namely, a common history of oppression. Appiah has objected to Du Bois's sociohistorical essentialism by pointing out that it fails to uniquely apply to black people, for African Americans share a history of oppression with many groups other than Africans or diaspora black people. This objection must be questioned, for I do not think it does much damage to Du Bois's suggestion that a commonly shared history of oppression provides a basis for African-American identity and for Pan-African unity.

What Du Bois was after with his reconstructed notion of race is best exemplified by considering its application to Jews. Membership in this group is determined mainly, but not exclusively, by a blood relationship (that is, matrilineal descent) with other members of the group.[60] Yet Jews are represented in all three of the biological races, most likely as a result of having intermingled.[61] Jewish identity does not seem to be strictly a matter of culture, that is, religion, or language, for during the Inquisition many people who were Jewish "by birth" were forced to convert to Roman Catholicism (hence the term "Jewish Catholic"), and, presently, there are many individuals who have chosen not to learn Hebrew, or practice a religion, yet in both cases they would still be considered Jews, and by and large they would themselves accept this designation. What then is essential to having a Jewish identity?

One very important factor which plays a major role in the construction of Jewish identity is the history of oppression commonly shared by Jews of all races and cultures.[62] With regard to this oppression there is a sociohistorical continuity to the consciousness which unifies the group that is perpetuated by the persistence of anti-Semitism. Moreover, this consciousness seems to extend uniquely throughout the Jewish diaspora and, since the holocaust, has provided a rallying call for the maintenance of a homeland in Israel.

What is important to notice in this regard is that contemporary Zionists in Israel have been accused of racism toward non-Jews, while anti-Semitism directed toward Jews seems to be virtually identical with other varieties of racism.[63] What this shows, I think, is that there seems to be some sense in which racist practices can be attributed to a multiracial ethnic group, and equally, a sense in which they can be considered the victims of racism.

In considering how Du Bois's reconstructed notion of race can be applied to multiracial ethnic groups, we must not assume that this is always by virtue of intermingling in the sense of some form of racial amalgamation. In the United States and in Latin American societies where so-called "miscegenation" has occurred, the mixed-blood populations are largely the result of involuntary sexual contact between white masters and their slaves.[64] In this historical context racism toward ex-slaves and their offspring has produced a value system such that "whitening" has become the racial ideal.[65] Although this is, understandably, a dominant tendency among oppressed Third World people generally, we must not allow the influence of racism to blind us to a quite different sense in which racial identities have been constructed.

Consider, for instance, the fact that British colonialists referred to the natives of India and Australia as "blacks" and "niggers." Pan-African nationalism may very well be viewed as a response to colonialism, but can it therefore be restricted to groups of people of black-African origin? There seems to be a clear sense in which people who are not of black-African descent share a common oppression with black Africans and diaspora black people. In Australia there has developed a black-consciousness movement among the aboriginals, who have appropriated a black identity heavily influenced by the 1960s' Civil Rights struggle in the United States.[66] In Britain the term "Black" is often used politically to include people of West Indian and of Asian descent. The reason for this development is that the Asian immigrant populations from Pakistan and India are politically aligned (in a way that is temporary and strained at times) with the West Indian immigrant population. The basis for the formation of this multiracial coalition under the rubric "black people" is the common history of oppression they share as ex-colonial immigrant settlers in Britain.[67] The extension of the racial term "Black" to non-African people in Australia, as well as to Asians in contemporary Britain, provides some indication that there is a sense in which a racial concept can be reconstructed to extend to a multiracial group that has not intermingled in the sense of having mixed blood.

Du Bois's proposal regarding group identity requires an adjustment in the biological essentialist criteria to account for intermingling in the sense of racial amalgamation, but what about multiracial group coalitions? By shifting the emphasis to sociohistorical consciousness, he wanted to modify the biological requirement (influenced by scientific racism) to specify only a vague blood tie. Given the fact of racial amalgamation in the United States, he rightly maintained that African-American identity can reside only in sociohistorical consciousness. It is far from clear that he would have embraced all that this implies, namely, that sociohistorical consciousness figures into the social formation of racial and ethnic groups on the model of multiracial group coalitions as well.

Racism and Color Stratification

What if a peculiar sort of cultural exchange were to suddenly occur such that the sociohistorical consciousness that once resided in the biological group now known as "black people" also begins to manifest itself in the biological group now known as "white people." Suppose further that, at some time in the future, the former group is exterminated (by genocide), or disappears (through amalgamation), and that the latter group inherits this consciousness. To what extent do we continue to apply the term "black people"? It seems that on Du Bois's account some such transference of consciousness would be allowed as long as there is, perhaps, a blood tie (say, "traceable") and the inheritors have a sociohistorical connection with their ancestors. If we treat Du Bois's stipulation regarding common blood as inessential, it seems that the sociohistorical criteria provide a sufficient ground on which to establish the black identity of this biological white group.[68]

While it may appear odd to speak of "white African Americans," such an expression could conceivably be applied in some sense that parallels the present usage of the expression "black Anglo-Saxons," which does not seem odd.[69] In each instance the respective expressions would be applied in virtue of a transference of consciousness from one biological group to another, even when there is no blood tie between them. The reason that the expression "white African American" may seem odd is because in the United States the concept of race applies strictly to blacks and whites in the sense that "traceable ancestry" really means that to be white is to have *no* non-white ancestry and to be black is to have *any* black ancestry. With few exceptions we can safely assume that there will be only a one-way transference of consciousness, that is, black people will acculturate into the dominant white mainstream.[70]

It would be a mistake, however, to rule out entirely the possibility of a group of white people appropriating something very much akin to the racial consciousness of African Americans. In 1880 Gustave de Molinari documented his observation that the English press "allow no occasion to escape them of treating the Irish as an inferior race – a kind of white negroes."[71] What is most interesting about this instance of bigotry by one white ethnic group directed toward another is that it was justified by appealing to the same scientific racism used to justify the oppression of black people, that is, the idea that the Irish were a lower species closer to the apes. Moreover, presently in Northern Ireland, the Irish Catholics are sometimes referred to by Protestants as "white niggers" – and, in turn, have appropriated and politically valorized this appellation. The link between African Americans and, say, black South Africans is largely sociohistorical such that an important feature of African-American identity includes a commonly shared history of oppression, but only in this attenuated sense. Similarly, there is no reason to suppose that Irish Catholic identity could not conceiveably include, as fellow colonial subjects, a commonly shared history of oppression, in this attenuated sense, with African Americans and black South Africans.[72]

The oddness of the concept of "white Negroes," or "white African Americans" is a result of a special norm that places black people into a rock-bottom category to which others can be assimilated for political purposes.[73] The simianized portrayal of white Irish Catholics figures into their oppression and degradation in a fashion similar to the function of such portrayals of African Americans. What must be noted, however, is that black people are the paradigm for any such category.[74] This indicates that racism is an ideology regarding the superiority of white people and the inferiority of non-white people. Du Bois made reference to the fact that this color spectrum is defined mainly by the black and white extremes. Although certain white ethnic groups, such as the Irish and the Jews, have experienced their own peculiar brand of racial oppression by other whites, they are not above engaging in racial discrimination against blacks.

The most telling criticism of Du Bois's attempt to reconstruct an African-American identity in terms of culture, rather than biology or physical characteristics, is the fact that so much racism is based on color discrimination.[75] Unlike other racial and ethnic groups, for black people physical characteristics are more fundamental than cultural characteristics with regard to racism. It is for this reason that black Jews experience discrimination by other Jews, or that there is a need to distinguish black Hispanics from all others.[76] Racism based on color indicates that black people occupy an especially abhorrent category such that even hybrid groups that include mulattoes discriminate against them.[77]

Although certain considerations regarding the intermingling of different racial and ethnic groups motivated Du Bois's revision of the notion of race, his main concern was with the impact of racism on African-American group identity. He aimed to address the problem of color discrimination within the group by providing a concept of race that would bring African Americans of different colors together.[78] To the extent that color was an indication of class position among African Americans he also dealt with the issue of group pride by rejecting the extremely divisive assimilationist racial ideal. He challenged the assimilationist doctrine of "whitening" by formulating the criteria of group identity in non-biological terms, a strategy designed to include African Americans from both ends of the color spectrum. Group elevation does not require amalgamation and self-obliteration. Instead, social progress for African Americans requires a conservation of physical characteristics (already multiracial) in order to foster cultural development. The strength of a group lies in its cultural integrity, which has to be situated in a dynamic historical process, rather than in a biologically fixed category.

Chapter 5

Black Consciousness in the Art of Sargent Johnson

Historians tell us that San Francisco was unlike many eastern cities that had heavily populated black ghettos in the 1920s and 1930s, as a result of southern migrations at the turn of the century. Two major studies of San Francisco's black community, Douglas Daniels's *Pioneer Urbanites* and Albert Broussard's *Black San Francisco*, employ demographic comparisons with eastern cities prior to World War II to account for the absence of a black ghetto in San Francisco.[1] The invisibility of the black community in San Francisco seems to have come full circle. With a noticeably shrinking black population, political gains wrought by the Civil Rights struggle, including the legislative career of Mayor Willie Brown, have not affected the rate of black migration from the city. One important political implication of the current demographic shift is increased marginalization of the black community, a consequence that is incongruous with San Francisco's image of itself as socially progressive.

The history of African-American political struggle in San Francisco is inextricably linked with demographic change. Harlem Renaissance historian, Nathan Huggins, speaking as a native of San Francisco, credits black San Franciscans before World War II with a political complacency that accommodated social inequality.[2] This complacency, as well as the myth of racial tolerance that has long been associated with San Francisco, can be viewed as a function of demographics. Prior to World War II, the much larger Chinese and other Asian groups suffered the brunt of racial violence in San

Francisco.[3] By comparison with the Asian experience, black San Franciscans appear to have been tolerated because they were not the focus of race riots and lynchings. Many of the early black migrants interviewed by Daniels seemed grateful that they were spared the experience of African Americans in other parts of the country. They escaped the fate of their more populous Asian brethren because, with a population of less than 5,000 until 1940, African Americans posed no political threat.

Huggins also noted that in the absence of "conspicuous numbers," black San Franciscans were more apt to submerge racial identity and to minimize difference. For African Americans living in San Francisco during the 1920s and '30s, acceptance by the mainstream was contingent on racial invisibility. The political leverage to begin demanding fair treatment and respect would not come until the black migration of the 1940s. Because resistance to discrimination required a strong assertion of racial identity, black San Franciscans were faced with Du Bois's classic dilemma of double consciousness. But, given their small numbers, the question of whether to assert racial identity or to seek absorption into the mainstream was not a genuine choice. Prior to 1940 they could do neither. To expose the city's image of racial tolerance as a false one, historians often cite employment and income data that clearly indicate discrimination against African Americans in San Francisco prior to World War II. I want to take a closer look at the manner in which this myth supports a system of racial discrimination.

Sargent Johnson, an accomplished Bay Area multimedia artist, negotiated the Du Bosian dilemma with great success. Born in Boston on October 7, 1887, Johnson moved to San Francisco in 1915 after spending his young adult years living in Pennsylvania and Chicago. He was a versatile and innovative artist who, in addition to sculpting, painting, and etching used enameled porcelain steel panels to create large murals. With African Americans virtually locked out of every skilled profession, how was it possible for a black artist aligned with the Harlem Renaissance to excel in San Francisco's elite artist community in the 1920s and 1930s? Although Johnson's art, especially in his later period, was not exclusively devoted to racial images, he gained early recognition through his prize-winning submissions in the Harmon Foundation exhibitions of the work of Negro artists, as well as in other local and national competitions.

He managed to assert a strong black identity in his art without losing the racial invisibility required for mainstream acceptance. This apparent contradiction reveals an important insight regarding the ideological function of San Francisco's myth of racial tolerance; namely, that by relying on political complacency it masks social inequality.

There were many personal, as well as philosophical, influences on Johnson's art and aesthetic view. Commentators often note the multicultural aspects of his art, but they have little to say regarding the possible influence of his mixed-race family background or his multicultural experience in San Francisco. Alain Locke's classic anthology, *The New Negro*, is often cited as a major philosophical influence on Johnson's view of African-American art, yet many of the details of Locke's view that are crucial to fully understanding the place of African art and southern black folk culture in Johnson's practice are ignored.[4] In addition to Johnson's African-inspired work, which focused on a rather tenuous conception of a "pure American Negro," Locke's teachings regarding African-American art also accommodated the mixed-race image of African Americans that Johnson sometimes constructed (perhaps inadvertently) on the model of a Third World hybrid. Johnson's multicultural orientation was in keeping with Locke's general view of the relation between African-American art and mainstream American art, as well as with some of his more specific claims regarding the role of the African-American artist in America's "cultural democracy." Indeed, the influence of Asian and Mexican art, quite prominent in Johnson's large-scale public art, never detracted from his desire to produce the African-inspired images he reserved mostly for galleries, collectors, and museum exhibitions.

In many respects Johnson's career provides a paradigm of Locke's "New Negro" artist, whose work would display elements that were racial, national, and universal. Locke outlined a twofold cultural strategy: a vibrant race tradition in art would contribute to American art and, in turn, this achievement would help bring about social equality. One of the writers Locke had mentored, Langston Hughes, deemed the Harlem Renaissance movement a failure because it was motivated by a fantasy that the race problem could be solved through art.[5] Hughes rightly questioned whether the contributions by an elite group of black intellectuals to American culture would bring about social change for the masses of African Americans. Johnson's art had very little impact on segregationist policies, yet the eventual incorporation of his "Negro" art into mainstream American art fulfilled the aesthetic mission that Locke had set for African-American artists in 1925.

A Colorful Art for a Colorful Race

More than any of the other Renaissance artists, including Locke's protégé Aaron Douglass, Johnson epitomized Locke's teachings regarding aesthetics and black consciousness in art. Locke was well known for his denunciation of propagandistic art. Johnson shared Locke's aversion to the social realism of other so-called New Deal black artists such as Jacob Lawrence, Elizabeth Catlett, and Charles White. Unlike these latter artists, the black consciousness displayed in his work was not meant to disturb *status quo* racial inequality. He is reported to have remarked that working people "are sure they don't look as awkward, as earthy, and as unbeautiful as that."[6] This apolitical aesthetic stance, one of the problematic aspects of Locke's philosophy of art, served Johnson well. His highly acclaimed "Negro" art peacefully coexisted with widespread racial discrimination against black San Franciscans in the 1920s and 1930s. When we consider the fact that, despite the influence on his art by Diego Rivera and the Mexican muralists, Johnson chose not to engage in social commentary for ostensibly aesthetic reasons, we must wonder whether his success as a black artist in San Francisco was predicated on his taking a strong position against propaganda in art.

The only surviving statement of Johnson's aesthetic view seems to be his often quoted remarks in a *San Francisco Chronicle* interview he gave in 1935.[7] In what appears to be a series of highly edited quotations, Johnson distinguished between the "culturally mixed Negro of the cities" and the "more primitive slave type," and insisted that Negro art is devoted to a study of the latter as representative of the "pure American Negro." He agreed with Locke regarding the need for a group-conscious art and with Locke's view that the African-American artist should turn to the American south to study his or her cultural roots, rather than to Europe to imitate the European masters. Some of his remarks clearly indicate that he remained committed to expressing a strong sense of racial pride in his art long after the official demise of the Renaissance. In a declaration that has been compared with Langston Hughes's famous manifesto, "The Negro Artist and the Racial Mountain," Johnson asserted, "I am concerned with aiming to show the natural beauty and dignity in that characteristic lip, that characteristic hair, bearing and manner. And I wish to show that beauty not so much to the white man as to the Negro himself." When we associate these remarks with the voice of a visibly mixed-race black man living in San Francisco in the mid-1930s, other readings are suggested. Why would a person of mixed-race ancestry insist that, of all things, the "pure" African American be represented? Perhaps Johnson's preference for the "pure" Negro of the south can be understood as a criticism of black San Franciscans and their aesthetic values, for his claim to want to reveal a black aesthetic to the African American ends with the added comment, "And this is not so easily accomplished." He may have realized that his task would be especially difficult to accomplish in San Francisco. With very few southern black migrants in the Bay Area in the mid-1930s, it was quite likely that his use of images of black southerners to represent the race would fail to be appreciated by San Francisco's more status-conscious black urbanites.

It is worth noting that Johnson speaks of black southerners as "primitive," based on his perception that they were not "culturally mixed." His use of "primitive slave type" comes quite close to Locke's notion of "racial types." Johnson further specifies an African identity for this type with the stipulation "as it existed in this country during the period of slave importation." His appeal to this image of southern black people to construct what he considered to be more authentic visual representations of the race follows many of Locke's stipulations regarding "genuine Negro portraiture" and "true Negro types." For example, Locke referred favorably to the painter Aaron Douglass's earlier "Negro type studies," but was critical of Ronald Moody for his inattentiveness to "racial types."[8] In visual art, as in ethnological studies, a racial type is constructed from certain physical features that are selected and idealized as a model for representing a particular group of people. For Locke, the visual representations of ideal racial types were meant to counter, not only the negative effects of racist stereotypes and caricature, but also "Nordicized" images created by African-American artists. Locke invoked the need for "representative" African-American art when he defended his choice of German artist Winold Reiss to illustrate the 1925 "Harlem" edition of *Survey Graphic*.[9] Just as Locke must have known that he would face heavy criticism from many who thought he should have commissioned an African-American artist to portray African Americans from the usual Eurocentric perspective, Johnson must have known in 1935 that his rejection of the "mixed Negro of the cities," in favor of representing the African "primitive" type, would confront similar expectations from San Francisco's black urbanites.

Following Locke, Johnson advocated the study of southern black folk culture and African art as sources of inspiration for African-American art. But, because Johnson never visited Africa and only traveled once to New Orleans, his own representations of the "pure Negro" were largely idealized physical features he copied from African Americans he encountered in the Bay Area.[10] This observation is not meant to diminish the critical praise he received for his use of African sources, as demonstrated by his numerous awards. With regard to Johnson's copper masks, for example, commentators have noted that, rather than merely imitate African art, as so many other artists had done, he employed a thorough knowledge of the structural aspects of African art and applied that knowledge to create representations of African-Americans.[11] The concern Locke often expressed regarding the superficial use of African art by European and by African-American artists did not apply in the case of Johnson.

Even as a mentor who pulled strings behind the scenes to arrange exhibitions of African and of African-American art, Locke often criticized the work of the Renaissance artists. He was primarily concerned with the development of Negro art and often stated his criticisms generally. Hence, it is not always clear whether he had Johnson's work in mind. His scant remarks specifically on Johnson's work were always favorable, but some of his criticisms of the Africanist school of African-American art, if applied to Johnson's art, would constitute a misunderstanding. This suggests that, at best, Locke's attitude toward Johnson's work was indifferent. There is a bit of irony in Locke's oversight of Johnson's work for, more than anyone else, Johnson demonstrated the veracity of the aesthetic principles Locke advocated.

The most telling criticisms of Johnson's art were leveled by other African-American artists. In some cases the criticism of his art impugns Locke's aesthetic theory as well. James A. Porter, a student of Johnson's aunt, May Howard Johnson, and a coexhibitor with Johnson in some of the Harmon Foundation exhibitions, praised Johnson's modeling technique but preferred to view him as a "ceramic artist," rather than as a sculptor creating works of fine art in various materials.[12] Needless to say, this charge presupposed a questionable theory of art to which neither Locke nor Johnson subscribed. Porter rejected Locke's call for a race tradition in African-American art. He argued that this would foster the segregation of African-American artists from other American artists. Putting aside the question of whether Locke's strategy for bringing about the incorporation of African-American art into mainstream art was sound, there remains a question of whether the work of artists who are inspired by African art to study ancient craft and decorative styles should be considered fine art. Although Locke did not want to grant primacy to museum art as a standard of aesthetic achievement, his mild praise for Johnson's art suggests that he expected African-American artists to produce work that surpassed the African and the European masters. He invoked one of the guiding principles of African decorative art, "beauty in use," to contest the idea that only museum art has aesthetic value, or counts as fine art. Locke even quoted art critic Roger Frye's comments regarding the technical superiority of African sculpture to support his own belief that sculpture would be the forte of African-American art.[13]

Locke praised Richmond Barthe's famous sculpture of a mother holding her lynched son as a work of fine art, and took special note that it contained non-propagandistic racial content. We can only speculate as to whether he would have said as much for Johnson's masterpiece, *Forever Free*, a wood sculpture covered with lacquered cloth. This piece, along with one of his lesser-known works, *Negro Woman*, were based on the mother-child theme in one of Johnson's earlier drawings titled *Defiant*, and in numerous abstract works from his later period. Both *Negro Woman* and *Forever Free* display Johnson's preference for the ancient technique of applying color to sculpture. According to Johnson, these forms allowed him to express a racial dimension in his art. "I am concerned with color not solely as a technical problem, but also as a means of heightening the racial character of my work. The Negroes are a colorful race. They call for an art as colorful as it can be made."

It was precisely this art deco feature of Johnson's work, along with complete disregard of his endeavor to develop techniques better suited to capture racial aspects, that provided the basis for Porter's low esteem. Locke instead seemed more dissatisfied that none of the African-American sculptors, including Johnson, had advanced beyond either the European or African masters. Perhaps, Johnson's attempt to transform ancient practices went largely unnoticed by Locke because he viewed decorative arts as a less-advanced cultural development. For him, decorative arts would constitute the "raw materials" for fine art. He argued that, in its mature stage, African-American art will display universal aesthetic principles derived from many different cultures. Unfortunately, Locke failed to realize the extent to which Johnson's study of ancient techniques of applying color to sculpture, his use of images of Third World people, as well as his commitment to representing the beauty and dignity of the southern black peasant, followed through on this proposal.[14]

Art Big Enough to Belong to Everybody

Although Johnson's interest in African art and the visual representation of African Americans was shaped largely by his association with the Harlem Renaissance artists and the influence of Alain Locke, his distant location on the west coast was an important factor in his development as an African-American artist. Commentators fail to consider the social significance of Johnson's mixed-race background in this context. With Johnson's African-American identity in mind, they often conclude that he was "isolated." If this claim is taken to mean either that he was not a part of the art scene (centered on the east coast), or that he was not connected with the black community, it is very misleading. Johnson participated in all ten of the Harmon Foundation exhibitions of Negro art, as well as in an equal number of local and national exhibitions. In newspaper articles from the 1930s and 1940s, either his identity as an African-American artist was taken for granted because of the racial content of his art or ignored as irrelevant. To use Dick Hebdige's phrase, Johnson seems to have been "hiding in the light."[15] Knute Stiles points this out in his review of the Oakland Museum's retrospective of Johnson's work. Stiles claimed to have "known Johnson for several years before he mentioned that he was a Negro; I hadn't noticed. I was to learn that he had publicized his blackness during the political thirties and always acknowledged his dedication to raising his black brothers out of poverty and misery."[16] Unlike some of his family members, who preferred not to identify themselves or live as African Americans, Johnson chose not to pass, although he apparently was not opposed to capitalizing on his status as ethnically indistinct. There were several reasons why Johnson's career in San Francisco during the 1930s and 1940s was not hampered by his racial background, but a paramount factor was that he was not perceived, in many circumstances, to be a black person.

Another important factor in Johnson's successful career was his close association with two well-known Bay Area sculptors, Beniamino Bufano and Ralph Stackpole. Johnson came to San Francisco specifically to pursue his career as an artist. He studied drawing and painting at the avant-garde A. W. Best School of Art. Even though his interest in sculpting can be traced to his earlier experience of observing his aunt, May Howard Jackson, as she modeled clay, he was 32 years old when he began studying at the California School of Fine Arts. There he worked for two years with Stackpole and for several years with Bufano. Even as a student, he won awards for his sculptures of *Elizabeth Gee* (a Chinese neighbor's child) and of *Pearl* (his daughter), and by the mid-1930s he was at par with his teachers, coexhibiting and serving on juries with them. Some of Johnson's sculptures were included in Stackpole's *Court of Pacifica* at the Golden Gate International Exposition in 1938. In 1940 he was selected by officials at the Works Progress Administration Federal Art Project (WPA) to replace Bufano, who had been fired from a project at George Washington High. The fact that this much-publicized scandal was never viewed in racial terms by the press, or by anyone directly involved, is a sure sign that Johnson had fully arrived in San Francisco's art community. In addition to training him to work in various media, Johnson's teachers, as WPA artists, also communicated a multicultural orientation that would have a lasting influence on his art.

Johnson's selection to replace Bufano was not the only indication of recognition by his peers. He was elected in 1932 to the San Francisco Art Association and, two years later, he was appointed a member of the council. In 1936 he was hired by the WPA as a senior sculptor, advancing almost immediately to the position of unit supervisor. Working from his shop at 15th Street and Shotwell, Johnson began producing large-scale public art. His first public art project was a 22-foot-long organ screen for the California School for the Blind in Berkeley. This screen was carved in redwood with a center panel that featured African-American singers whose faces resembled some of his earlier masks. Johnson is known to have produced at least four other works for the WPA, including a two-part work comprised of a 30-foot-long, 14-foot-high, greenish-gray slate facade titled, *Sea Forms*, which was placed over the main entrance to the Maritime Museum on Polk Street, and a 125-foot-long, 14-foot-high, glazed tile of green and white abstract patterns resembling sea forms that covered the stairwells to the promenade deck. His group of animals of cast terrazzo (a camel, burro, grasshopper, duck, hippopotamus, and elephant), colored coral, green, and gray, were placed in the child-care center playground of the Sunnydale Housing Project. Ten years later he was commissioned by the architect, Albert Williams, to create an abstract pattern incorporating pots and pans with fired enamel on iron 14 feet wide and 28 feet long. This facade was designed to be placed over the entrance of the Dohrmans building, located on Geary Street in Union Square. What is important to notice in connection with Johnson's work for the WPA is that his large-scale public art projects required him to collaborate with other Bay Area artists in the public and in the private sector while, in some cases, supervising their work.

Johnson is sometimes depicted in art-history books working on the massive 185-foot-long, 12-foot-high relief frieze of cast stone he installed on the retaining wall across the back of the football field at Washington High School, at 32nd Avenue and Anza.[17] When he was selected by the WPA to replace Bufano, his design had to be submitted for approval to the San Francisco Art Commission, which initially rejected it. Some of the committee members went on record declaring support for the retention of Bufano, whose design they had already approved. Johnson eventually won approval by creating a clay model 12 feet high and 3 feet long. It is worth noting that, while the Art Commission was split on the merits of Johnson's plans for the Washington High frieze, this same group voted unanimously to accept Diego Rivera's mural for the yet-to-be-built San Francisco City College Library. This is extremely important to consider in connection with the political aspects of Johnson's dispute with Bufano.

Bufano and Johnson jointly contributed to other public art projects for the WPA prior to Bufano's dismissal. Bufano had created two stylized animals carved in brown and black granite, "Seal" and "Frog," for the promenade deck of the Maritime Museum, which were not installed until 1942. A 1938 photograph of Bufano working in his studio with four of his assistants, including Johnson, accompanies an essay Bufano wrote for Francis O'Connor's anthology of essays by WPA artists.[18] Less than two years after this photograph was taken, Johnson would literally betray his former teacher and collaborator. Several commentators have erroneously reported the circumstances surrounding Bufano's dismissal. For example, we are told by Romare Bearden and Harry Henderson that "Johnson's design won him the commission for this athletic frieze. . . . The award outraged Beniamino Bufano . . . who felt his own design should have won, and ended their friendship."[19] The only truth in this assertion is the fact that their friendship ended. It is not at all true that Bufano became bitter because he lost a competition to his former student. Rather, what really happened was that the Art Commission had already commissioned Bufano to do the frieze, but WPA officials objected to the political content in Bufano's design and assigned Johnson to take over the project. According to Richard McKinzie, Bufano was fired when WPA officials learned that he had used the Marxist labor leader Harry Bridges as a model for the frieze.[20] The *San Francisco Chronicle* reported that "When [Joseph] Allen changed the locks on Bufano's workroom, to impress on him that he was fired, the clay that Bufano was molding into the heroic figures of the frieze became Johnson's to work with."[21] Keeping in mind that the workroom from which Bufano was barred had been a training ground for Johnson's development as a sculptor, the official story repeatedly told by politically naïve commentators evades many of the important issues raised by Johnson's betrayal of Bufano.

Although Johnson clearly benefited from his collaborations with Bufano and Stackpole on public art projects, he was highly critical of some of his more politically minded colleagues – in particular, the Coit Tower muralists. His ability to relate to the art establishment, especially collectors, was to a large extent due to his well-known political neutrality. His opposition to political messages in art places him closer to Locke than to Bufano on questions of ideology and aesthetics. In his essay on public art, Bufano presents a philosophy of contemporary art that is thoroughly political.[22] Bufano maintained that art must become democratic by being "big enough to belong to everybody, too big for anyone to put in his pocket and call his own." Rather than produce art to fit over some patron's fireplace, he invoked a notion of public art that is created for the benefit of the masses. He maintained that the function of art is to create a universal culture "that will guide the future course of world destiny to a better way of living." When Bufano spoke of guiding the future course of world destiny, he assigned a political role to artists in combating the rise of fascism and modern warfare.

Unlike Johnson, who is reported to have shrewdly studied the tastes of patrons by working in an art gallery to meet them, Bufano maintained an anti-patron stance. He quoted the "whining complaint and recrimination" in a letter he received from an ex-patron to illustrate the need for artists to be less dependent on patrons to survive. The patron was incensed at Bufano for proposing a monumental St Francis made of stainless steel and copper overlooking the bay, insisting instead that Bufano's best work was represented by his little statues of children, rabbits, deer, and puppies. Bufano then asked, "How can such a man understand the Sun Yat-sen or the Statue of Peace"? "How can a cultural pattern be developed for America if art and the artists are subjugated to the whims and idiosyncrasies of a few overfed decadent merchant princes, carryovers from the days of feudalism"?[23] Rather than capitulate to the economic pressure of survival, Bufano advocated the radical practice of offering his service to any community that could simply pay him day wages and supply the materials. He wanted to produce art for the masses with materials and designs that would "reflect public service and functional objectives." He maintained that public art allows artists to give something to the world and enables

their voices to be heard beyond the provincialism of their immediate locales.

According to Johnson's own testimony, the desire to produce
public art that would be available for future generations motivated
him to paint murals in large buildings.[24] As in the case of his abstract
design for the Dohrmans building, he sought white patronage to
paint religious murals in several black churches in Oakland. Because
Johnson's reliance on patrons contrasts sharply with Bufano's
teachings, Locke's view of the WPA seems more relevant to understanding Johnson's relationship with his patrons. Bufano believed
that the WPA would lay the foundation for a renaissance of art
in America, whereas Locke viewed it as a means of sustaining the
earlier generation of Harlem Renaissance artists. Given Locke's influence on Johnson's identity as a black artist, Johnson was placed
in the predicament of having to negotiate the black quest for self-
esteem that he shared with the Harlem Renaissance artists and his
own recognition of the cogency of Bufano's antipatron stance. Under
the rubric of "cultural democracy" Locke aimed primarily to include
the African-American image in mainstream American art, but he
expected African-American artists to earn the recognition and esteem
of rich patrons. Bufano's notion of "democratic art" was a rejection of Locke's elitism. The renaissance Bufano spoke of would move
art into the public domain, whereas Locke conceived the Harlem
Renaissance as a means of changing the image of black people in
art and socially elevating black artists.

Certain aspects of Bufano's view of art seem to coincide with that
of Locke. For example, Bufano criticized American artists, claiming that they have "borrowed some decadent European form and
have pursued it in true merchant fashion." He advocated a more
"universal" art that included ancient and non-Western practices.
I have already noted traces of this doctrine in some of Johnson's
remarks. His view, however, involves a more complex blending of
the teachings of his mentors. The technical aspects of his art – for
example, applying color to sculpture – were heavily influenced
by Bufano, but his turn to Africa as a source of inspiration was a
consequence of Locke's influence. Bearden was critical of African-
American artists such as Johnson because he believed they had
not progressed beyond the influence of their teachers. Bearden's
criticism exposes Johnson to one of his own criticisms of other

African-American artists; Johnson was in no position to criticize them for going to Europe only to imitate the masters, when he seems to have imitated some of his white teachers – specifically Stackpole and Bufano.

Bearden's criticism seems misguided in the case of Johnson, even if he was right to note traces of Bufano's influence on Johnson's style. The fact that Johnson's technique was indebted to Bufano is not sufficient reason to dismiss his art as imitative. Even though Johnson's sculpting technique was acquired from Bufano, the content of his art was considerable different. Bufano's penchant for creating statues of "great men" contrasts sharply with Johnson's preference for African-American "primitive types" and ordinary people of all races. With regard to the politics of representing southern black folk culture, Johnson's practice seems to have been influenced by Locke and by Bufano. Both advocated a return to folk sources; only Locke had mainly ideological concerns in mind, whereas Bufano was more concerned with technical issues pertaining to the use of what he called "pure forms" in modern art. Johnson followed Bufano's teachings regarding the use of ancient and of modern materials as a matter of technique, but he also wanted to meet Locke's demand for African-American art with a racial content. He accomplished both by using the technique he acquired from Bufano to emphasize universal themes in his WPA projects, while reserving the expression of black consciousness for his pieces geared to collectors.

Johnson's art reflects many Asian-Pacific elements that can be found in the work of other Bay Area artists, including his teacher Ralph Stackpole. Lizzetta LeFalle-Collins maintains that Johnson's statues of the Incas, which were created for Stackpole's installation at the International Exposition on Treasure Island, represent his attempt to depict the "pure Indian."[25] What might be considered by critics as imitative in Johnson's style enabled him, in fact, to collaborate on public art projects with other Bay Area artists. LeFalle-Collins notes, for instance, a striking similarity between the divers and swimmers in Johnson's athletic frieze at Washington High, and the swimmers shown standing and diving in Rivera's mural at City College of San Francisco. Johnson's plans for the frieze were rejected by the art commission for reasons having to do with aesthetics. One sculptor on the committee, Ruth Cravath, is reported to have complained "It looks fine except for that diving group down there. I have a psychological reaction to that group – they appear to be going to hit the water ker-plop and at once. But that could be corrected, I like it." Another architect on the committee, Paul Ryan, also chimed in with the following suggestion "We might have that jackknife diver taken out, and space the other two divers. That would give it movement over and across."[26] In the face of such criticism, Johnson's knowledge that Rivera's mural with divers had already been approved without dissent by this same committee was no doubt an inducement to submit a similar design. But to suppose that he was interested only in pre-Columbian or contemporary Mexican art as a marketing-networking strategy would be misleading. It makes more sense to suppose that he actually found a style, in the work of Stackpole and Bufano, most suitable to expressing a multiracial perspective. Indeed, his own Indian background provided a motive for his interest in the art of the Zapotec. His interest in Third World cultures was not limited to African and pre-Columbian Indian art. In addition to his travels to Mexico to learn technique from the Zapotec Indians, he also visited Shinto shrines and studied Japanese art.

What is the relevance of Johnson's success as a Harlem Renaissance artist and as a WPA artist for understanding the myth of racial tolerance? This question involves several issues pertaining to the relationship between elitism in art and the politics of representation.

When Locke advocated the appropriation of black folk culture by artists, he had a European model of nationalistic art in mind. Harlem would be a Mecca for the black renaissance in art just as Dublin and Prague were centers where European artists gathered to mine their national folk cultures. But what about the excavation of folk culture by intellectuals, black or white? Johnson's art is not to be confused with the folk expression of the Africans or the Indians, whose technique and imagery he appropriated. But if Johnson was black and Indian, why should we construe his use of folk techniques as an "appropriation"? Both Locke and Bufano expected modern art to rely on folk cultures as a source of inspiration for contemporary ideas. When Johnson began working in the black Oaxacan clay used by the Zapotec Indians, he was not interested in making pottery or sculptures that were a part of their traditions. Neither were any of the African masks in his series meant to be part of African religious tradition. Rather, he aimed to incorporate ancient principles of aesthetics regarding sculptural forms into a transformative practice by combining Western with non-Western elements. This hybrid form is not to be confused with any of the folk forms from which it is derived. We can best understand Johnson's appeal to folk sources as appropriation in the sense that African art forms were used by European artists such as Georges Braque, Pablo Picasso, and Amedeo Modigliani.

There is a certain amount of ambivalence that can be associated with Johnson's appropriation of folk art, as well as his representations of southern black folk. He was quite aware of the political thrust of his images of African Americans in an era of legal segregation and racial oppression. For this reason he subscribed to Locke's philosophy and attempted to create a new black aesthetic in contemporary American art. His peer acceptance by other Bay Area artists bodes well for the social objective Locke had set for the renaissance artists. Johnson was a perfect instance of Locke's notion of "cultural democracy," whereby American artists of all races are at liberty to draw on native folk sources for raw materials and inspiration. The problem with this notion, as we have seen in connection with Bufano's philosophy, is that the inclusion of African-American images in mainstream art is quite compatible with the denial of social equality to African Americans. Brazilian culture provides a case for comparison. The inclusion of the African and Indian cultures of Brazil into the national culture has not resulted in any significant social change for blacks and Indians in Brazil. This criticism seems to apply to the lack of impact Johnson and the Harlem Renaissance artists had on the institutionalized practice of racial discrimination in the United States.

San Francisco's myth of racial tolerance is much like Brazil's myth of "racial democracy."[27] If we situate Johnson's art in the context of what Bay Area artists were doing, it clearly reflects a cultural pluralism that did not exist in other parts of the United States. It is in this sense that the myth is sustained by Johnson's success. But if we consider the fact that Johnson consciously avoided raising political issues in his work, we come closer to understanding why the idea of racial tolerance in San Francisco is only a myth. Johnson's role in the silencing of Bufano is unforgivable, for Bufano was a very strong voice for social change in America. He produced art that advocated resistance to oppression. "I sculptured 'Peace' in the form of a projectile, to express the idea that if peace is to be preserved today it must be enforced peace – enforced by the democracies against Fascist barbarism. Modern warfare, which involves the bombing of women and children, has no counterpart in a peace interpreted by the conventional motif of olive branches and doves."[28] The ambivalence that those of us who take ourselves to be progressive sometimes feel toward Johnson's art derives from his refusal to use his art to advocate social change. When we consider Johnson's relationship with the black community, the question arises as to whether he trained any black artist to paint murals in black churches or, whether, as a WPA unit supervisor, he included any black artists on any of his projects. Virtually nothing has been written about his relations with other Third World artists in the Bay Area. When we celebrate Sargent Johnson as one of San Francisco's great artists we must not fail to consider his success in relation to the social environment from which he emerged – including the community of black artists with whom he associated in San Francisco.

Chapter 6

Black Vernacular Representation and Cultural Malpractice

The unfortunate thing about American thought is the habit of classifying first and investigating after. As a result this misrepresentation of the temper and spirit of Negro folk lore has become traditional, and for all we know, permanent.

Arthur Huff Fauset
"American Negro Folk Literature" in Alain Locke (ed.), *The New Negro*
(New York: Atheneum, rpt. 1925/77), p. 241.

If we are a race we must have a race tradition, and if we are to have a race tradition we must keep and cherish it as a priceless – yes as a holy thing – and above all not be ashamed to wear the badge of our tribe.

Alain L. Locke
Lecture on Paul Laurence Dunbar delivered at Fisk University,
(date unknown) Locke Papers, Box 125, File # 46, pp. 12–13.

Witnessing black comedians perform acts of self-denigration sometimes can be a painful experience for black spectators. Many prominent black leaders expressed outrage at Ted Danson's use of blackface comedy in his roast of Whoopi Goldberg. Several black celebrities in attendance claimed to have been deeply offended by Danson's minstrel show humor, which they thought viciously objectified and ridiculed black people whether it was intended to do so or not. Being told that Whoopi Goldberg collaborated with Danson to write the skit did not affect this judgment. Some maintained that such humor perpetuates racism whether presented by a white or a black comedian.[1] This public outcry by black leaders marks a recent break with a familiar pattern of officially protesting apparently racist humor by white performers, while refraining from officially protesting a very similar humor by black performers. A major difficulty faced by those who believe that an official protest ought to be possible in either case is the lack of agreement, especially in the latter instances, about what constitutes racism and self-denigration. By focusing on some of the perennial criticisms of black vernacular representation I aim to highlight a much-neglected discussion of this problem in the discourse on black culture. I want to draw attention to the inadequacy of the criteria used to identify self-denigrating aspects of black vernacular culture. Political ideology is a major factor influencing judgments of this sort. I argue that to identify a particular instance of black vernacular representation as self-denigrating is tantamount to rendering a judgment regarding the ideological orientation of the artist.

The term "black vernacular" refers primarily to the oral and paralinguistic activity of the speakers of a black dialect. Here I use it to include the idioms employed in various media to represent these speakers. Black artists have been charged with cultural malpractice whenever they have been taken to employ these idioms in a fashion that misrepresents black people. This misrepresentation occurs at several levels. The material image might include phenomena – such as misspelled or mispronounced words, sambo and mammy caricatures, simianized portrayals or even gorillas themselves – as a sign of the inferiority of black people. The material image, however, does not always reveal its underlying ideology; that is, whether beneath this surface there are elements of accommodationism, resistance, or perhaps even both. On the view I shall advance in support of the black cultural norm against malpractice, the accusation that black vernacular culture has been misrepresented at a deeper ideological level is most often a perceptual claim standing in need of a justification. Historically, the change of cultural malpractice has been leveled by an illustrious group of intellectuals. To what criteria did they appeal to justify their various *perceptions* that a misrepresentation of black vernacular culture had occurred?

The Cultural Malpractice Charge

One type of vernacular misrepresentation at the material level of transcription involves the spelling of the words used to represent a black dialect. Sojourner Truth's famous quote, for instance, is sometimes rendered as *Ain't I A Woman* or *Ar'n't I A Woman*, depending on the author.[2] If Truth spoke with a Dutch accent, however, it is a misrepresentation to attribute a black southern speech pattern to her. Moreover, if it is racist for a white transcriber to impute a black literary dialect to her, it seems equally racist for a black transcriber to do this. Sojourner Truth's speech will be misrepresented if rendered in standard English, in a conventional literary black dialect, or in any other dialect we invent for her.[3] This is because an accurate transcription of her lost dialect is needed to gain access to the idiom captured by her manner of speech. But is this generally so?

Sterling Brown, an accomplished dialectal poet, wrote a cautionary note to the WPA regarding the collecting of slave narratives in dialect.[4] He made two recommendations. He insisted that standard English be used, arguing that because most Americans speak with a dialect there is no need to adopt a special spelling of words for African-American speech patterns. He even provided a list of words that were not to be used. Unlike the Sojourner Truth case of a lost dialect, Brown's recommendation seems to presuppose a common familiarity among the readers of the WPA narratives with the pronunciation used by speakers of a black dialect.

Brown also insisted that the editorializing should be minimal, with the words "darky" and "nigger" omitted. He stipulated that these words are permitted only where the ex-slave herself used them. Apparently, Brown was addressing not only an issue of transcription, or the spelling of words, but also a political concern with racism. Notwithstanding a common awareness that, in the context of a legally segregated south, the connotation of terms such as "nigger" or "darky" were quite different when stated by a white person, it is remarkable that Brown remained more concerned with the representation of black dialect than with the racial identity of the transcriber. He maintained that "Truth to idiom is more important . . . than truth to pronunciation" and cited Erskine Caldwell, Ruth Suckow, and Zora Neale Hurston as authors who could "get a truth to the manner of speaking without excessive misspellings."[5]

In his book, *The Cool World*, Warren Miller recorded the speech patterns of the black urban males he observed on the streets of Harlem.[6] Critics have suspiciously viewed Miller's book not only with regard to his literary representation of black dialect, but with equal regard to his reproduction of popular mainstream conceptions.[7] Because, for most, the dialect he employed requires translation, undoubtedly, his story would have been more accessible had he followed Brown's advice regarding the spelling of words in standard English. Although, just as in the above cases, Miller's use of black dialect can be criticized by specifically citing the linguistic criterion of spelling, he might have replied that he used a particular spelling in order to capture the black urban idiom more accurately. This shows that disagreement about whether the spelling Miller adopted constitutes a misrepresentation is not precluded, and perhaps further that what is really at issue is a question of ideology. Given the social norm that dictates that a white-authored version of a black dialect is always to be suspected of latent racism, such disagreements cannot be resolved on wholly scientific grounds.[8]

There have been occasions, however, on which scientific evidence has been persuasively employed to resolve such disagreements when suspicions about a black person's use of dialect were raised. In her typical eloquence, Anna Julia Cooper accused Paul Robeson of misrepresenting black dialect. According to Cooper,

The story has gone the rounds of the press that Paul Robeson, who himself tells us that he has toiled and spent to attain the accent not offensive to Mayfair, sometimes slips into the "soft slur of the Southern Negro" and even at the tragic moment of Othello's sublime fury demands: "Where am dat handkerchief, Desdemona?"

Reporters and critics must sell their stuff and one should not grudge them their little joke. Nothing helps like a bit of local color to heighten tone effects. This story listens well for heart interest on this side of the Atlantic, where a black man is not true black unless he says "am dat". Mr. Robeson in his impersonation of the noble blackamoor may on his own part deliberately allow himself the racial touch, not at all inconsistent to my mind with a highly artistic effect. If he did so, be sure it was not a slip; he had been instructed and believed that such a departure would give just the original flavor he was expected to create. Buy speaking *ex cathedra* I claim, as one who ought to know, that no artist who has intelligently analyzed the Negro folk-speech, whether he be poet, novelist, or impersonator, can ever accept "am dat" as a possibility in Negro or Southern vocalization.[9]

Cooper goes on to provide a detailed physiological explanation of the impossibility of this verbal construction in southern black speech. She supported her cultural malpractice charge against Robeson's use of dialect by relying on sociolinguistic evidence and facts about the physiological production of speech. Her insight was derived from her long experience as a southern black teacher, as well as from her formal study of languages at the Sorbonne.[10]

Notice that Cooper accused Robeson of using an invented dialect to emphasize his black identity. This is similar to the cultural malpractice charge against Sojourner Truth's transcribers. In both cases the pronunciation is deliberately changed to accord with a more stereotypical representation. Further, the misrepresentation originates with a white author but it is perpetuated by a black author or performer. The black cultural norm against accepting white-authored black dialect by writers such as Warren Miller must be viewed in the light of a history of deliberate misrepresentations by white transcribers. Cooper's cultural malpractice charge against Robeson makes clear that such misrepresentations involve more than a matter of misspelled words, but rather involve a political problem of idioms being manufactured to fit a certain stereotype of black people.

Alain Locke's Remarks on the Representation of Black Folk Culture

In his analysis of the literary uses of black dialect, J. L. Dillard noted that, among all of the black writers he had surveyed, Zora Neale Hurston and Richard Wright were the best at reproducing authentic black dialect.[11] But how do we square this praise from a sociolinguist with the well-known criticisms of Hurston's use of dialect by some of her literary cohorts?[12] Given Hurston's training as an anthropologist, it is difficult to imagine how she could have either produced an inaccurate transcription of black dialect or misrepresented the southern black idioms of her hometown. Yet her mentor, Alain Locke, had the following to say in his review of her book, *Their Eyes Were Watching God*:

Her gift for poetic phrase, for rare dialect, and folk humor keep her flashing on the surface of her community and her characters and from diving down deep either to the inner psychology of characterization or to sharp analysis of the social background. It is folklore fiction at its best, . . . But when will the Negro novelist of maturity, who knows how to tell a story convincingly – which is Miss Hurston's cradle gift, come to grips with native fiction and social document fiction? Progressive southern fiction has already banished the legend of these entertaining psuedo-primitives whom the reading public still loves to laugh with, weep over and envy. Having gotten rid of condescension, let us now get over oversimplification![13]

Locke's criticism has an aesthetic and a political dimension. From his aesthetic standpoint he praised Hurston's ability to accurately represent the dialect and idioms of her folk characters. What he questioned was her lack of social consciousness in presenting these characters. He was concerned that she merely perpetuated the sentimentalist dialectal tradition of caricature, rather than what he considered to be "genuine folk portraiture."[14] Locke's distinction between caricature and portraiture, however, is far from clear.

Scholars have sometimes conceived certain folkloric aspects of black vernacular culture as retentions traceable to West Africa.[15] In his book, *The Signifying Monkey*, Henry Louis Gates juxtaposes black vernacular oral literature and a "formal black Literature."[16] This dichotomy of folk culture and high culture sometimes conveys a transhistorical notion of dialectal speakers as bearers of an authentic black culture.[17] This idea was quite prominent in Alain Locke's social theory and a cornerstone of his account of the evolutionary development of African-American art. With regard to African-American drama, he claimed that "the timeless beauty of Negro folk life and tradition, including that tap-root of it which leads back to the vast traditions of Africa, must someday yield its dramatic treasures."[18] Locke was keenly aware of the social transformation of African retentions under the brutal influence of slavery and their continual transformation as the ex-slaves developed an African-American folk culture from their peasant lifestyles. He recognized that, owing to the large migrations of blacks from the rural south to urban centers in the north at the turn of the century, most of their preindustrial folk beliefs and folkways would be lost.[19] His theory of folk art aimed to provide an account of the metamorphosis of surviving Africanisms from their earliest forms as folklore to their more mature forms as high tragedy or comedy. According to Locke, "One can scarcely think of a complete development of Negro dramatic art without some significant artistic reexpression of African life, and the tradition associated with it."[20]

Locke's concern with African retentions in African-American folklore is most vividly presented in a series of manuscript notes he sent to Hurston regarding her field studies of southern black folklore.[21] In some cases he rejected her stories as being of a non-African origin or he requested a more accurate or more complete explanation of an alleged retention, whereas, in other cases, he endorsed their African elements or origin. Taken as a whole, Locke's remarks suggest that he thought the authenticity of African-American folk culture is ultimately established by reference to verifiable African retentions.[22]

In his Fisk University lecture on Paul Laurence Dunbar, Locke explained the importance of field studies such as Hurston's for the advanced development of a black literary tradition. "[T]he Negro must reveal himself if the true instincts and characteristics of the race are ever to find their place in literature. In Ireland now some of the greatest literary men of our time are hard at work, visiting the lumber cabins of the Irish peasants collecting their folk tales, their stories, and writing them into literature."[23] Locke often drew this parallel between African-American folk culture and other folk cultures throughout the world. He held that to carry out the social function of revitalizing the cultural life of the race, African-American art must develop an organic tradition by drawing on the "ancestral sources of African life and material."[24]

Although Locke believed there were African retentions, he rejected the notion of an atavistic "race-soul" that contributed to the primitivism formula so prevalant in American fiction and drama about black people.[25] He maintained that "the Negro's primitivism is nine-tenths that of the peasant the world over and has only a remote tropical flavor."[26] He held a strictly sociohistorical notion of race that emphasized cultural, rather than biological, traits. Hence, he used the notions of "race" and "folk" interchangeably, identifying African Americans as a race with the spoken tradition that developed from their isolation in the rural south and the rigors of agricultural life.[27] According to Locke, "We are a race because we have a common race tradition, and each one of us becomes such just in proportion as he recognizes, knows and reverences that tradition."[28] He considered Dunbar to be an exponent of this race tradition because of Dunbar's interest in preserving the plantation folk beliefs and folkways that were gradually vanishing. Locke believed that maintaining this tradition was the only means of transmitting the valuable lessons of the forebears to a younger generation.

Locke's criticism of Hurston does not seem to square with his praise of Dunbar's contribution to the African-American literary tradition. He attributed to Dunbar a sense of social responsibility concerning the race tradition. Given that Hurston could easily be viewed as having Dunbar's sense of social responsibility, Locke's point had more to do with the relation between her work and its social context, than with the work itself.[29] During the period of Dunbar's writing career his poetry served the useful purpose of adding an absent black voice to the sentimentalist plantation literature, whereas several decades later, at the time Hurston wrote, the dialectal tradition had degenerated into minstrelsy.

In his critique of minstrelsy Locke recognized that the sentimentalist tradition, fostered by white authors such as Joel Chandler Harris, as well as Dunbar, included portrayals of the southern black peasant that were really "vital."[30] He also recognized that the influence of the public demand for more and more stereotypes had led to disproportionate caricature. His criticism of Hurston meant to draw in question her intention in presenting characters who simply perpetuated this caricature. Perhaps the force of this objection to Hurston can be appreciated by comparing it with his equally nuanced criticism of white authors who wrote in dialect. For example, he criticized DuBose Heywood for using the primitivism formula of an atavistic race-soul, while in the same breath he claimed that "Porgy was the first Negro play that moved with real primitive force instead of the fake primitivism imposed on the Negro cast by directors trying to force them into preconceived moulds."[31] But with regard to Gershwin's opera version of "Porgy" Locke protested that the director "was guilty of overworking his own discovery with set mannerisms."[32] The dissatisfaction Locke expressed here with the representation of black folk culture by white authors seems to parallel his criticism of Hurston.

Locke was critical of white dramatists for relying on stock formulas that produced "an overstudied situation lacking spontaneity and exuberant vitality."[33] Many of his reservations about the black folk drama of white playwrights stemmed from his belief that only the black playwright can reveal the inner stresses and dilemmas of black folk characters. For Locke, this was "not a question of race, but of intimacy of understanding."[34] Although white dramatists such as Paul Green had "unimpeachable artistic motives" and came close to a genuine representation of black folk idioms, Locke believed that only a black dramatist could provide the requisite touch.[35] In his review of Hurston's play, *Moses: Man of the Mountain*, however, he again gave a scathing critique of her treatment of black folk characters. "What if the stereotyping is benign instead of sinister, warmly intimate instead of cynical or condescending, it is still caricature for all that instead of portraiture."[36] Locke generally expected something more from black playwrights than from white playwrights. His criticisms of Hurston, nevertheless, seem somewhat unfair by comparison with his more favorable comments on Heywood's *Porgy*.

Given his dismissal of Hurston, what more did Locke expect from black dramatists? He claimed that Hurston's treatment of black folk characters was caricature rather than portraiture. This criticism was tantamount to his political objection to minstrelsy. Keep in mind here that Locke does not object to Hurston's characters as such; rather he thought Hurston's shortcoming was that she failed to provide "a sharp analysis of the social background."[37] This objection, however, is out of line with Locke's more notorious criticism of black writers whose work he considered to be political propaganda.[38] Locke seems to have commented more favorably on white dramatists because he considered the black dramatist's advantage of psychological intimacy to be more than offset by the disadvantage of insufficient aesthetic distance which inclined so many to seek racial vindication in their work.

To clarify Locke's political concern with minstrelsy, some explanation is needed of the discontinuity between his commentary on Hurston's black folk characterizations and his commentary on similar folk characterizations by white authors. He seems to have criticized Hurston inconsistently for not providing a social analysis he labeled as propaganda in the work of other black writers, leaving us to wonder about some of the political implications of his aesthetic notion of genuine folk portraiture for his general view of high folk art. When he spoke in praise of the "dramatic treasures" that would come from "the timeless beauty of Negro folk life and tradition" and more harshly of the "un-actable propaganda plays" of black dramatists, he set up a time-honored dichotomy between aesthetics and propaganda. He believed, however, that there was a social and political justification for "the more purely aesthetic attitudes."[39] His periodic evaluations of the growth and development of Negro artistic expression rested on his sociological view of group progress. Because he believed that life was becoming less of a problem and more a "vital process" for the younger black person, Locke thought that the purely artistic point of view and vision were also becoming more of a possibility.[40] In this regard Locke's criticisms of Hurston seem to reflect his dissatisfaction with her lack of artistic maturity. In his earlier review of her first novel, *Jonah's Gourd Vine*, he stated, "For years we have been saying we wanted to achieve 'objectivity': – here it is."[41]

There was a political dimension to the aesthetic principle underlying Locke's critique of minstrelsy. He saw his view of folk drama as being compatible with Marxism.[42] In response to the criticism that his view was a reversion to aestheticism and art-for-art's-sake, he pointed out that "a reawakening of an oppressed people is spiritually impossible without restored pride and cultural self-respect."[43] He compared his proposal that folk culture provide a source of materials for high art with the policy of the Soviet national theaters. According to Locke, "The social yield of such ethnic art is as great or greater than its artistic yield."[44] But what exactly was the social yield Locke had in mind?

As the drama of "free-expression and imaginative release," according to Locke, folk drama, "has no objective but to express beautifully and colorfully the folk life of the race . . . to cover life with the illusion of happiness and spiritual freedom."[45] While it is far from clear how this would break down false stereotypes and stimulate black cultural life, Locke's remarks regarding the objectives of folk drama nonetheless help shed light on his notion of genuine folk portraiture. He tells us that, "But when our serious drama shall become as naive and spontaneous as our drama of fun and laughter, and that in turn genuinely representative of the folk spirit which it is now forced to travesty, a point of classic development will have been reached."[46] Here we are again left to wonder what, if anything, could possibly have satisfied Locke's criteria for a genuine representation of the folk spirit.

Surprisingly, his clearest statement of this achievement is reserved for the Hollywood film, *Hearts in Dixie*.[47] After noting certain lapses in the film, Locke cited several outstanding features of its representation of black folk culture. He claimed that "[t]he absence of the clownish leer and the minstrel's self-pity are real steps toward the genuineness of Negro emotion."[48] He also claimed that in a film such as this, which managed to "cut away from all dependence on stock pantomine, the Negro voice achieves an artistic triumph, and for the reason that it is purely Negro than ever, a fine peasant thing in a genuine setting."[49] Locke's praise of this film is quite remarkable when compared with the views of film critics who straightforwardly dismissed it as minstrelsy. Consider, for example, Locke's claim that "Stepin Fetchit in this picture is as true as instinct itself a true mirror of the folk manner."[50] Film critic Gary Null saw something different. According to Null, "Stepin Fetchit led the songs and played the very incarnation of the irresponsible nigger who knew his place, loved his master, and just grinned for joy every time his laziness was rewarded by a kick in the pants."[51] The fact that Locke's judgment of the representation of black folk culture in this film is contested in almost the same terms as his own criticism of Hurston shows, I think, that his attempt to ground his critique of minstrelsy on aesthetic principles was inadequate. The disagreement betweeen Locke and Null indicates that what Locke considered genuine portraiture is sometimes viewed by others as caricature. Locke's aesthetic criteria for identifying genuine portraiture failed to render it distinguishable from caricature. In what follows, I will argue that this failure is due to the highly politicized nature of black vernacular representation.

The Paradox of Minstrelsy

Despite Locke's desire to use wholly aesthetic criteria to distinguish between racist and non-racist white authors who wrote in the folk-dialectal tradition, he invariably made reference to their *intentions*. Saunders Redding followed Locke's rationale regarding this distinction, showing even more concern with the political motivation of white authors who used black dialect. In a manner that echoed Locke's commitment to genuine folk representation, Redding championed a view of integrity and honest exploration of the black experience. Much more than Locke, however, he viewed the folk-dialectal tradition as a manifestation of Washington's accommodationist ideology, which perpetuated the image of the contented ex-slave and supported the views of white apologists for segregation.[52] For this decidedly political reason Redding's view quickly shifted from a criticism of individual practitioners of the folk dialectal tradition to a rejection of the dialectal genre entirely, whereas Locke saw in the genre the aesthetic possibility of a transformation of folk expression into high art. Hence, Redding dismissed Dunbar's dialect poetry while Locke saw worthier elements in it.

Does the intentionality criterion invoked by Locke and Redding against white authors who wrote in black dialect apply to black authors as well, and to what extent? Interestingly, Redding was critical of Dunbar's dialectal poetry, but not of Dunbar. He acknowledged that Dunbar was urged by his sponsor, William Dean Howell, to write in dialect against his wishes.[53] Dunbar was against writing in dialect because he understood that his dialectal poetry functioned socially to reinforce the stereotype of illiterate blacks who lack the intellectual capacity to use language properly. Redding tells us,

Thus a Negro character, like Black Samson of Brandywine, could be ever so heroic and noble so long as he "talked nigger" and was ignorant of what nobility meant. Thus, too, the loftiest precepts could fall from the lips of a black woman, so long as she was in the white folk's kitchen and spoke her maxims in dialect. This was incongruous, like a monkey with table manners, and just as amusing, and therefore, so far as whites were concerned, permissible.[54]

To the extent that Dunbar produced dialectal poetry under social pressure, his cultural malpractice can be excused on the intentionalist ground that he wrote in dialect against his will.

There is no reason to suppose, however, that an appeal to Redding's intentionalist criterion can always succeed in distinguishing between representations of folk dialect by black and white authors. Redding supported his malpractice charge against Dunbar by comparing Dunbar's representation of black dialect with that of his African-American predecessor, James Edwin Campbell. He concluded that "Paul Dunbar's dialect is a bastard form, modeled closer upon James Whitcomb Riley's colloquial language than upon the speech it was supposed to represent. Campbell's ear alone dictated his language. Dunbar's five senses (as they should) controlled his."[55] Even in the absence of overt social pressure, as in the case of Robeson's invented dialect, a black-authored representation of folk dialect can sometimes voluntarily display the oppressive aspects of a racist white author.

Although minstrelsy always carries the burden of proof, from the standpoint of black audiences, there is sometimes disagreement about whether to count it as a misrepresentation of vernacular culture. In some instances, where audience reactions are divided along class lines, the charge of cultural malpractice is grounded on a judgment about the representation's underlying political ideology. Cinematic representations provided by minstrel characters from television programs such as *Amos "n" Andy* or *In Living Color* can project ambiguous images that suggest at once both accommodation and resistance. By signifying on themselves, these characters will sometimes elicit a favorable response from an appreciative segment of the black audience.[56] The audience split arises from the perception by a dissenting segment that a social critique employing certain images can function as another form of minstrelsy, despite any element of resistance it sometimes ambiguously may express.

To speak of a given minstrel performance, or work, as constituting or expressing resistance is to make an implicit appeal to some intentionalist criterion. For how do we know whether a particular instance of minstrelsy should count as resistance unless we also know the intention of the author or performer? The use of dialect itself does not signal this, given that some representations of black vernacular culture aim to empower oppressed black people while others aim to perpetuate their oppression. The paradoxical nature of minstrelsy derives from its dual social function as well as from the fact that minstrel behavior alone is an inadequate sign of the

agent's intention. Subversive elements often entered the performances of black minstrels.[57] On what basis, however, can we attribute an act of resistance to a minstrel's performance given that, to
succeed, the behavior has to be sufficiently ambiguous for the subversive intent to go unnoticed?

A similar consideration applies to the question of whether
Dunbar's dialect poetry was minstrelsy. The underlying presupposition of this question is that minstrelsy is by its very nature
accommodationist and therefore always stands in juxtaposition
with more oppositional acts of resistance.[58] This presupposition can
be challenged, however, when we take into account the manner
in which minstrelsy can be employed to resist racial oppression.
Some interpreters of Dunbar, for instance, take his use of dialect
to implicate him as a plantation apologist, whereas others maintain that his use of dialect was a subversive means of raising black
consciousness.[59] What must be acknowledged by proponents of the
view that Dunbar's dialect was, as it were, a mask is that once this
guise was adopted it may have functioned as accommodationism,
despite Dunbar's intent to use it for subversive purposes.

There is not much disagreement about whether the use of
blackface, whether for derogatory purposes or not, is inherently
offensive to a majority of black people. In the minds of most black
spectators, however, dialect can range from closely representative
to crudely manufactured. Even among scholars, there does not
seem to be a settled view of whether the various forms of dialect
used in minstrelsy were historically accurate representations of black
speech patterns. Dillard, for instance, claims "Everyone knows
that the minstrel shows used phony dialect, although some of the
earlier ones might have been more nearly accurate."[60] Mahar is
less reserved in his claim that "The discovery of common characteristics in blackface song and black English shows that there was
much truth to the contention that the early minstrels borrowed from
black culture."[61] What exactly did the early minstrels "borrow" from
black culture? To understand this disagreement as only a debate
about whether certain speech patterns have been accurately represented, I think, is to overlook the political-economic role of white
intervention.

Consider, for instance, ex-Los Angeles Police Chief, Daryl Gates's
response to a statement that his new video game, *Police Quest: Open*

Season, might be viewed as racist, given the Amos 'n' Andy-style dialect of the game's black suspects. Gates pointed out that he was against using some of the dialogue written by Tammy Dargan, a former segment producer for *America's Most Wanted*. According to Gates, "I told [Dargan] that these people use the same language that you and I use. A lot of that was changed. It's not intended to offend anyone."[62] Apparently, Dargan won out and much of the potentially offensive dialect remained. Dargan justified keeping it in by claiming that it was "inspired" by Fab 5 Freddy's record, *Fresh Fly Flavor*. What if, however, we were to view the dialect used by Fab 5 Freddy as only an adopted dialect, a mask used for signifying, or even for theatrical purposes. This has been an option for many rap artists seeking to profit from the large white audience demand for the latest, most controversial, rap records. Gates's video game responds to a strong market incentive to exploit mass-media constructions of hip-hop culture as a criminal underclass.[63] Dargan's decision to use a black dialect to represent black people appears somewhat pernicious in the context of Gates having insisted that blacks and whites use the same language.

Dargan's appropriation of Fab 5 Freddy's dialect for minstrel purposes shows the difficulty that underlies the question of whether Dunbar's dialectal poetry was minstrelsy. To provide an answer we must first determine for whom the dialect was written. Because so much of Dunbar's dialectal poetry was heavily influenced by the plantation tradition, even when he employed it as a subversive mode of resistance, it ran the risk of being interpreted as accommodationist.[64] We know from his public testimony that Dunbar preferred not to write in dialect.[65] Moreover, his protest literature makes clear that he was not entirely an accommodationist.[66] But to resolve the ambiguity of Dunbar's dialectal poetry on the side of resistance by appealing to various documentations of his nonaccommodationist political ideology is to choose to treat his protest literature as a better indication of his real aims.[67] The debate about whether Dunbar's dialectal poetry was a form of minstrelsy indicates quite clearly that each poem has to be judged separately. Given that Dunbar's dialectal poetry exemplifies the ambiguity of the minstrel, Locke's endorsement of it as a form of race-conscious literature was tantamount to an endorsement of minstrelsy.

The Aesthetic of Cultural Resistance

What about Dunbar's lyric poetry written in conventional English? Because Dunbar preferred to write in standard English, it seems odd to consider his nondialect verse to be a less "authentic" form of African-American cultural expression than his dialectal poetry. "Authentic" cultural expression means here a genuine dialect spoken by black people on the plantations. Dunbar's dialect was not genuine in this sense. But, given the political thrust of Dunbar's appropriation of white-authored literary black dialect, perhaps his political orientation was on a par with the dialectal form of expression for which he was known. Insofar as Dunbar's poetry written in conventional English aimed to express the true sentiments and aspirations of African Americans, whether or not he employed dialect as a sign of blackness seems irrelevant.[68]

Consider, for instance, slave narratives written by African Americans in standard English. By comparison with those written in dialect, they offer another paradigm of African-American cultural resistance. House slaves were enabled by their class position within the social system of slavery to acquire the skills by which to document their aspirations. In the narratives of Harriet Jacobs and Frederick Douglass, many of the ideas expressed, as well as their general style of expression, were thoroughly Eurocentric. Douglass's discussion of his consciousness as a slave, his references to the natural rights of slaves, as well as the structure of the narrative itself is closer to an Anglo-American tradition in literature, distinguished only by the fact that the author is a black person.[69] In a very similar fashion, Jacobs patterned her narrative after the sentimental Victorian novel. Both works, nonetheless, constitute a form of cultural resistance to slavery by African Americans.

There seems to be something both correct and misleading about the reference to these narratives as a form of African-American cultural resistance. Given their Eurocentric mode of expression, they do not represent what is commonly understood to be a distinctive idiom of African-American culture. If, however, African-American-authored slave narratives played an important consciousness-raising role in the abolitionist movement, the political agenda of the authors seems sufficient to alleviate the concern about the status of their narratives as a form of cultural resistance. This worry seems to derive from the misguided idea that cultural assimilation and cultural resistance are contrary notions. Jacobs and Douglass represent highly assimilated African Americans who employed their acculturated status to engage in resistance to slavery. Although their narratives constituted a form of cultural resistance by African Americans, they do not count as an African-American form of cultural expression where this implies some unique form of expression.

Spirituals and coded sermons presented in the social context of the slave's religious practices are often touted as unique forms of African-American cultural resistance.[70] The Harlem-based negritude movement, spearheaded by Locke, is also sometimes taken to be a form of African-American cultural resistance because of its appropriation of the black southern folk traditions, some of which already had been transplanted to the north.[71] The use of dialect by Zora Neale Hurston and Langston Hughes aimed to capture in literary fashion a distinctive feature of the African-American oral tradition. Dialect earmarks a distinctive aspect of African-American culture by representing an African linguistic component that has been syncretized, along with other mainstream elements, into African-American cultural practices.[72] Spirituals, sermons, and literature written in dialect are held to be forms of cultural expression that are distinctly African American because they contain elements of African-American culture (namely, transformed retentions) that are distinguishable from the Eurocentric mainstream.

This notion of a unique form of African-American cultural expression fits the prevailing characterization of rap music as a distinctly African-American cultural practice whose roots can be traced to the oral and music-making traditions of West Africa.[73] By contrast with slave narratives written in standard English, rap music provides a paradigm of African-American cultural resistance involving transformed African retentions. For obvious political reasons, cultural resistance cannot always be overtly oppositional. In the nineteenth century the sentimentalist dialectal tradition was overtly racist, hence, many black writers were politically motivated to eschew it as a form of cultural expression. To the extent that the aim of Dunbar's appropriation of black dialect was to foster group consciousness among black people and institute a race tradition in literature, we can allow a subversive reading of his works. A similar line of argument can be applied to various forms of twentieth-century minstrelsy. The era of legal segregation provided the social context for the legal battle waged by the NAACP to ban the television version of *Amos 'n' Andy*.[74] Ironically, in the racial climate of post-desegregation, black urban youth has appropriated a black dialect as an overtly oppositional form of cultural expression. The sign of blackness used in an earlier era by mass media to rationalize the oppression of African Americans, when appropriated and incorporated into hip-hop culture, implies a form of collective resistance to the cultural hegemony sustained by mass media.

Unlike slave narratives that were authored by a single person, rap music involves the joint activity of a group of artists. The fact that rap music-making is a shared cooperative activity, however, does not mean that it can be taken as a whole to be a form of cultural resistance. To do so would be to treat a cultural practice that ranges over twenty years as though it were a single collective act. The creation of conventions regarding the use of various idioms including dress, dance, and posturing involve activity that rap artists as a group have engaged in over a certain period of time. Although the making of records by various rap artists throughout the history of rap music involves a series of specific collective acts, such acts are a part of the shared cooperative activity constituting a musical tradition. The cultural practice established by many groups of rap artists over a long period which constitute a hip-hop tradition can be distinguished from a collective act of a particular group at any given time during this period. This distinction is important if we are to remain clear about which specific performances or recordings should count as resistance and which should not.

A similar distinction has been made within hip-hop culture itself between so-called "hardcore" rap and "commercial" rap. Hardcore rap is sometimes viewed as more "authentic" in the sense that it emanates directly from the streets and does not disguise, or "sell out," its messages to increase record sales. Commercial rap is supposed to be less "authentic" in the sense that it eschews the politics of opposition expressed so frequently in hardcore rap and, instead, attempts to be more appealing to a mainstream audience. This distinction has proven to be somewhat untenable given that hardcore artists such as Snoop Dog, Ice Cube, Ezy-E, Niggaz With Attitude, and Naughty by Nature have had phenomenal record sales. Politics accounts for the distinction between the lyrical content of hard-core and commercial rap. Hence, hardcore rap tunes deliver messages of a gritty reality, sometimes even revolution, and thereby embody acts of resistance when performed or played. Commercial rap tunes emphasize style over substance to avoid such messages in an effort to gain a wider appeal with mainstream audiences. A rap tune's status as resistance turns on whether the intention of the artist is to communicate a political ideology that addresses issues of concern to black urban youth.[75]

What about some of the messages in hardcore rap that seem to denounce politics? Ezy-E, a member of the gangsta rap group, Niggaz With Attitude, has been quoted as having made the statement "Fuck that black power shit: we don't give a fuck. Free South Africa: we don't give a fuck," with reference to tunes by politically motivated artists from the Afrocentric school.[76] The group's producer, Dr. Dre, elaborated by pointing out that he valued being crazy more than he valued being political. Bev Francis, the host of *Our Voice*, a talk show on Black Entertainment Television, expressed a black middle-class concern with some of the lyrics in hardcore rap. She asked her two women guests from the rap group, Bytches With Problems, about the potentially destructive influence of their music on black youth. Francis was concerned with the rap group's embracing of, and communicating, nihilistic values that, when internalized by black youth, might exacerbate the violence that plagues black communities. This concern indicates, whether we share it or not, that the idea that hardcore rap music is a form of cultural resistance stands in need of further examination.

Whether groups such as BWP and NWA are engaged in an oppositional form of cultural resistance can be ascertained by considering more generally the target of resistance in hardcore gangsta rap. There seem to be several: the black nationalist focus on Africa by politically minded rappers (rather than a greater focus on the local situation of African Americans), the government's role in the international drug trade, the racist hypocrisy of capitalism, the success of the black middle class, and the problem of police brutality. The recent controversy, resulting from black women and black political and religious organizations publicly protesting the mass marketing of the violence and pornography in hardcore gangsta rap, has shifted the media's overriding focus to gender issues.[77] Because a critique of global capitalism sometimes may be given by the same artist who also performs tunes that are extremely misogynistic, each tune must stand on its own, rendering it extremely difficult to ascertain the political significance of a gangsta rap artist.

Matters are made even more difficult by the fact that the aesthetic qualities of a rap tune can sometimes overshadow the politics it displays. When asked what he thought of the latest album by NWA (*Niggaz 4 Life*), former group member Ice Cube responded by pointing out that it was not well conceived from the standpoint of its political message. He added, however, that he thought "[t]heir production is dope."[78] This expression metaphorically captures the problem of musical technique dominating political content and reveals the difficulty that the aesthetic aspects of rap music poses for ascertaining elements of resistance. Many progressive people enjoy dancing to rap music. Are young women "hypocritics," for instance, when they denounce the misogyny in the lyrical content of a hardcore rap tune while deriving pleasure from its other musical qualities? How are we to understand this phenomenon of progressive people enjoying music they would otherwise find objectionable for political reasons? The key to resolving this puzzle is to understand an important implication of the claim that the production is dope, namely, that the music has the aesthetic power to cause pleasure, perhaps even against the wishes of the listener.

This suggestion about rap music's aesthetic appeal also accounts for a related phenomenon that the premier political rap group Public Enemy has the status of being the favorite rap group in racist white communities such as South Boston and Bensonhurst. The truth contained in Ice Cube's remark is that rap messages need not be the only reason certain audiences listen to rap music. The aesthetic qualities of the music can be an overriding factor. He points out that "[t]o white kids rap ain't nothing but a form of entertainment, for blacks it's a strategy on how to manoeuvre through life."[79] How then do we assess rap music as a form of cultural resistance when the mediating role of its aesthetic characteristics can sometimes guide us away from political messages we might want to endorse or condemn?

The Political Ambiguity of Bad Nigga Narratives

Some commentators have argued that we should view the practice of making rap music in relation to the record industry.[80] By sampling, scratching, and remixing recorded music, rap artists are engaged in a political struggle with the commercial culture industries that control the production of African-American music. The difficulty with this line of thought is that the recording industry seems to have accommodated the production of rap music with very little difficulty. Even the so-called underground channels for rap music have been incorporated into a distribution network that permits the calibration of record sales.[81] With the commercializing of gangsta rap we can no longer speak in a totalizing manner of rap music as a form of cultural resistance. Instead, this designation must be reserved for specific rap tunes.

The denial of values that prevades the worldview presented by gangsta rappers has sometimes perplexed commentators who view rap as a form of cultural resistance.[82] At other times this amoral lapse in gangsta rap is taken to be only a certain phase in hip-hop culture's evolution towards becoming a genuine social movement.[83] The Afrocentric values in New York-centered hardcore rap represent elements of cultural resistance that promote a political agenda consistent with a legacy of black political struggle dating from early nineteenth-century slave revolts and abolitionism to the more recent civil rights movement and urban riots. The emergence of a nihilistic school of Los Angeles-centered gangsta rappers represents a break with this tradition, an unparalleled rupture that is to be understood in terms of the social conditions that fostered it.

The nihilism expressed in gangsta rap music is deceptive. A much-celebrated element of resistance in gangsta rap, for instance, is the appropriation of the term "nigga." Gangsta rappers have effectively recoded the social meaning of this term. In public discourse its use is a social taboo, although what the term connotes is reiterated on daily newscasts of crime and violence. On the news program, *Nightline*, Ice T, a popular gangsta rapper, engaged in a long-drawn-out debate with Harvard professor, Alvin Poussaint, about whether the use of the term "nigger" by any group of black people, even among themselves, is always self-denigrating.[84] Finally, Ice T drove home the point of his disagreement by capping on Poussaint's view with the signifying expression, "Nigga, please"! Poussaint's self-hatred account of the black vernacular use of the term "nigger" was challenged by Ice T's *demonstration* of its appropriateness as a term of defiance. When used in black vernacular culture such a reversal of meaning allows this term to function as a source of pride rather than denigration.[85]

Poussaint, of course, was also concerned that, although the appropriation of the term "nigger" by gangsta rappers aims to recode its racist meaning, there remains a question of whether such an appropriation can change the racist connotation, or whether it serves instead only to reinforce a negative image of African Americans. This concern, however, tends to ignore the social significance of the term's newly acquired meaning. The appropriated use by gangsta rappers adds an ambiguity that shifts, depending on whether the term is used in a white racist discourse or whether it is constructed as an idiom of a resistive mode of African-American cultural expression. To capture the class consciousness of a distinctly black male lumpenproletariat, gangsta rappers revised the spelling of the racist version of the term "nigger" to the vernacular version, "nigga." The vernacular version permits a distinction to be made between black urban youth who constitute a so-called "black underclass" and other black middle-class professionals. Poussaint's analysis failed to acknowledge that gangsta rappers such as Ice T have been extremely outspoken about their belief that some African Americans in positions of institutional authority are responsible for perpetuating the plight of the black urban poor. The appropriation and respelling of the term "nigga" by gangsta rappers displays resistance by embracing and rejecting the social meaning of this term. NWA's top-selling *Niggaz 4 Life* was spelled backwards on the record cover to avoid censorship. This maneuver succeeded in subverting, by means of a socially transgressive black idiom, the taboo Poussaint defends.

A political distinction remains between hardcore and non-hardcore rap music, despite the commercial success of gangsta rap. The fury over Ice T's "Cop Killer" tune reflected the cultural politics governing the relationship between rap-music production and the record industry. Although Ice T "voluntarily" withdrew his album *Body Count* from distribution, the incident called to attention the constitutional ground of free speech. The subsequent suppression of rap music by corporate decision-makers has been justified by their judgment of whether the lyrical content is socially harmful. The economic factor also seems to have been of some importance to Ice T and Time-Warner, a sure indication that profit was the bottom line for their "agreement" to renege on the First Amendment. Ice T's capitulation to the record industry's economic pressure contrasts sharply with the "no sellout" aspect of his bad nigga persona.[86]

The fact that Ice T aimed for a white youth audience with a heavy metal album that contained socially transgressive lyrics regarding interracial sex and retaliatory violence against racial bigots was, no doubt, a factor contributing to the corporate pressure to suppress "Cop Killer." But, once we acknowledge that some of the controversies surrounding hip-hop personalities frequently serve to increase the market value of their records, it is difficult to ignore the question of whether the bad nigga persona adopted by gangsta rappers is mostly an exaggerated defiance feigned for commercial purposes. When gangsta rap is viewed in its political-economic context, it displays an ambiguous mock nihilism that parallels the ambiguous accommodationism displayed in subversive forms of minstrelsy.[87]

One important consequence of the transnational commodification of hip-hop culture is that it made possible the introduction of an ambiguous meaning of the term "nigga" into a global context. Alain Locke's claim that "the Negro's primitivism is nine-tenths that of the peasant the world over" is borne out by the international appeal of rap music. There is reason to believe that its widespread appeal is due to more than just the music. Even cross-culturally the political ideology expressed in some of the bad nigga narratives that dominate gangsta rap's lyrical content are often perceived to contribute to an emancipatory political agenda.[88] Within the local context of black urban youth, however, the gangsta rapper's appropriation of the term "nigga" as a source of pride rather than degradation resonates with a tradition of black urban folklore in which the counterpart to the gangsta rapper's "real nigga" is the "bad nigger" who personifies defiance, brutality, and ruthlessness.[89] The corporate suppression of Ice T's "Cop Killer" was an acknowledgment that, by exceeding the social limits of gangsta rap's bad nigga, this tune had disrupted the music industry's transnational system of commodification.[90]

There is an aesthetic dimension to this disruption that is of equal political significance. Locke's praise for Richard Wright's "Zolaesque" style of social realism in *Native Son* shows Locke's willingness, by the early 1940s, to allow a notion of the urban proletariat in place of the rural peasant as the subject of black literature and art. It also indicates the extent to which he continued to place a greater value on aesthetics. Although, in his review of *Native Son*, Locke quotes a crucial passage from Wright's essay, "How Bigger Was Born," he failed to appreciate the fact that Bigger Thomas was conceived by Wright as a "bad nigga," a character Wright intended to be aesthetically displeasing.[91] In the passage Locke quotes, Wright claims that Bigger Thomas was capable of becoming either communist or fascist, but was neither. According to Wright, "But, granting the emotional state, the tensity, the fear, the hate, the impatience, the sense of exclusion, the ache for violent action, the emotional and cultural hunger, Bigger Thomas, conditioned as his organism is, will not become an ardent, or even a lukewarm, supporter of the status quo."[92] Locke completely disregarded Wright's stated aim to write a book that no banker's daughter could weep over. His criticism of *Native Son* urged a more romantic tragedy in the face of Wright's explicit rejection of that. With regard to Locke's proposal to elevate black folk expression to high art, it was held in abeyance by Wright's construction of Bigger Thomas as a "bad nigger" who unromantically profanes mainstream values.

Locke's frequent references to Emile Zola indicate his strong commitment to a nineteenth-century European standard for judging the aesthetic merit of black social realist literature.[93] He believed that the portrayals of black urban existence by social realists, such as Wright, were aesthetically limited due to their preoccupation with sociology and psychoanalysis. When Locke's concern with aesthetic pleasure is applied to gangsta rap it has an interesting political twist, for Wright's appropriation of the bad nigga figure from black urban folklore was in keeping with Locke's urging of black writers to return to folk culture as a source for artistic self-expression. In a manner similar to Wright's Marxist framing of the nihilism represented by Bigger Thomas, the gangsta rapper's image of the bad nigga is often employed for political purposes. The point of Locke's critique of minstrelsy was that it was not a form of genuine folk expression that was representative of the true sentiments of the southern black peasant. This critique was consistent with his objection to Wright because he considered both to be distortions of authentic folk expression. It seems that, as in the case of Hurston, Locke is committed to endorsing the use of bad nigga narratives by authors, or artists, who aim solely to produce aesthetic pleasure.

The political ambiguity of bad nigga narratives in gangsta rap arises from the fact that the nihilism represented is only a mask employed by various rappers for political and for commercial purposes.[94] For this reason we must be wary of equating all of the gangsta rap music offered under the rubric of cultural resistance simply because of the nihilism expressed. As an oppositional form of cultural expression, gangsta rap music is constituted by inherently resistive elements. But how does this aspect of the aesthetic of gangsta rap fit with the fact that not every tune aims to engage in resistance? The political use of a form of cultural expression does not rule out other uses. The mock nihilism in gangsta rap music is an inherently resistive element that also has been a key element in its commercial exploitation. The choice of title for MC Ren's album *Kiss My Black AZZ*, shows the extent to which, as a resistive element, the representation of nihilism in gangsta rap has been commodified.[95] The aim of MC Ren's version of the bad nigga seems to have been to provide aesthetic pleasure for a thrill-seeking audience. Commodification of gangsta rap's bad nigga idiom leaves unclear how the concept of resistance can provide a basis for a distinction between tunes that are political and those that are commercial.

Jon Michael Spencer appeals to a well-known distinction between various genres of black folklore to provide a ground on which to condemn the nihilism in gangsta rap. Spencer claims "the black community knows how to tell the difference between the 'bad nigger' and the heroic badman."[96] Following John Roberts, he maintains that, unlike the badman, the "bad nigger" is motivated by a narcissistic hedonism that is genocidal and threatens the safety and moral stability of the black community. For this reason, the "bad nigger" is never viewed as a hero by the black community. This claim does not appear to be well grounded given that some gangsta rappers who have adopted this guise are quite popular with black audiences.[97] Roberts and Spencer have failed to realize that, under the influence of mass media, their highly questionable distinction between the badman and the "bad nigger" lapses into a troublesome

conflation given that both are sometimes represented indiscrimin-
ately as violent criminals. We can notice this conflation, for example,
in the film *Trespass*. The heroic badman is Ice T, portraying a gang
leader who considers himself a responsible businessman, while
the sociopathic "bad nigger" is Ice Cube, portraying an impetuous
gangbanger who values nothing but ruthless violence. In accordance
with the film's existentialist theme, both die violently as black criminals in the end.

The conflation of the figures of the moralistic badman and the
amoral "bad nigger" into a composite image of the violent black
criminal occurs in the context of mass media's politicizing of the
image of the "bad nigger." By appropriating the term "nigga" and
recoding its social meaning, gangsta rappers have imbued mass
media's criminal image of black urban youth with a political ambiguity akin to all the subversive nuances of the minstrel's Sambo
image. What clearly distinguishes Ice Cube's use of bad nigga
narratives from their use by other gangsta rappers, such as Ezy-E,
is his well-known intention to promote a political agenda. The
gangsta idiom nonetheless remains the same in both cases. In the
case of Ezy-E, this idiom facilitates an accommodationist ideology
that appears as a form of cultural resistance. Because the bad nigga
idiom encompasses Ezy-E's amoral "I don't give a fuck"! attitude,
as well as Ice Cube's strongly felt nationalist desire, resolving the
political ambiguity of bad nigga narratives in gangsta rap music trades
on a judgment regarding the intention of the artist.

The black cultural norm that justifies a suspicion of the intention of a white author, or artist, when a racist material image, such
as the black criminal stereotype, is employed rests on the underlying assumption that, in a racist social context, this image will serve
to perpetuate racism. But what distinguishes a black author's or
artist's employment of a similar image? The cultural malpractice
charge raises a similar suspicion regarding the intention of a black
author, or artist. In unclear cases involving subversive strategies,
the audience orientation of the author or artist is paramount.
With regard to concerns about the social harmfulness of gangsta
rap, there is no need to deny that the black criminal image may
very well reproduce, accommodate, or perpetuate a racist ideology
among some white audiences. For this concern does not outweigh
the consideration that, at the same time, its recoded ideology

can be emancipatory for some black audiences. Ice Cube's album *The Predator*, provides a politically conscious gangsta rapper's interpretation of the 1992 uprising in Los Angeles.[98] Similarly, Da Lench Mob's album, *Guerrillas in the Mist*, appropriated the racist police image of black people as gorillas to provide a view of the Los Angeles rebellion as guerilla warfare. It seems undeniable that, by articulating an ideological frame for urban rebellion, gangsta rap music such as this has moved the hip-hop generation toward social action.

Chapter 7

Marooned in America: Black Urban Youth Culture and Social Pathology

In his mid-1960s' study of the plight of the black family Daniel Moynihan drew the rather untoward conclusion that,

It would be troubling indeed to learn that until several years ago employment opportunity made a great deal of difference in the rate of Negro dependency and family disorganization, but that the situation has so deteriorated that the problem is now feeding on itself – that measures which once would have worked will henceforth not work so well, or work at all.[1]

Although Moynihan's speculation emerged from a liberal perspective, ironically, his pessimistic concern has since become a cornerstone of the neoconservative opposition to liberal-sponsored government intervention on behalf of black urban poor people.[2] It is with this realization in mind that William J. Wilson's recent discussion of the problems faced by the black urban poor has attempted to salvage liberal public policy from this hoisting by its own petards.[3] In keeping with Moynihan's rather bleak assessment, neoconservatives have employed a culture-of-poverty thesis according to which the black urban poor are conceived of as an isolated group of individuals whose behavior is aberrant and dominated by pathological cultural values. Although on Wilson's account so-called "ghetto" culture is to be viewed as a by-product of socioeconomic conditions in extreme-poverty neighborhoods, his rejoinder to the neoconservative culture-of-poverty thesis offers no criticism of their view of black culture. Instead, he maintains that changes in the oft-cited destructive aspects of so-called "ghetto" culture can be brought about by addressing more fundamental economic problems.

Wilson rightly wants to connect policies designed to ameliorate the problems of the black urban poor with policies that address broader issues of socioeconomic organization, but it is unfortunate that he needlessly acquiesces to the neoconservative contention that the culture of black urban poor people is pathological.[4] I want to call into question the claim that the culture of black urban poor people is pathological, and as such, is somehow responsible for the perpetuation of their plight. Unlike his neoconservative detractors, Wilson is less inclined to draw this conclusion; nonetheless, many of his remarks about the Moynihanian tangle of pathology lend credence to their viewpoint and, further, suggest that he has not given sufficient attention to the conceptual scheme embedded in the expressive culture of black urban poor people.[5] I aim to rectify this shortcoming in Wilson's account to some extent by examining the social and political orientation of the popular culture of black urban youth.

Debates about the so-called black underclass typically presuppose the legitimacy of the American capitalist social order, and employ the notion of a pathological black "underclass" culture to reiterate the hegemony of the dominant group's one-way assimilationist ideology.[6] I present an analysis of the social and political consciousness reflected in the music and practices of rap artists and their audiences to show that some of these cultural manifestations fit into a system of meanings around which political action and struggle can be organized. On the basis of criteria that indicate the manner in which certain cultural practices of black urban youth attempt to valorize notions of affirmation and resistance, a distinction can be drawn between the pathological social conditions under which the black urban poor live and the culture they have created to help cope with those conditions. I will argue that, contrary to the prevailing image of black urban youth as pathological, black popular culture is understandably in many ways a recoding of various elements of mainstream culture that have been adapted to fit the circumstances of extreme-poverty urban neighborhoods.

The Elevation of Black People

Wilson's rather narrow focus on the social conditions of the black urban poor since the mid-1960s is undoubtedly motivated by his polemic with neoconservatives. As Moynihan's successor, he is concerned primarily with explanations of the recent "deterioration" of socioeconomic conditions in extreme-poverty neighborhoods at a time of increased government-funded poverty programs and civil rights legislation. Of course, this limited concern justifies his use of the term "underclass" so as to only remotely connect the problem of jobless black urban youth in the 1980s with the fact that large numbers of unemployed black people have never been fully absorbed into the labor force since emancipation from slavery.[7] But if the term "underclass" is meant to refer to the group of black people who have been permanently on the fringe of the job market, the question of what to do about their plight simply cannot be limited to the scope of Wilson's study. In fact, this question has long been a major preoccupation in black social thought.

In the nineteenth century there were several, quite different, ideologies about how best to address the socioeconomic plight of black people. I will refer to these views categorically as race-uplift theory because, despite their differences, in every case advocates were chiefly concerned with the elevation of black people as a group. Interestingly, some of the most influential notions of race uplift involved various suggestions regarding the role of culture. I want to note a competing tendency either to reject or to affirm the intrinsic worth of African-American culture in several versions of race-uplift theory.

The prominence of a bootstrap version of race-uplift theory in nineteenth-century black political thought is hardly surprising, given its appropriateness as a theory of social change well suited to meet the needs of a large group of ex-slaves. What is surprising, however, is the persistence of this notion into the late twentieth century.[8] Perhaps, as I shall suggest, this is because the conditions to which race-uplift theory initially applied have also persisted. Whatever the reason for the notion's longevity, I shall question the account its recent neoconservative advocates want to offer for its relative inefficaciousness as a theory of social change.

When Martin Delany wrote about the elevation of black people in the mid-1800s, he proposed emigration as the best option.[9] He spoke of black people escaping class oppression in America by finding a place that would permit their socioeconomic development. Edward Blyden added to Delany's argument for emigration the idea of slavery being a manifestation of divine Providence.[10] Unlike Delany, who was not especially committed to any particular place, Blyden emphasized a missionary role for black Americans in Africa. Through enslavement Africans would become Westernized, and through recolonization they would be returned to their homeland to impart this newly acquired culture to their African brethren. According to Blyden, slavery was to be viewed as part of God's plan to civilize Africa. Although Delany and Blyden shared a similar nationalistic diaspora consciousness regarding the fate and destiny of black Americans as a group, Blyden wanted black Americans to work to elevate Africans, whereas Delany, with little emphasis on culture, wanted to find a place where conditions would permit the elevation of black Americans. Despite their ideological differences with regard to culture, for Delany and Blyden, the notion of elevation meant, for the most part, escape from the socioeconomic conditions under which black people were oppressed in America.

Blyden's talk of a civilizing mission for black Americans in Africa seems to presuppose that African culture was less valuable than that which had been acquired by slaves in America.[11] This conception of the positive influence of Western culture on African slaves can appear a bit odd when we consider that Frederick Douglass was much more deeply concerned with the deleterious effects of slavery than with its alleged benefits. He believed that, through its dehumanizing effects, slavery destroyed black people's sense of self-worth and dignity, and that, once slavery ended, a period of rehabilitation would be required to rectify this. Needless to say, Douglass wholeheartedly believed that assimilation into the American mainstream would someday be possible once black people were educated and allowed to demonstrate their social equality with whites. Consequently, he vigorously opposed emigration as a policy for elevating black people because he saw ex-slaves as Americans. For Douglass, then, the notion of elevation meant the acculturation of black people into the American mainstream.[12]

What about the fact that the legal segregation which followed slavery would prevent the mass acculturation of black people? Faced with this question, Douglass's assimilationist view found a new expression in the philosophy of Booker T. Washington. Assimilationism required a strategy for changing the socioeconomic conditions of black people. By appealing to the self-interest of whites, Washington advocated economic development as a key to the elevation of black people as a group.[13] Unlike Douglass, he believed (or, at least, preached) that social equality was not a priority and that black people should not demand it. Rather, it would come eventually with the economic progress of the group.[14]

Washington's emphasis on group economic development as a means by which to achieve social equality provides the classic formulation of the bootstrap version of race-uplift theory. His strategy involved the incremental transformation of the black southern peasantry into a working class that, several generations later, would be superseded by a group of entrepreneurs who would comprise a full-fledged middle class ready for assimilation.[15] Although Washington was well known for his commitment to political accommodationism, the most interesting aspect of his bootstrap social philosophy was the role he assigned to the working class in the process of elevating the group. By following his dictum, "Cast down your bucket where you are," the black middle class would develop from that segment of the working class who managed to gain a foothold in the economy. Hence, Washington's political accommodationism was a social philosophy that reiterated the ideals of the American class system.[16]

W. E. B. Du Bois placed a greater emphasis on the cultural status of black people. He argued against "a servile imitation of Anglo-Saxon culture" on the ground that black people have a unique cultural contribution to make and that to accomplish this they must not assimilate.[17] Hence, for Du Bois, social equality would be achieved through the distinctive cultural achievements of black people. When Alain Locke appropriated the concept of the New Negro in the 1920s, and spearheaded the Negro Renaissance Movement in Harlem, he seems to have followed through on the Du Boisian agenda of developing a talented tenth to produce a black American culture that would be on par with European cultures. For Locke, this meant that the southern black folk culture, which was brought to northern urban centers at the turn of the century, would be rehabilitated and transformed by a vanguard group of artists who would give it expression in higher art forms.[18]

Paradoxically, Locke's New Negro would emerge as an assimilated black person who proudly displayed the southern folk heritage of black people.[19]

In race-uplift theory, the idea of social equality is quite ambiguous with regard to whether black people ought to pursue a path of maintaining a distinct culture, or whether they ought to acculturate into the mainstream. But, even when assimilationism is rejected, the theory often assumes that black American culture figures into elevating the race only as something that itself has to be elevated.

The Black Middle Class's Obligation to Contribute to Group Progress

Many of the turn-of-the-century black writers I have mentioned argued that black people have a duty to perpetuate black culture, albeit face-lifted to meet European standards. Their arguments aimed largely to sustain the moral imperative of race uplift, namely that all black Americans are under some (perhaps different) obligation to endeavor to elevate the group. This special obligation derives from sharing a cultural heritage. The specific nature of this obligation depends, of course, on what it means to speak of "elevating" the group, but also on what it means to speak of preserving one's culture.

Although they can be clearly distinguished, there is a tandem relationship between the duty to perpetuate black culture and the duty to seek to elevate the group. For instance, when black writers such as Frances Ellen Watkins Harper and Pauline Elizabeth Hopkins employed their literary output in the service of race uplift, their focus was primarily on the obligation of a certain group of black people, namely mulattoes, to refrain from marrying whites, or passing, and instead to devote themselves to the betterment of the masses of black people.[20] In this case, there was a special duty requiring a sacrifice of social privilege by some members of the group in order to devote themselves more fully to elevating other members of the group. This norm proscribing intermarriage emerged from a social context, namely legal segregation, in which the biological boundaries of race were understood to be necessary for group identity.

Harper and Hopkins explicitly raised the issue of race uplift as a duty and, within the context of their fiction, attempted to shed light on the nature of the educated black elite's special obligation. While Harper and Hopkins focused more on the role of literature in shaping the consciousness of the black middle class to be more receptive to assuming responsibility for various family, educational, and occupational endeavors that would benefit black people as a group, Du Bois and Locke tended to emphasize the uplift of black cultural practices. They seem to have been more concerned with the duty of an educated black elite to elevate various expressions of black folk culture to the status of high art.[21] Taken together, these turn-of-the-century views of race uplift imply that the black middle class has a special obligation not to assimilate into the American mainstream, but as an educated elite seek to transform black cultural expression into some European equivalent.

Proponents of the culture-of-poverty thesis, who maintain that only with significant change in the culture of the black urban poor will the economic opportunities for them improve, seem to have adopted Washington's accommodationist view of politics. Despite both thinkers' adherence to a doctrine of social separation, Du Bois was, at times, anti-assimilationist in a sense that Washington was not.[22] Du Bois's notion of social equality entailed a view of cultural pluralism that he thought could be realized only through political agitation. Unlike Washington, whose focus was on economic development, Du Bois called into question the existing social order that excluded black culture. Hence, for Du Bois, culture was a means of gaining social equality.[23]

What happens, however, when bootstrap uplift is combined with social protest? Neoconservatives err in their criticisms of the civil rights vision by supposing that a self-help philosophy precludes a denunciation of America's racism.[24] Marcus Garvey, a self-proclaimed disciple of Washington, keenly recognized that black people were being systematically subordinated to the bottom of the American social order with no chance of eventual assimilation. His emigrationist philosophy explicitly acknowledged that black people would never achieve social equality under America's apartheid.[25]

The reason bootstrap uplift, as a theory of social change, has not produced the desired results is because it is a very misleading success myth. Its advocates present their arguments on the assumption that the existence of what some Marxists refer to as a reserve army of unemployed workers has nothing to do with the nature of capitalism.[26] But, if Marxists are right that unemployment is inherent to an advanced industrial capitalist economic arrangement, and if Garvey is right that institutionalized racism operates to keep as many black people as possible in the group of unemployed workers, the creation of the so-called black "underclass" can be viewed as a matter of economically structured racism. Although quite different in many respects, these radical perspectives suggest an alternative framework from which to question the fundamental assumption of Washington's theory of social change, namely, that America's existing socioeconomic arrangement can be made to work such that black people as a group will gain social equality.

These radical perspectives imply that, regarding the black middle class's obligation to contribute to group progress, a certain kind of assimilationist role-modeling can be objected to on political grounds. When the black middle class deliberately role models its economic success, as if to suggest that the masses of black people would also be assimilated into the American mainstream if only they were, in some sense, more acculturated, this practice fosters a social myth regarding what is required for group progress.[27] To what extent would the mere possession of mainstream cultural attributes solve the problem of large numbers of black urban poor people inhabiting the ranks of the unemployed? Neoconservative advocates of bootstrap uplift, who denounce the culture of black urban poor people, cannot draw upon its historic appeal as a theory of social change because, among a group of twentieth-century Maroons, there is by now a common understanding of how, as ideology, bootstrap uplift utilizes token models of success to *rationalize* the exclusion of the masses of black people.

The Concept of the Underclass and Mass Media

The neoconservative critique of liberal social policy is based on the idea that the problems of the urban poor are cultural rather than socioeconomic in origin. By emphasizing "socially dysfunctional behavior," neoconservatives have used the culture of poverty to frame the debate with liberals such that the socioeconomic *structure* of American society is not at issue. We are constantly reminded that, given the new black prosperity, and the ability of the class system to deliver on its promise of opportunity for everyone, the system itself is no longer to blame. Responsibility for their plight must be placed more squarely on the poor themselves. Hence, Wilson's structural argument regarding the erosion of the industrial base, as well as other concentration effects, on extreme-poverty neighborhoods, has begun to appear to the American public less salient than the cultural explanations offered by neoconservatives. I suspect that this development has a lot to do with the influence of mass media on the prevailing mainstream conception of black urban poor people. As the site of the debate about the underclass shifts more from the academic arena into mass media, structural accounts such as Wilson's have lost ground.[28] Consequently, even Wilson now believes he must argue within a culture-of-poverty framework.[29]

Mass media operate at many levels to influence public opinion about the plight of black urban poor people, most often with a characteristic ideological posture of subordination.[30] The social construction of the "underclass" concept has been profoundly influenced, not only by the presentation of various notions by social scientists, including Wilson, in popular print media, but also by television programs such as Bill Moyer's documentary, *The Vanishing Family*, and Bill Cosby's weekly situation comedy. The ideological framing of issues in terms of the culture-of-poverty thesis has been emphasized in print and electronic media.

A recent survey of popular new journals appearing over the past ten years or so revealed that, between 1977 and 1988, the prevailing definitions of the underclass moved from a general reference to poverty that included whites, to an exclusive emphasis on the behavioral, cultural, and moral characteristics of black urban poor people.[31] This conception of the underclass as exclusively black has become an assumption that is regularly reinforced by television. *The Cosby Show*, for example, indirectly displays the culture-of-poverty frame by role-modeling mainstream corporate values. In this case, the underclass is represented in the program's subtext, that is, the program's images indirectly speak to issues that have been presented in nonentertainment sources such as daily newscasts. By contrast, documentaries such as Bill Moyer's *The Vanishing Family* have more blatantly argued the culture-of-poverty thesis, making a grandstand effort to establish it with visual proof. These television images of the culture of black urban poor people as pathological have been among the more powerful validations of neoconservative bootstrap ideology.

But what about the culture of black urban poor people as viewed from their own perspective?

The Crime Metaphor in Rap Music

The voice of black urban poor people is best represented in black popular culture through rap music.[32] As a dominant influence on black urban youth, rap music articulates the perspective of a black lumpenproletariat. For this reason, class lines have been drawn around it within the black community.[33] This "underclass" status of rap, however, tends to conceal the fact that it has certain social and political dimensions that suggest that something other than pathology is occurring in black youth culture.[34]

Black urban males have been depicted in mass media as the number-one criminal threat to America. In George Bush's presidential campaign, Willie Horton was used as a cultural signifier to perpetuate the time-honored myth of the black male rapist who deserved to be lynched.[35] The social and political function of mass media's image of the so-called "underclass" is to routinely validate this claim, a practice that reached a pinnacle at the time of the Central Park gang rape when the demand for a lynching was published by Donald Trump in a full-page ad in the *New York Times*. Trump's ad is a noticeable manifestation of the mass media's general tendency to employ a Girardian script when dealing with such potent racial fears.[36] News reporting of incidents such as the Central Park Rape and the Charles Stuart Murder Case were cultural spectacles that validated the consciousness responsible for racist lynchings, a consciousness already prepared by history. The mass media's labeling of black men as criminals serves in the consciousness of many whites as a justification of antiblack vigilantism including the Goetz-styled slayings and the police beating of Rodney King.[37]

The response of the black community to this media onslaught has been divided along class lines. The black middle class denounces as a negative image any association of black people with crime by media. In hip-hop culture, however, crime as a metaphor for resistance is quite influential. Unfortunately, the generation of this new meaning frequently has been misunderstood.[38] The point of the rap artist embracing the image of crime is to recode this powerful mainstream representation.

In their reflections on the social and political significance of their music, rap artists have sometimes likened their cultural practice to a kind of alternative media, that is, "black America's TV station."[39] What this means is that rap music is a cultural reaction to the hegemony of television's image of black people. The crime metaphor in rap culture serves notice on mass media's ideological victimization of black men. Rap artists have declared war against the dominant ideological apparatus. Their purpose is to invalidate, on a constant basis, the images of black men in mass media with various recoding techniques that convey other meanings to their largely black audience.

Scholars in cultural studies have noted that the deconstructive aspects of rap music lay bare the anatomy of other black music that has been mediated by the record industry and transform it through reorganization.[40] Deconstructionism, as applied to rap music, means literally to take on every aspect of the record industry from production to marketing. The techniques involved in the production of rap music are inherently oppositional because, not only do they aim to dismantle the record industry by scratching, sampling, and remixing records to create new meanings, but they threaten the very legitimacy of claiming ownership of black music through copyright laws. Television advertising agencies have appropriated black 1960s' and 1970s' soul music to sell their products as a result of their power to purchase copyrights.[41] But when rap artists use sampling devices to reappropriate the same music, they are accused of copyright violations. In response, they have ingeniously claimed to be engaged in the African custom of ancestor worship, thereby rebutting this legal charge from the self-consciously adopted perspective of a diaspora people who desire to retain their African identity.

This exchange reflects the dialectical relationship between black popular culture and mainstream society. The outlawing of rap music in certain places, as well as its exclusion from the radio, has only helped it to flourish in an underground market, much in the same way as other illegal goods are bought and sold in that segment of the economy. The political implication of this is that rap artists are subject to the political constraints imposed by the mainstream culture industries only to the extent that they participate in main-stream media. For better or worse, control and censorship of the messages in rap music are limited.

The crowning achievement of hip-hop culture and rap music is that, within the American system of apartheid, the victims have restructured their reality with quite deliberate opposition to mass media's representations. Hip-hop culture is the basis of an authentic public sphere which counterposes itself to the dominant alternative from which black urban youth have been excluded. Middle-class social uplift has been exposed by rap artists as inauthentic role modeling. Such role models lack validity among black urban youth who are fully aware that they face structurally based unemployment. This is poignantly illustrated in one of the tunes by the very popular rap group, NWA, who offer their critical assessment of middle-class role models by giving advice to a black male child: they straightforwardly inform him that the name of the game is "bitches and money." I submit that NWA's characterization of success in these terms is a black male lumpenproletarian reading of the *The Cosby Show*. As inhabitants of extreme-poverty neighborhoods, many rap artists and their audiences are entrenched in a street life filled with crime, drugs, and violence. Being "criminal-minded" and having street values are much more suitable for living in their environment.[42] Without either glorifying or condemning this attitude toward the mainstream, I want to draw attention to the sense in which rap music has shown the potential to engender a liberating consciousness in black urban youth.[43]

Although rap artists appear to be totally free to say whatever they please, in practice this is not entirely so. They must demonstrate through their music that they "know what time it is." This knowledge can come only from one's experience on the streets. Although, at its worst, this knowledge is manifested through egotistical sexual boasting, the core meaning of the rapper's use of the term "knowledge" is to be *politically* astute, that is, to have a full understanding of the conditions under which black urban youth must survive. In many cases, rap artists are exchanging largely *inspirational* messages to reinforce self-respect, a measure that is an essential means of coping with their oppression.

Cultural Resistance and Social Pathology

As long as black urban youth in extreme-poverty neighborhoods see themselves trapped under America's apartheid their cultural expressions will continue to exhibit elements of resistance. The role of the black middle class in helping to alleviate the pathological conditions under which black urban youth must live by seeking to eliminate their cultural practices, especially when these practices provide a means of coping, is misguided. Moreover, it is futile for the black middle class to role model bootstrap uplift in a system of apartheid. Instead, what is needed is a strong black middle-class leadership engaged in the dismantling of this system.

The social isolation Wilson speaks of involves more than just the geographic relocation of black working- and middle-class families. As the economic gap has widened, there has been a psychological distancing by members of the black upper strata from other black people living in extreme-poverty neighborhoods that violates the historically determined cultural imperative to contribute to the elevation of the group.[44] What seems to facilitate this tendency toward class division is the perception that many middle-class black people have of black urban poor people. They frequently adopt the mainstream view, namely, the culture-of-poverty frame, and see the black urban poor as lacking the cultural attributes that the black middle class had to acquire to succeed. But to what extent do black urban youth lack mainstream values?

The culture-of-poverty frame prevents us from seeing that many of the values held by black urban youth are quite similar to those held by mainstream society. In white America social mores have progressed to the point where childbearing out of wedlock and female-headed households are no longer stigmatized, where involvement with drugs and drug trafficking is quite widespread, where in foreign and domestic affairs violence is regularly espoused by political leadership as a ready-made approach to conflict resolution, and where criminality runs rampant from Wall Street right through Congress and the White House. Hence, there should be little surprise in discovering that these mores have been replicated in other echelons of American society.

To see the drug trade that has devastated so many black neighborhoods as anything other than illegitimate capitalists operating under the auspices of a multinational cartel is to blindly follow the hypocrisy of mass media's racial hype.[45] As an equal-opportunity employer the drug business is an essential part of the infrastructure of black neighborhoods that have been wrecked by economic dislocation. Black youths who enter the drug trade are frequently as ambitious and as highly motivated as any prep-school graduate entering Harvard's Business School.[46] From a mainstream perspective, the mere illegality of drug dealing is sufficient to warrant its condemnation, but that perspective is clearly influenced by the fact that those in the mainstream have access to options not available to black youth living in extreme-poverty neighborhoods.

Given the multinational status of the drug trade, when we speak of pathology there is a need to distinguish between the social conditions that induce black teenagers to get involved with drugs and the cultural practices they have developed to cope with their sense of oppression. With regard to drug abuse, as with any other aspect of the social conditions which define the material existence of black urban youth, we must be able to condemn the pathology without condemning the culture.[47] So-called criminal behavior as such is not necessarily pathological.[48] Mainstream observers of black urban youth tend naively to overlook the fact that under the conditions of anarchy that prevail in most extreme-poverty neighborhoods the role of law enforcement is quite dubious with regard to crime.[49] It is simply a fact of daily life that any black man is subject to police harassment and brutality, whether he is criminal or not. This point is vividly captured in NWA's revenge fantasy, "Fuck the Police," which engendered a campaign by the FBI to get authorities to prohibit their concerts. The politically oppressive function of police departments in the black community is a common theme in much rap music, including Boogie Down Production's, "Who Protects Us from You," L. L Cool J's "Illegal Search," M. C. Trouble's, "Got to Get A Grip," and Public Enemy's, "Anti-Nigga Machine." Black youth shares a widely held view that police departments are simply regulating the drug traffic and often profiting from it. This is some of the "knowledge" that rap artists speak of when they extol the virtues of being criminal-minded.

The destructive aspects of drug dealing and drug-related lifestyles have not been overlooked in rap music. Even some of the most nihilistic rap artists have urged their listeners to see where drugs will lead them. In the music of more prominent artists, such as Ice Tea, Ice Cube, and The Geto Boys, the woes of addiction, violence, and prison life, all of which accompany drug dealing, have been well touted. Contrary to the prevailing mainstream perception, rap artists sometimes quite consciously recode mainstream values by employing so-called "negative images" to communicate very powerful messages to each other about issues of self-respect.[50]

Despite their status as a group of Maroons in America's urban centers, ironically, black urban youth, through their culture, have had a major impact on mainstream popular culture. The idea of black urban youth being intelligent users of nonstandard English can no longer be doubted – the large-scale infusion of black street language into mainstream culture is a clear testament to its powerful appeal. By paying attention to the tenacity of rap music and hip-hop culture to withstand ostracism, as well as legal condemnation, we can better understand why the retention of a distinctive black identity has it over assimilation for many black youths. The principles of music-making that have been passed on through generations of black musicians, from blues and be-bop to contemporary rap, attest to the perpetuation of a syncretic African culture.[51]

The Neoconservative's Dilemma

The duty of black people to maintain their cultural heritage was an integral part of Du Bois's version of race-uplift theory. He assigned to the black middle class the role of propagating the cultural ideals of the group. But there are other reasons, apart from the dictates of a race-uplift theory, for thinking that black people ought to retain their cultural heritage and not assimilate.

In a classic study of the black middle class, E. Franklin Frazier presented a portrait of a black middle class that had degenerated into social pathology.[52] According to Frazier, their particular malaise involved gross self-deception and the fabrication of a world of make-believe largely derived from inauthentic cultural values. Frazier's black bourgeoisie were presented as the epitome of a group of people who have developed a false consciousness because they had rejected their cultural heritage. Although Frazier never spells out what he would have considered a more authentic black culture,

I suggest on his behalf that the idea of eliminating black culture altogether to pursue assimilation seems to be at odds with the fundamental human right of self-determination. Hence, no theory of social change can justifiably require black people to do this.

Some neoconservatives seem only to be regurgitating a bootstrap version of race uplift when they maintain that an assimilated middle class is necessary for the socioeconomic progress of black people as a group.[53] A dilemma can be posed, however, for subscribers to the culture-of-poverty thesis who have insisted that the culture of black urban poor people is pathological. On the one hand, given the alleged pathology of so-called "ghetto" culture, we are led to believe that the black middle class *ought* to assimilate, and in some way help the "underclass" by doing so. On the other hand, given Du Bois's argument about propagating black cultural ideals, as well as Frazier's observations regarding the pathology of a black middle class that has failed to do this, there is some reason to suppose that the black middle class *ought not* to assimilate.

This dilemma arises from the presupposition of bootstrap uplift that the problems faced by the black urban poor, as well as the success of the black middle class, is somehow connected with their different levels of acculturation. According to bootstrap uplift, the role of the black middle class in the elevation of the black urban poor is to transmit mainstream culture to them. This suggests, of course, that America's capitalist social order need not be changed and that the problems of the black urban poor are a result of their own cultural maladaptation.

Neoconservatives, who have adopted the culture-of-poverty frame to condemn black culture as pathological, have failed to realize the nature of the cultural imperative that obligates the black middle class to endeavor to elevate the masses of black people. In the late twentieth century this imperative must be understood to allow the masses of black people to assimilate with their culture intact, that is, without rehabilitating it to meet the standards imposed by the mainstream society.

Chapter 8

Black Marxist in Babylon: Bayard Rustin and the 1968 UFT Strike

Reading Dan Perlstein's account of Bayard Rustin's involvement in the 1968 United Federation of Teachers (UFT) strike against community control in Ocean Hill-Brownsville brought to mind the ambivalence I experienced while watching a recent televised roundtable discussion during which Sister Souljah verbally attacked Cornel West for advocating interracial coalitions as a political strategy.[1] Sister Souljah's line on the virtues of Pan-Africanism was forcefully delivered, yet it was her bitter denunciation of the white liberals and feminists with whom West proposed to create an alliance that carried the debate. The exchange between Sister Souljah and Cornel West represents an ongoing ideological dispute in black political discourse between Marxism and nationalism. My ambivalence regarding this dispute arises from wanting to agree with the kind of Marxist vision Cornel West advocates, while acknowledging that Sister Souljah's criticisms of interracial political coalitions must be well taken.[2]

Although Rustin would reject Sister Souljah's separatist ideology, he would be first to endorse much of her criticism of the role whites have played in the civil rights movement. He would strongly agree with her claim that the success of the civil rights movement has not made a difference in the lives of the black urban poor.[3] Rustin's first-hand experience with the frustration sometimes violently expressed by a younger generation of black activists brought him to the brink of despair. Perlstein suggests that, although Rustin's despair was induced by the riots, there were a host of factors that culminated in his realizing the ineffectiveness of interracial political coalitions to bring about radical social change.[4] I want to emphasize an important nuance in Rustin's realization – in particular, his belief that the frustration and violent outrage expressed by urban rioters (and, hence, by community activists such as Sister Souljah) was *justified*. I will suggest a way to understand the ideological grounds for Rustin's support of the UFT in terms of his effort to accommodate the black nationalist critique of interracial political coalitions within his Marxist view. While I sustain Perlstein's negative assessment of Rustin's political ideology, I distinguish various components of his ideology so as to allow a more sympathetic reading of his argument for interracial political coalitions.

Although Rustin's support of the UFT strike was in keeping with the Marxist principles underlying his social democratic view, the rationale for his commitment to interracial political coalitions seems to have been influenced as much by his analysis of the history of the civil rights movement. If we distinguish Rustin's social democratic political philosophy from his historical view of the civil rights movement we can see that race is not eliminated from his social analysis, as Perlstein suggests. The class analysis he derived from his Marxist view was coextensive with his historical account of the civil rights struggle. Rather than reduce race to class, he instead argued that the civil rights movement's later shift of focus to the economic injustice suffered by an alienated underclass of urban blacks in the north was the "natural outgrowth" of its success in eliminating legalized racial discrimination in the south. This argument was based on what Rustin identified as the three phases of the black struggle for social justice. He maintained that, in earlier phases of the struggle, race was a more salient factor because the massive interracial political coalitions of the post-World War II civil rights movement were not yet possible.[5] What should be noted here is that Rustin employed his political view to explain certain historical developments such as the evolution of the black power ideology in the civil rights movement and the outbreak of widespread urban violence. His Marxist critique of nationalism was a major theme of his historical view. For example, he criticized Malcolm X on the ground that "he never clearly understood that, as progress was made toward social integration, the problem for America's Negroes would become just as much one of class as of race" (MM, 139).

The convergence of Rustin's Marxist view with his historical view of the civil rights movement provided more than adequate ideological grounds for his shift from his earlier career as a civil rights activist to his later affiliation with labor organizations. In his Dewey Award acceptance speech to the UFT he asserted that "the trade union movement is the only mass institution in our society that is making the social and economic demands which, if enacted, will eradicate poverty" (ID, 216). The whole point of Perlstein's objection to Rustin's appeal to his social democratic political philosophy to support the UFT in the 1968 New York school crisis was to show how Rustin's Marxist politics went awry. But, because integration was such a key ingredient in Rustin's argument for interracial political coalitions, it is not at all clear that his Marxist view was at fault. Some of Rustin's remarks suggest that he was far from convinced that there could be a majority coalition of the sort he envisioned.[6] There is, however, another important lesson to be gleaned from his argument that interracial political coalitions provide the only winning strategy to achieve economic objectives. Whatever the shortcomings of Rustin's view of coalition politics, his advocacy of a colorblind social policy of massive government intervention to deal with the plight of black urban poor people is noteworthy for having presaged William Julius Wilson's recent proposals along the same lines.[7]

Perlstein's Criticism of Rustin's Support of the UFT Strike

Perlstein's narrative of Rustin's career as a political activist accords fairly well with Rustin's own account in his Radner Lectures. The crucial element missing from Rustin's account is any mention of how his gay lifestyle may have been a factor influencing his break with civil rights activists as well as his adherence to a social democratic political philosophy. In this regard Perlstein supplies the following conjecture. "[T]he social democratic vision allowed Rustin to transcend his own conflicting identities and disassociate his problematic personal life from his political work."[8] The problematic personal life Perlstein refers to is the scandal caused by his 1953 arrest and conviction for sodomy, which led to his resignation from the Fellowship of Reconciliation and his subsequent ill treatment by other civil rights leaders. Perlstein suggests that this untenable situation may have impelled Rustin towards the safe haven provided by the labor movement with its social democratic vision.

It seems undeniable that Rustin's shift away from his former ties with civil rights organizations to an alignment with labor was partly motivated by the scandal caused by his gay lifestyle, but Perlstein indicates that there were equally important ideological motives as well. Indeed, Perlstein criticizes Rustin's ideology and his support of the UFT strike as a "failure of strategic thinking."[9] We must be wary, however, of this tendency to indict Rustin's social democratic vision along with his failed strategy. According to Perlstein:

As civil rights concerns gave way to economic issues, Rustin and other civil rights leaders were caught between the demands of the grass-roots activists they hoped to lead and the allies they sought to nurture.[10]

Rustin's calls for race-blind socialist organizing masked the modesty of social-democratic efforts to transform the social order.[11]

Perlstein rightly understood that (1) and (2) are related given that Rustin justified his alignment with labor by reference to his social democratic political philosophy.[12] Moreover, Rustin's ideological shift from emphasizing a social analysis based on race to one based on class after 1964 seems to have emanated from his concern with (2) as a response to (1). Even though I think Perlstein is right about Rustin's failure of strategic thinking, I want to caution against throwing out the baby with the bathwater.

An assessment of the merits of Rustin's social-democratic vision should not be limited to a consideration of it only as a justification of his support of the UFT for, as Perlstein makes clear, there were no compelling Marxist arguments favoring the UFT position against community control.[13] To fully understand the shortcoming of Rustin's general view of coalition politics, as well as his ideological reasons for supporting the UFT, several components of his political view must be distinguished. In his Radner Lectures he tells us:

The movement which enabled blacks to surmount the twin handicaps of racial and class discrimination was rooted in three basic principles: a belief that racial progress could only be achieved in an integrated framework, a commitment to the tactics of nonviolence, and a realization that broad, permanent change cannot be achieved by a movement confined to blacks – a belief, in other words, in coalition politics (SF, 1–2).

Although the political strategy Rustin outlines here alludes to his *social-democratic vision* and to his *critique of black nationalism* as well as to his *commitment to nonviolence*, it was the latter that would become most closely associated with his use of the term "coalition politics." Perlstein rightly claims that Rustin's strategic thinking was a failure, but perhaps the chief ideological defect of his political strategy was his overriding commitment to nonviolence.

Rustin's Social-democratic Vision

To the extent that the Marxism underlying Rustin's social-democratic political philosophy offers a remedy to poverty, that vision, and the reform agenda Rustin derived from it, were not inappropriate to addressing the economic concerns of black urban poor people. In 1965, Rustin endorsed A. Philip Randolph's ten-year plan to eliminate poverty with an estimated $100 billion Freedom Budget.[14] While this proposal was not specifically aimed toward the black community, Rustin quoted Randolph's claim that it "leaves no room for discrimination in any form because its programs are addressed to all who need more opportunity and improved incomes and living standards, not to just some of them" (BPCP, 163). Rustin went on to point out the need for "a legally binding commitment" to the goal of guaranteeing "full and fair employment to all Americans" (BPCP, 163–4).[15]

As Perlstein has argued, these proposals are color-blind. Randolph and Rustin, however, were claiming that a race-blind economic policy is the best strategy to end the poverty of African Americans. The color-blind feature of an economic proposal does not seem to be a sufficient reason to reject it especially if, *in fact*, the net effect of adopting such a proposal would be to address the economic dimension of racial injustice. Perhaps Perlstein is right about Rustin's painful realization of the modest effort by social democrats to bring about these reforms.[16] This should not be taken to mean, however, that Rustin's economic proposals were modest.[17] To the contrary, Rustin's social-democratic vision yielded a quite radical economic proposal to deal with "race and poverty," especially his call for "a national plan to eradicate the ghetto" (MBM, 212).[18]

Consistent with his belief that the black power movement filled a void left by the failures of interracial political coalitions, Rustin criticized the latter for their weak effort in pushing for more radical reform. He was keenly aware of the radical political implications of his decidedly Marxist proposals, and cited this as a reason for the liberal-labor-civil rights coalition's lack of support for the Freedom Budget:

It is one thing to organize sentiment behind laws that do not disturb consensus politics, and quite another to win battles for the redistribution of wealth. Many people who marched in Selma are not prepared to support a bill for a two-dollar minimum wage, to say nothing of supporting a redefinition of work or a guaranteed annual income (BPCP, 164).

Rustin frequently reiterated his criticism of white liberals for their reluctance to support radical economic reforms that would go beyond the judicial and legislative measures that have had little impact on the economic conditions of black urban poor people.[19]

Rustin viewed the reaction of white liberals to the hostility expressed by a small percentage of black power advocates as only an excuse to give up the fight for social justice. He publicly bemoaned the fact that the once liberal Daniel Moynihan, as a member of the Nixon administration, had written a memo recommending a policy of " 'benign neglect' of the issue of race" (BN, 309). Similarly, he criticized white liberals for promoting Malcolm X, and other black nationalists, who had no viable economic program.[20] In his reply to an open letter written by Thomas Billings, the national director of Project Upward Bound, Rustin leveled a scathing criticism that was aimed towards white liberals in general: "Negroes have been used and exploited in many ways by white Americans, but it is only recently that they have been asked to satisfy the masochistic craving of disenchanted liberals for flagellation and rejection" (TB, 285). Against the liberal interpretation of the Kerner Commission's

Report, he insisted that "It is institutions – social, political, and economic institutions – which are the ultimate molders of collective sentiments" (PP, 117). He denied that fighting racism is a matter of changing peoples' hearts. Given the Kerner Commission's indictment of institutional racism, liberals should focus more on institutional change rather than worrying about the private attitudes of racists, black and white.[21]

Rustin's Marxist reading of the crisis in education led him to castigate members of interracial political coalitions "who think that string, Scotch tape, and spit will get us out of our present dilemma" (MBM, 212). On the basis of his concern with fundamental economic change he asserted that, without "a *master plan* to cover housing, jobs, and health, every plan for the schools will fall on its face!"[22] He understood his Marxist view to be consistent with the view of "Ghetto radicals" who "see the problems of housing, schools, jobs, health, and police as so interrelated and so complex that it appears to them that *no* program is, in fact, workable" (BPCP, 211) [his emphasis]. In his later reflections on what went wrong with the civil rights movement, he remarked that "the separatist impulse emerged precisely when the need for a new and sophisticated approach to coalition politics was greatest" (SF, 12). He maintained that the black power movement challenged American society "to live up to its proclaimed principles in the area of race" (BPCP, 164). By advocating the social-democratic vision of "a national program to eliminate poverty and racial discrimination," he sought to accommodate the black nationalist challenge by explicitly connecting race and economics.

Rustin's Critique of Black Nationalism

Rustin's concurrence with grass-roots activists as to the scale and complex interrelatedness of the problems faced by black urban poor people did not preclude his criticism of their nationalist political agenda. His criticism of the black power movement consisted of several overlapping strands derived largely from his strongly held belief in racial integration. For example, he appealed to his integrationist view to oppose the separatism espoused by black power advocates, rejecting their concept of black unity as an illusion. He argued that in a pluralistic democracy racial unity is a meaningless goal. Given the class divisions among black people, the interests of the urban poor would be better served by their forming alliances with other groups who have common interests: "It is pointless to talk of unity between Roy Wilkins, who advocates integration, and Roy Innis, who wants to resegregate black schools. Nor does it make sense to pursue unity between blacks who favor national health insurance and a black medical association that opposes it" (SF, 65). Talk of black unity presupposes that divisions by wealth and status are irrelevant and, hence, diverts attention from "more substantive issues" (SF, 65).[23]

Rustin's criticism of black electoral politics was consistent with his historical view of the civil rights movement. He identified class as more of a factor "when the goals of the movement evolved from the juridical to the political and economic" (SF, 66). Here his Marxist view of economic class division coincided with his historical view of the civil rights movement to provide a ground for his condemnation of black elected officials who were under the control of machine bosses and working against the interests of black urban poor people. Although he considered "Negro machines" to be an improvement over the situation of African Americans having no power at all, he was concerned that the aim of black power advocates was "to create *a new black establishment*."[24]

He insisted that, rather than race, the question of class was more relevant to determining what interests a politician will serve, whether that politician is black or white. For instance, he employed an analysis based on class interests to distinguish Whitney Young's leanings toward the business community from A. Philip Randolph's leanings toward the labor movement. These two quite divergent views of how to meet the political and economic challenge of eliminating black poverty represent the development of factions along class lines among "the traditional allies of racial progress in the liberal and labor arenas" (SF, 66). Although Rustin cites class as a factor influencing the divisions among black and white civil rights activists, his bottom-line objection to the black power movement's emphasis on race as the most important criterion in electoral politics was that the few African-American elected officials can do nothing alone. He held that a majority coalition, with labor organizations and the Democratic party playing a central role, would make the electoral process truly responsive to the needs of black urban poor people.[25]

Rustin on Nonviolence

On Perlstein's interpretation, Rustin's ideology is construed to entail a moderate reform agenda which prevented his affirmation of a more radical activism.[26] Perlstein does not make clear, however, which component of Rustin's ideology was responsible for his opposition to the militant tactics of a younger generation of grass-roots activists. Rustin's view of nonviolence was a key ingredient in his ideology. Hence, his proposals for radical economic reform were always presented in conjunction with his view of nonviolence. Although Rustin claimed Gandhi's teachings as the ideological source of his own view of nonviolence, his affiliation with A. Philip Randolph provided direct experience of its effectiveness as a political strategy.[27]

There were nonetheless two aspects of Gandhi's teachings that shaped Rustin's view of nonviolence. Rustin adopted Gandhi's belief that a social movement relying on a nonviolent political strategy cannot succeed unless it can convince the majority that its cause is just.[28] He criticized "the confrontationist tactics" of the New Left by pointing out their failure to win over the majority, instead provoking a counterreaction (SF, 24). He also held Gandhi's belief that nonviolent protest becomes effective "to the degree that it elicits brutality and oppression from the power structure" (SF, 24). He attributed the early success of SCLC to its strict adherence to nonviolence. According to Rustin, the contrast of the nonviolence of the civil rights movement with the vicious display of southern brutality forced many ambivalent Americans to take a stand.

The conjunction of a radical economic reform agenda with a doctrine of nonviolence was a source of tension in Rustin's Marxist view, a tension that was reflected in many of his own remarks. In his account of the evolution of the civil rights movement, he offered the following explanation of the failure of interracial political coalitions: "What had previously been a movement seeking exclusively racial goals was now called upon to challenge the fundamental class nature of the economic structure. To be sure, the majority of civil

rights leaders, except for the most extreme and ineffectual militants, did not define their goals in terms of class struggle" (SF, 72–3).

Here, the conclusion he draws from his historical view of the
civil rights movement is couched in terms of his Marxist view.
The tension this creates for his political ideology emerges when we
consider his Marxist interpretation of the urban uprisings, for this
consideration generates the question of how his radical economic-
reform proposals are related to his view of nonviolence. He spoke
of the post-World War II phase of the civil rights movement as "the
period when nonviolent protest was the major weapon of civil rights
forces," whereas he characterized the post-1960s phase in terms
of a class struggle.[29] But, if in an earlier phase of the civil rights
movement the racial goal of ending legal segregation had been
achieved, thereby paving the way for economic goals to become
paramount in a later phase, why not expect that the strategy to
achieve the more difficult goal of eradicating poverty would require
something different, more radical even, than nonviolent protest?

Although Rustin saw the necessity of developing new tactics and
a new agenda once the objectives of the civil rights movement had
shifted from the legal to the economic and political, he preferred to
speak of these matters in terms of a nonviolent "social revolution."
"But the term revolutionary, as I am using it, does not connote
violence; it refers to the qualitative transformation of fundamental
institutions, more or less rapidly, to the point where the social and
economic structure which they comprised can no longer be said
to be the same" (PP, 118).[30]

In his Dewey Award acceptance speech to the UFT he quoted
Matthew Arnold's remark, "where ignorant armies clash by night"
as a metaphoric reference to the strike in Ocean Hill-Brownsville.[31]
The anguish he referred to in his speech was an indication of
his concern with the potential for violence in the Ocean Hill-
Brownsville situation. Because of his fear of the consequences for
African Americans of a race war, he could not envision a class
struggle in America that involved violence as a political strategy.[32]
He referred to the advocacy of violence and revolution by so-called
"militants" as "extreme tactics" adopted out of frustration (AF,
234). He rejected the comparisons drawn by media commentators
between "the ghetto uprisings" and other "independence revolu-
tions" (WOEG, 179). The equating of black urban rioters with the

Viet Cong was mistaken because the two basic preconditions for an independence revolution do not exist in the United States: first, African Americans lack a geographic focus for nationalist sentiment and, secondly, they do not constitute a popular majority struggling against a ruling minority of white settlers.[33]

Motivated by his fear of a white backlash that would usher in an era of repression, Rustin invoked his Marxist view to condemn the rioters and other advocates of violence. "Upon what classes do the advocates of rioting, the voices of the apocalypse, base their revolutionary perspectives?" (WOEG, 180) He cited Daniel Moynihan's data to identify the rioters as "lower class." Unlike the working class, the lumpenproletariat are unemployed petty criminals who lack a sense of having a stake in society. For this reason, he argued, they "cannot be a central agent of social transformation" (WOEG, 180). In keeping with his Marxist interpretation of the urban uprisings, he at one point likened them to a child's tantrum that aims to get attention. Because the actions constituting the riots "were detached from political policies, programs, and goals" he denied their status as full-fledged rebellions. He rejected the suggestion that the black power ideology played a role other than "an after-the-fact justification" and claimed that, given their lack of political coherence, the urban uprisings were only "riotous manifestations of rebellion" (WOEG, 183).

Rustin's use of Marxist theory to deny the revolutionary potential of dozens of major urban riots occurring in the same year seems rather tenuous. Although he eschewed the nihilism that led to urban violence, he strongly identified with the frustration experienced by the black power advocates of urban rebellion. He complained, however, that the rioters were being rewarded with only token benefits, and that this policy had the effect of undermining the efforts of "more responsible leaders" who were fighting for long-term changes (MBM, 210). What seemed to motivate his complaint, that the younger generation was being taught "that violence is the only effective force for social change" was the realization that that generation was also being taught that "when liberal forces of this nation join in coalition and urge that something be done, they are ignored" (AF, 230). Rustin understood that American society responded to urban violence in a manner that could not be matched by the efforts of coalition politics and the electoral process.[34] He was not above averring to the portent of futher rioting to bolster the case for his economic proposals as a more "practical choice" (WOEG, 186). He must have also realized the hopelessness of developing an effective majority "coalition of labor forces, of religious forces, of businessmen, of liberal and civil rights groups standing together" (AF, 237). For, as his own remarks make clear, he clearly saw that the class divisions between these different groups would present an insurmountable barrier to maintaining a coalition.[35]

Chapter 9

A No-theory Theory of Contemporary Black Cinema

When film scholars are asked to decide which are best among a body of films they identify as "black," what is at stake is something more than merely the aesthetic question of what counts as a good black film. Indeed, they must consider a more fundamental definitional question regarding the nature of black cinema, a question that raises deeper issues concerning the concept of black identity as well as the concept of cinema itself. I suspect that the reason film criticism has not offered much assistance in clarifying the concept *black cinema* is because there exists no uncontested criteria to which an ultimate appeal can be made to resolve these underlying issues. This scholarly morass must be understood in terms of the inherently political context in which the concept of black cinema has been introduced.

In his book, *Black Film As Genre*, Thomas Cripps demonstrates how difficult it is to provide an adequate definition of black cinema. He employs a notion of black cinema that refers almost exclusively to theater films about the black experience that are produced, written, directed, and performed by black people for a primarily black audience.[1] But this leaves us to wonder what to do with a well-known group of films about black people by white film-makers. Although Cripps displays a rather tenuous allegiance to his initial statement of an essentialist paradigm, he has nonetheless presented an idea that lends credence to those who would exclude films, such as King Vidor's *Halleluja*, Shirley Clarke's *The Cool World*, Michael

Roemer's *Nothing But A Man*, Charlie Ahearn's *Wild Styles*, and John Sayles's *The Brother From Another Planet*, from the newly emerging black canon. On strictly aesthetic grounds, however, these films may strike some critics as being a lot better than many others which would more adequately satisfy Cripps's essentialist criteria.

Some black film catalogers have sought to avoid the essentialist problem of being overly restrictive by opting for all-inclusive criteria. Phyllis Klotman's *Frame by Frame: A Black Filmography* and James Parish's and George Hill's *Black Action Films*, for instance, seem to identify films as black if they meet *any* of Cripps's several criteria.[2] As to be expected, some critics have complained that not all of the films they list ought to count as black cinema.[3]

Missing from the narrowness of essentialist criteria and from the broadness of nonessentialist criteria are criteria that would account for the political dimension of black film-making practices. Although audience reactions may vary from film to film, black people have a deep-seated concern with their history of being stereotyped in Hollywood films, a concern that provides an important reason to be skeptical of any concept of black cinema that would include works that demean blacks. Some would seek to abate this concern by specifying a set of wholly aesthetic criteria by which to criticize bad films about black people by black and by white film-makers. Unfortunately, this approach contains undesirable implications for black film-making practices. We need only consider the fact that low-budget productions (for example, *Bush Mama*, *Bless Their Little Hearts*, and *Killer of Sheep*) frequently suffer in the marketplace, as well as in the eyes of critics, when they fail to be aesthetically pleasing, or the fact that a film's success will sometimes be due largely to its aesthetic appeal, despite its problematic political orientation (for example, *Roots* and *Shaka Zulu*).

For this reason, such commentators as Teshome Gabriel and Kobena Mercer have urged the need for film criticism to address the politics of black film-making practice with an awareness that, what is often referred to as "aesthetics," is linked with important issues pertaining to the control of film production and distribution.[4] Incorporating aesthetics into a more politicized account of black film-making practices would seem to allow critics to evade the narrowness of the essentialist view, but there still is some reason to wonder whether this move toward aesthetics would allow the accommodation of a strictly cultural criterion for the definition of black cinema without invoking a notion of "black aesthetics," upon which some reconstituted version of biological essentialism may again be reinstated.

The political aspects of the notion of aesthetics in film theory is sometimes shielded by the latent connection between biological essentialism and issues of control in film practice. We can see a tendency to racialize the political concern with control of the black film image in August Wilson's recent demand for a black director for the movie version of his play, *Fences*: "Let's make a rule. Blacks don't direct Italian films. Italians don't direct Jewish films. Jews don't direct black American films. That might account for about 3 percent of the films that are made in this country."[5] Although Wilson's claim can easily be taken to commit him to accepting any director who is biologically black, he clearly would not want a black director who lacked the cultural sensibility required for a faithful rendering of his play. But if even a black director could prove un-satisfactory for aesthetic reasons, how do we make political sense of Wilson's demand for a black director, given that there could be some white director who might be more suitable from a cultural standpoint?

I want to advance a theory of contemporary black cinema that accords with the fact that biological criteria are neither necessary, nor sufficient, for the application of the concept of black cinema. I refer to this theory as a no-theory, because I want to avoid any commitment to an essentialized notion by not giving a definition of black cinema. Rather, the theoretical concern of my no-theory is primarily with the complexity of meanings we *presently* associate with the political aspirations of black people. Hence, it is a theory that is designed to be discarded when those meanings are no longer applicable.

The Aesthetic Critique of Blaxploitation

The history of black cinema can be roughly divided into the fol-lowing four periods: Early Silent Films (1890–1920), Early Soundies and Race Films (1920–45), Post-war Problem Films (1945–60), and Contemporary Films.[6] With regard to the history of black cinema, the so-called "blaxploitation" period is a relatively recent, and short-lived, phenomenon. Although there has always been a siphoning-off of black audiences since the early days of race films, nothing approximating the Hollywood onslaught of the early 1970s has occurred at any other time.

The term "blaxploitation" has been used to refer to those black-oriented films produced in Hollywood beginning in 1970 and continuing mainly until 1975, but in various ways persisting until the present.[7] In addition to its being an historical index, however, the term is a way of labeling a film that fails in certain ways to represent the aesthetic values of black culture properly.[8] Mark Reid, for instance, expresses this view in his account of the short-comings of blaxploitation-era films:

Having established the fact that there was a young black audience recept-ive to thoughts about violence, it should have been possible to create black action films that appealed to this audience while satisfying a black aes-thetic. The commercial black action films of the 1970s, however, never reached this ideal because they were not independent productions or because black independent producers relied on major distributors.[9]

Although, as I shall indicate shortly, Reid's criticism rests on a misleading dichotomy between independent and non-independent films, his remarks inherently acknowledge the role that produc-tion and distribution play in shaping the aesthetic characteristics of a film. At a time of financial exigency, some Hollywood studios discovered that there was a large black audience starving for black images on the screen. This situation provided an immediate inducement for them to exploit the box-office formula of the black hero (first male, and later female) which, subsequently became the earmark of the blaxploitation flick.[10]

Although there are many issues raised by blaxploitation-era film-making that deserve greater attention, I want to focus on the prob-lem of commercialism in order to highlight the influence of the market on certain aesthetic characteristics of black movies.[11] First of all, it needs to be stated, and clarified, that not all blaxploitation-era films conformed to the box-office formula. Some were not com-mercially oriented, while others were very worthwhile from a social and political standpoint.[12] To reduce them all to the hero formula, provided somewhat inadvertently by Melvin Van Peebles's *Sweet, Sweetback's Baaadasssss Song*, is to overlook their many differences in style, audience-orientation, and political content.

Secondly, given the history of black cinema, there is a certain logic to the development of the box-office formula. The idea of depicting black men as willing to engage in violent acts toward whites was virtually taboo in Hollywood films all the way through the 1960s. Once the news footage of the 1960s' rebellions, along with the media construction of the Black Panther Party, began to appear, mainstream films such as *In the Heat of the Night* made an effort to acknowledge (albeit to contain) this "New Negro."[13] Even within these limits, however, what had made Malcolm X appear so radical to mainstream television audiences at that time was the fact that he had *publicly* advocated self-defense.

When *Sweetback* was shown in 1971, it was an immediate success with black audiences because it captured an image of self-defense that gave on-screen legitimation to violent retaliation against racist police brutality. Black heroic violence against white villains rapidly became a Hollywood commodity, and literally dozens of films were produced for black audiences that capitalized on this new formula. It is worth noting here that it was, in many respects, a Hollywood-induced taboo that created a need for such images in the black audience, a need that was then fulfilled by Hollywood. The ultimate irony is that, once these films began to proliferate, there was an organized effort in the black community to demand their cessation.[14]

It is also worth noting that *Sweetback* provoked a critical response that varied among different political factions within the black community, as well as among film critics. Community-based activists, who opposed the film's image of black people, ranged from cultural nationalists, who wanted a more culturally educational film, to middle-class black protesters, who wanted a film that projected a more positive image of the race.[15] As Reid has noted, the film's political orientation, quite interestingly, received "high praise" by Huey Newton and the Black Panther Party newspaper in Oakland and "denunciation" by a Kuumba Workshop nationalist publication in Chicago.[16] Although Newton was not alone in giving the film critical praise, his allegorical interpretation of the film's sexual imagery was not widely shared among critics, especially feminists concerned with its portrayal of women.[17]

The critical controversy around *Sweetback*'s image of black people is not amenable to resolution on strictly aesthetic grounds, for *Sweetback* clearly represents some version of the black aesthetic. A political debate seems to have transpired between the film's supporters and detractors in an attempt to make the case for either accepting or rejecting the film. Indeed, some critics have argued that *Sweetback* lacked a politicized image, while others have argued that it politicized the image of black people to the point of lapsing into propaganda.[18]

With regard to the role of aesthetics, blaxploitation-era films pose a rather peculiar problem for a theory of contemporary black cinema. Can a film count as black cinema when it merely presents a blackface version of white films, or when it merely reproduces stereotypical images of black people?

Commentators have maintained quite different views in answer to this question. James Snead has argued for a very sophistocated notion of recording that requires of black cinema what he calls the 'syntagmatic" revision of stereotyped images through the selective use of editing and montage.[19] According to Snead, the syntax of traditional Hollywood cinema must be reworked to recode the black image effectively. Against the backdrop of Hollywood's pre-blaxploitation-era stereotype of black men as sexually castrated buffoons, however, what rules out the less-sophistocated blaxploitation practice of substituting a highly sexualized black male hero who exercises power over white villains as an attempt to recode the Hollywood image of black men? Reid asserts, with little hesitation, that "blacks who would find psychological satisfaction in films featuring black heroes have just as much right to have their tastes satisfied as do whites who find pleasure in white heroes such as those in Clint Eastwood and Charles Bronson films."[20] If the creation of black heroic images through role reversals can be considered a recoding technique utilized by blaxploitation film-makers then how does this practice compare with the other, more avant garde, recoding practices of black independent film-makers?

It can be quite troublesome, for a theory of black cinema that relies too strongly on aesthetics, to give an account of the influence of blaxploitation films on subsequent independent black films.[21] Given that aesthetic-based theories, such as Snead's, want to contrast independent black films with Hollywood-produced films about black people, where do blaxploitation films fit into such a juxta-position? How do we make sense of the charge, brought by an independent black film-maker, of a fellow independent black film-maker having irresponsibly produced a blaxploitation film?[22] The fact that the charge was made suggests that independent black film-making is not immune from the aesthetic pitfalls of blaxploita-tion cinema.

For present purposes, I am less interested in deciding the ques-tion of what films to count as blaxploitation than I am interested in the implication that the appeal to aesthetics, inherent in the accusation, seems to carry for our understanding of the place of aesthetics in a theory of black cinema. To denounce a film, such as *Sweetback*, as exploitative is to suggest that aesthetic criteria provide the highest ground of appeal for deciding definitional questions regard-ing black cinematic representation, for the charge presupposes that there is some sense in which to produce a blaxploitation film is to have compromised black aesthetic values. What must be explained, however, is how such films stand in relation to independently made films that were not constrained to violate black aesthetic values in this way. Apparently, the term *independent* does not always mean that a film-maker has eschewed market concerns. When a blax-ploitation film is independently made by a black film-maker for a black audience, however, to whom has the film's aesthetic orienta-tion been compromised, and, further, to what extent do such com-promises affect a film's status as a black cinematic work?

Recently there has been a major shift towards independently produced blaxploitation films. This practice makes clear that the biologically essentialist view of black cinema (those films about black people, produced by a black film-maker, for a black audience) is much too simplistic. One important implication of the aesthetic critique of blaxploitation is that certain aesthetic qualities of a film can sometimes count as much against its being inducted into the canon of black films as the film-maker's race or the film's intended audience. While the insights derived from the aesthetic critique of black film-making practices are undoubtedly healthy signs of sophistication in black film commentary, we must not overlook the fact that these critiques also give rise to many difficulties connected with the problem of how film criticism should relate to a plurality of standards by which black films are evaluated.[23]

One such difficulty that must be faced by aesthetic-based theories of black cinema arises from the fact that, since the mid-1980s, there has been a growing interest in black-oriented cinema, especially black comedy, by white audiences. The success of black television sitcoms, as well as Arsenio Hall's nightly talk show, provides some indication that white audiences are more willing to indulge not so completely assimilated black people than network executives had previously supposed. Spike Lee's humorous social commentary has opened the door for other, similarly inclined, black film-makers and television producers. All of this comic relief in the television and movie industry has been spearheaded, of course, by the mass appeal of Richard Pryor, Eddie Murphy, and Bill Cosby. Given their influence on the present context for black film-making, it seems that a theory of contemporary black cinema cannot postulate the black audience as a necessary ingredient.

A related difficulty, that carries greater significance for our understanding of the influence of the crossover audience on the aesthetics of certain films about black people, arises from the manner in which Eddie Murphy's attempt to signify on black minstrelsy has simply replaced the old-fashioned minstrel show. Murphy's success in Hollywood was quickly followed by his "black pack" cohort, Robert Townsend, whose humorous criticism of Hollywood in his very popular film was largely reduced to a shuffle with a critique of itself.[24] As though the hegemony of the Hollywood industry were not enough to contend with, more politically astute film-makers working in the realm of comedy, such as Spike Lee, are now challenged with finding ways to distinguish themselves from such neominstrelsy. Indeed, some film-makers, who were formerly aligned with the counterhegemonic practices of the post-sixties' black independent movement, seem to have allowed the white audience for black-oriented humor to so influence their film-making that we now have a new generation of blaxploitation cinema. We see this influence displayed in the Hudlin brothers' film, *House Party*, which seems to rigorously avoid dealing with certain very pressing issues raised in the film (for example, police brutality) in order not to offend the potential white audience. Unlike Spike Lee's probing satire, which engages in a black-oriented humor that sometimes seems intended to offend white audiences, *House Party* is closer to mindless slapstick.[25]

Although some film commentators have attempted to acknowledge the disparity between the aesthetic values of back audiences and the aesthetic values of film-makers and critics, film criticism generally tends to adhere to a top-down view of aesthetics, as though audiences have no role to play in the determination of aesthetic values. What the black audience appeal of blaxploitation films (old and new) indicates, against the wishes of many film critics, is that it is misguided to suppose that a filmic work of art, or entertainment, has black audience appeal simply because it aims for a black audience by promoting certain black aesthetic values. In the case of the independent black cinema movement of the 1970s in America, as well as the 1980s' black workshop movement in Britain, the attempt to reclaim and reconstruct a black film aesthetics, that would somehow counteract the influence of Hollywood's blaxploitation film-making, has by and large not been well received by black audiences, although many of these films have been frequently presented at international festivals, in art museums, and in college courses devoted to film study.[26] How can we best understand the fact that films which aim to present a more authentic black aesthetic are largely ignored by, and unknown to, black audiences, while being extremely well received in elite white film circles? Despite their admirable political orientation, such films seem to have achieved the status of art-for-art's sake, with mainly an all-white audience appeal.

This lack-of-a-black-audience problem shows the need to resist the tendency of aesthetic-based theories of black cinema to position the aesthetic values of the black artist above those of the black audience. For black film commentary to acknowledge more pluralistic criteria by which to assess the artistic value of cinematic works, some weight must be given to the viewpoint of black audiences, inasmuch as it seems strange continually to posit a black aesthetic which very few black audiences share.

Some of these considerations regarding the audience crossover phenomenon in contemporary black cinema argue against the cultural essentialist attempt to define black cinema in terms of aesthetics. As the divisions between independent and Hollywood-produced films about black people begin to dissolve, as a result of the mainstream market for both, it has become extremely difficult to maintain that either a black film-maker, or a black audience, is required for a film with a black orientation. To see this we need only consider the fact that, in addition to his crossover status in the record industry, Prince is virtually neck and neck with Spike Lee as a film-maker, each having four major releases. There is no reason to suppose that, despite a preference among commentators for Spike Lee's version of the black aesthetic, the aesthetic in Prince's movies has any less box-office appeal to much of the same audience.[27]

The need for an essentialist theory diminishes, along with the idea of a monolithic black film aesthetic, once we realize that there is no monolithic black audience. There certainly are black-oriented films, some of which are much better than others, but not all of those approved by critics manage to touch base with black audiences (for example, *To Sleep with Anger*) and many of those condemned by critics have become black audience classics (for example, *Superfly*). These facts may be difficult to accept, but to advocate a "better" cinema which is significantly different requires a political argument. I will now turn to consider the argument I think is presently most viable in a politically confused era dominated by neoconservative ideology.

Black Identity and Black Cinema

Before I take up the question of how politics and aesthetics can be situated into a theory of black cinema, I would like to add here a word of clarification regarding the prevailing use of the term *cinema* to refer to films as such, that is, movies that were made to be shown in theaters. I believe that this restricted usage is rather unfortunate because some quite good films about black people have been made for television.[28] The misconception that underlies this narrow focus on box-office movies is exacerbated by the fact that some of the most innovative black film-making is currently occurring in music videos. Indeed, the dominant influence of television on black popular culture has some rather interesting implications for black film practices that no theory of black cinema can afford to overlook. Because black urban youth culture has been visually promulgated primarily through television, this segment of the black movie audience has been heavily influenced by black images presented on television. Added to this television orientation is a large black youth market for blaxploitation films on video cassettes. These influences are displayed quite regularly in what Nelson George refers to as "blaxploitation rap," that is, rap lyrics that have been heavily influenced by blaxploitation films.[29] It is, to say the least, perilous for film-makers interested in reaching black youth to ignore the single most important medium of visually representing their cultural values.

In Britain, black film-making and television are much more structurally connected because the workshops produce their films for Channel 4.[30] Undoubtedly, this structural relation between film-making and television will eventually obtain in America once high-definition television is introduced because, with the advent of this new technology, movies, as such, will be superseded by television. For all these reasons, I think it wise at this point to expand the concept of cinema to include television.

With regard to politics, there is a very good reason why the biological version of the essentialist definition of black cinema will invariably fall short. Any definition which requires films to be made by black film-makers in order to be included in the category of black cinema will simply not match the ambivalence engendered by having to place biological over cultural criteria in deciding questions of black identity. This does not mean that, generally speaking, most of us have no idea of what to count as a black film. Indeed, the definition of black cinema is a problem by virtue of the fact that, whether it is based on biological or cultural criteria, its viability can easily be called into question.

The Du Boisian worry about the adequacy of biological criteria as the ultimate ground of appeal when faced with questions of black identity poses the greatest difficulty for the essentialist notion of black cinema. For Du Bois, the problem stems from the fact that there is no agreement about how best to define a black person, although there is some sense in which we all operate with some ideas about what constitutes black identity.[31] We need only consider the manner in which we must still grapple with the age-old problem of the "non-black" black person, that is, the person who, though biologically black, does not identify with black culture. Although there can be little doubt that, in the context of the American system of apartheid, the question of whether a particular person counts as black is most often decided by skin color and physical appearance, there are numerous instances in which this honor is withheld strictly on cultural grounds. It is far too common for black people to feel the yoke of oppression at the hands of a white-identified black person. Consequently, as someone perceived to be disloyal to the group, an overly assimilated (Eurocentric) black person can sometimes lose his or her standing in the eyes of other black people. In such cases we can notice how the tension between biological and cultural criteria of black identity is resolved in terms of a *political* definition of black people.[32] It is for some reason such as this that I am motivated to develop the concept of black cinema within the context of a political theory.

The Concept of Third Cinema Revisited

Without any pretense that I can offer a replacement for the essentialist definition of black cinema, I want to suggest why I think the Third Cinema movement of the 1960s seems to have been on the right track, although, as I have indicated, in America certain mainstream cooptational factors have basically derailed it. According to various conflicting reports, the advocates of Third Cinema have come under heavy criticism lately for being, of all things, overly nationalistic.[33] Unfortunately, in an attempt to address this worry, some commentators tend needlessly to equate nationalism with the essentialist view.[34] But the concept of Third Cinema should not be saddled with the myopic vision of essentialists who are constrained by an overemphasis on biological criteria for resolving questions of national identity.[35] What makes Third Cinema *third* (that is, a viable alternative to Western cinema) is clearly not exclusively the racial make-up of either a film-maker, or a film's aesthetic character, or a film's intended audience, but rather a film's *political* orientation within the hegemonic structures of postcolonialism. When a film contributes ideologically to the advancement of black people, within a context of systematic denial, the achievement of this political objective ought to count as a criterion of evaluation on par with any essentialist criteria.

The best way to meet the criticism that the concept of Third Cinema is too vague because it allows under its rubric many diverse cultural groups is to recognize that this objection misleadingly imputes an uncontested essentialist paradigm.[36] The Third Cinema movement represents a break with, and resistance to, the cultural imperialism fostered by the global expansion of the Hollywood industry. There is an important sense in which it aims to do what Hollywood has done; namely, it attempts to reach beyond national boundaries. There is no reason to deny that cultural diversity is a problem among the many ethnically distinct black people living together in America, much less a problem among various Third World people from widely different backgrounds in faraway places. But clearly, if Europeans, who for centuries have waged war against one another and are still caught up in their own ethnic rivalries, can construct a concept of themselves as a globally dominant white group, how can it be so much more objectionable for nonwhite people to construct a global counterconcept by which to defend themselves? The white cultural nationalism of Hollywood's Eurocentric empire requires something like a Third Cinema movement to help nonwhite people survive the oppressive and self-destructive consciousness that empire seeks to perpetuate.

With regard to black film-making practices, the concept of Third Cinema provides the rudiments of a theory of black cinema that is most conducive to this political function. As a primarily oppositional practice engaged in resistance and affirmation, black cinema need not be presently defined apart from its political function.[37] I call this a no-theory theory because I see no need to resolve, on aesthetic grounds, the dispute over what counts as blaxploitation. Neither do I see a need to choose between realism and avant-garde film techniques.[38] I am more interested in understanding how *any* aesthetic strategy can be employed to challenge, disrupt, and redirect the pervasive influence of Hollywood's master narrative. To accomplish this decidedly political objective, black film-making practices must continue to be fundamentally concerned with the issues that currently define the political struggle of black people. Hence, I want to advance a theory of black cinema that is in keeping with those film-making practices that aim to foster social change, rather than participate in a process of formulating a definition of black cinema which allows certain films to be canonized on aesthetic grounds so as to occupy a place in the history of cinema. The theory we need now is a political theory of black cinema which incorporates a plurality of aesthetic values that are consistent with the fate and destiny of black people as a group engaged in a protracted struggle for social equality.

Chapter 10

Prime-time Blackness

How can those of us who consider ourselves progressive make sense of the ambivalence we sometimes feel toward black television programs such as *The Cosby Show* and *In Living Color*? In *Watching Race*, Herman Gray provides an analysis that allows us to understand our tendency to praise and to criticize these shows.[1] With a focus on black programs appearing on prime-time commercial television (ABC, CBS, NBC, and FOX) in the 1980s, most of Gray's text is devoted to issues pertaining more generally to cultural politics. Indeed, his discussion of the politics of representation proceeds on the assumption that questions regarding the television representation of black people require a consideration of the complex interplay between mass media and black culture. This interplay involves the television industry's production of blackness as a market category and oppositional moments within its discursive confines. Gray effectively argues that "commercial culture operates as both a site of and a resource for black cultural politics."[2]

The idea that prime-time television programs have oppositional potential has been discussed by other commentators such as Douglas Kellner, John Fiske, and Todd Gitlin.[3] Gray extends this discussion to four noteworthy black programs: *A Different World*, *Frank's Place*, *Roc*, and *In Living Color*. He critically examines the multiple views of blackness set forth by white liberals and Reaganites, as well as by black nationalists, progressives, and neoconservatives. Following Stuart Hall, he maintains that, within the realm of television representation, "we are constantly being constituted and positioned, as well as reconstituting ourselves collectively and individually."[4] This claim has several facets. With the notion of a dialogical relation between the programming and the viewing of these programs, Gray distinguishes *The Cosby Show* from earlier situation comedies as well as from certain programs that followed. He points out how *Frank's Place* and *A Different World* presented black perspectives that were new to commercial television. This sets up a pre- and post-Cosby analysis that challenges the orthodoxy, championed by Michael Winston, that commercial television is inherently (structurally), and hopelessly, white oriented. The endeavor by black producers to create a space for blackness involved these programs in a more-complicated negotiation of the politics of representation that govern commercial television.

In a chapter devoted to the influence of Reaganism, Gray draws an analogy with the conservative strategy in the 1880s and the way blackness was used in the nineteenth century to support the white hegemonic order. The sign of blackness in the Reagan era was constructed from the discursive organization of television news images of a criminal underclass. To a large extent, the manner in which Bill Cosby attempted to counter this construction was over-determined. Without giving in to the inclination to support *The Cosby Show* for its rejection of this image of black people, Gray positions Cosby's complex appropriation of a discourse of assimilation alongside a pluralist discourse and a discourse of multiculturalism. Armed with these three categories, he attacks the long-standing assumption that authentic representations of black people can occur only outside the commercial realm.

The assimilationist discourse of invisibility has the longest history dating back to programs such as *I Spy, Julia,* and *Room 222*. It was succeeded by the pluralist discourse of separate-but-equal in programs such as *Family Matters, 227, Amen, Fresh Prince of Bel Air, The Jeffersons, What's Happening, Sanford & Son,* and *That's My Mama*. The multiculturalist discourse of diversity within the black community is the most recent development represented by programs such as *Frank's Place, A Different World, Roc,* and *South Central*. Black producers such as Debbie Allen and Tim Reid operated within a multiculturalist discourse to avoid the zero-sum game of presenting a "universalism versus difference within blackness."[5] Instead, their discourse on blackness was party to an *internal* struggle by African Americans for the sign of blackness.

With regard to the external struggle over the sign of blackness, Gray indicates how the conservative demonization of Willie Horton and rap artists, such as Ice T and NWA, served a political objective. The black urban poor became a sign of cultural erosion and menace that legitimated the conservative shift in policy. Of course, the conservative political agenda aimed to redistribute wealth from the middle class to the already wealthy and to eliminate entitlements from the "undeserving" inner-city populations. As television began to frame this shift, the poor and underprivileged were presented more and more as deviants, dependants, and threats.

There was at the same time, however, a different view produced by African Americans, who not only contested the conservative claims, but who also sought to reposition the traditional view and imagine new ones as well. These counterimages were presented in black theater, cinema, literature, music, dance, and sports. According to Gray, this constituted a powerful counterhegemonic force. American cultural politics then must be understood in terms of the *intersection* of the conservative construction of blackness and the multiple representations of blackness by African Americans. For this reason representations of blackness are often contradictory, yielding ambivalent responses. Gray's theory acknowledges that representations of black people derive their meanings (and countermeanings) from their circulation in popular discourses and the commercial media. He concludes that "conservative claims and uses of the sign of blackness necessarily produce different effects and meanings for blacks and whites."[6]

This notion of the relational meanings of the sign of blackness is at the heart of Gray's theory, according to which the meaning (and power) of black representations in television and in popular culture is not contained in the image alone. Rather, representations of black people gain significance from "the ways those images situate, activate, and structure alliances of identification and pleasure."[7] Television representations of black people, as well as those in popular culture, are resources that different constituencies within the black community employ in their struggle to affirm their humanity and counter the denial of this. Rap artists, for example, employed the sign of blackness as a cultural resource to contest social invisibility and cultural condemnation by white racists, women, gays, and other blacks and minorities. The meaning of the sign of blackness can no longer be defined only in relation to whiteness. Neither can it be defined only in terms of Utopian desires for a monolithic black identity. The African-American cultural struggle over the meaning of blackness challenged the claims of Reaganism as well as the totalizing constructions from inside the black community.

In a chapter on the social production of blackness, Gray turns to a consideration of the political economy of the television industry to explain the proliferation of black-oriented situation comedies in the mid- to late 1980s. There were structural transformations that positioned black audiences as a key element in the industry's operation.

In the mid-1980s, television representations of black Americans proliferated when the big three television networks, ABC, CBS, and NBC, experienced a decline in total viewers as a result of competition from cable programming, increased use of videocassette recorders and video games, the rise of a fourth television network, and an increase in original programming on independent stations.[8]

There was also a displacement of Arbitron and Nielson rating systems that allowed network executives to target specific markets and remain profitable. Most important, however, was the success of *The Cosby Show*. By "narrowcasting" networks followed NBC's success and focused their marketing strategies to reach black audiences. Despite the fact that most of the black-oriented shows resonated with conservative views of individualism, responsibility, and morality, they nonetheless displayed an increased interest by networks in black popular culture. Gray insists that, given the new bottom line, programs that failed to acknowledge changing attitudes towards race, gender, and class were no longer profitable.

Gray's outline of the structural changes that facilitated "narrowcasting" includes a discussion of the increasingly symbiotic relationships among film, music television, and advertising that influenced the transformation of the film and of the television industries. Another important aspect of this transformation was the dramatic changes in ownership – especially the emergence of the Fox Broadcasting Company as a fourth television network in 1986 – which

changed the way audience shares were split. Prior to this development, the traditional three networks had evenly divided the market but, with Fox as a new player in the ratings game, the pricing
structure of advertising changed. It was within the context of
these economic changes that networks began to target black audiences as a source of low-risk profit.

It is not surprising that the sudden interest in black culture by
network executives was economically motivated. Black audiences
often had fewer options and could almost guarantee advertisers a
profit from their commodification of black culture and black celebrities. Along with black-oriented programs, there was an increase
in black-oriented commercials that marketed fast food, sneakers,
cars, personal grooming, and household products to black audiences.
This economic incentive nonetheless allowed a small number of
black producers, writers, directors, actors, and comedians to gain
entry into the television industry. The outcome was mixed. Either
the black directors and producers worked on programs that were
not focused on black themes, or black culture (for example, *Equal
Justice* and *Lonesome Dove*), or the programs that dealt with black
themes, or black culture (for example, *Sanford & Son*, *The Jeffersons*,
Good Times, *Amen*, and *227*), were under the control of white producers and directors. Gray cites the 1989 report of the National
Commission on Working Women that stated that only 7 percent
of all producers working on shows with minority characters are
minorities, and minority female producers comprised only 2 percent. The introduction of African-American cultural perspectives
that challenged conventional television representations of blackness
was accomplished by only a few black producers, such as Bill Cosby,
Keenen Ivory Wayans, Debbie Allen, Arsenio Hall, Tim Reid, and
Quincy Jones.

The story Gray tells about the history of the black image on television prior to the 1980s is quite fascinating. Although a lot of the
information he imparts has been gone over by J. Fred MacDonald
in his encyclopedic study, *Blacks on White TV*, Gray marshals this
history to garner a novel insight.[9] The success of *Roots* in the wake
of the Civil Rights struggle, for instance, is given a political reading:
"I would place *Roots* in dialogue with the reactivation and renewed
interest in black studies and the development of African-centered
rap and black urban style, especially their contemporary articulation

and expression in popular culture and mass media."[10] Gray goes on to point out that, despite its evasion of issues that stem from slavery (namely, the social organization of racial subordination, the cultural reliance on human degradation, and the economic exploitation of black labor) *Roots* was an acknowledgment by commercial television of black subjects that interrupted momentarily the gaze of the white middle-class audience.

The most culturally significant development in the history of television was *The Cosby Show*, for it created the space for a new aesthetic treatment of black culture. Cosby's dissatisfaction with the black image in film and television had been voiced in the 1968 documentary, *Of Black America I: Black History: Lost, Stolen, or Strayed?*, which he narrated. Rather than make the race of the characters an object of derision as had been done throughout the history of Hollywood, Cosby instead used the situation comedy genre to present a more complex representation of African-American life. Following Michael Dyson, Gray criticizes *The Cosby Show* for its failure to build on the image of diversity and complexity of black culture that it had introduced to television audiences.[11] Cosby's stance against indulging racial issues generated the ultimate contradiction when the show's final episode was juxtaposed with news coverage of the post-Rodney King riots in Los Angeles.

Gray expresses ambivalence towards *The Cosby Show* that is no doubt shared by many. He cites the pleasure he derived from his regular viewing of this program and confesses that, despite his own criticism of its drawbacks, he has been unwilling to stake out a position on the show. Instead of registering a judgment of absolute praise or condemnation Gray offers an analysis of the contemporary image of African Americans on television by identifying three kinds of discursive practices (referred to above). In an effort to come to grips with his own ambivalence towards *The Cosby Show*, he acknowledges that the program succeeded in recoding the traditional representations of African Americans and broke with assimilationist and pluralist practices by attempting to explore the interiors of black life from an African-American perspective. Yet, he believes that elements of these practices continued to structure certain aspects of the show. He considers *Frank's Place*, *Roc*, and *South Central* to be better examples of the movement away from assimilationist and pluralist discourses.

These comparisons suggest that Gray has a view of the chrono-logical development of black-oriented television that is inherently evaluative. Clearly he considers programs that fall within the multiculturalism/diversity category to be preferable to those that never reach this level. Indeed, Gray's ambivalence towards *The Cosby Show* can be understood to be a consequence of that program's failure to break more completely with assimilationist and pluralist discourses. Gray relies on his distinction between the three kinds of discursive practices to critically examine some of the post-Cosby programs. He clearly likes *A Different World, Frank's Place,* and *Roc,* but has strong reservations regarding *In Living Color.* He is keen on noting certain nuances in the way some of these programs nego-tiated mainstream television conventions to present black life.

In the case of *A Different World,* he notes that it almost always operated within the confines of the standard television plot struc-ture of stasis, conflict, resolution, stasis. How then did this program manage to tell stories about black life through the conventions of television? Gray runs down a list of radical changes that occurred after the show's initial season as a *Cosby Show* spin-off that are tell-tale. Originally conceived as a show about the second-oldest Huxtable daughter, Denise (Lisa Bonet), attending a fictitious black college, the show was centered on Denise's relationship with her white room-mate. Gray tells us that, after quickly degenerating into a black television version of *Animal House,* Cosby was so embar-rassed he threatened to have it taken off the air. But, instead of cancellation, Debbie Allen (a Howard University graduate) was brought on as the new director. Denise and her white room-mate, Maggie, were replaced by Whitley Gilbert (Jasmine Guy) and Dwayne Wayne (Kadeem Hardison) as the program's central characters. The opening theme song that was sung by the racially indistinct Phoebe Snow was replaced with another version by Aretha Franklin. The show made an explicit turn toward black culture.

Gray attempts to shed light on how the show's producers adapted the conventions of casting, writing, setting, and narrative to fit African-American social experiences and cultural sensibilities. The casting deliberately aimed to show the diversity within the black community, and break with television's conventional construction of African Americans as monolithic. The program's diverse repres-entations included, not only differences in complexion among

African Americans, but also differences pertaining to gender, age, and class.

The major achievement of the program was the manner in which the producers used the conventions of television writing to examine issues facing African Americans. Multiple and overlapping plot lines were used as devices to explore these issues.

By using minor themes, characters, and settings in this way, the show's production team was able to saturate the show with cultural knowledge central to African American life without necessarily being didactic, exclusive, or derisive. This use of minor plots, characters, and settings enabled the writers to construct and represent the sensibilities of an African American youth culture full of intertextural references to black popular culture, current events, and contemporary debates about blackness.[12]

Although Gray may be quite right about the program's use of B stories to represent the sensibilities of black youth culture, he seems to undermine his own analysis, or at least renege on most of it, by further claiming that these emblems of blackness are easily found throughout commercial television in music videos, sports events, advertising, and even in other situation comedies. What seems unclear here is whether the adaptations of the conventions of casting, writing, setting, and thematic content actually "saturated" the show with what Gray calls black "cultural knowledge," or whether the result was only the addition of "subtle nuances that heightened the look and feel of the show."[13]

Gray avers to the fact that the writers earned a reputation in the industry of not being labeled "message" or "issue" oriented, yet there were many controversial issues presented, including stories about AIDS, South Africa, racism, sexual harassment, date rape, violence against women, and affirmative action. The account he provides of this puzzling aspect of the program seems to cut both ways. On the one hand, he points to the program's attempt to subvert the television conventions it employed while, on the other hand, he acknowledges the program's inability to succeed in this regard because it was too firmly tethered to conventional practices. For example, at one place in his analysis, he seems to downplay the manner in which the story of the underground railroad is sneaked in as a B plot. Later on, however, he cites as a major shortcoming the program's inability to move beyond the confines of a liberal commitment to presenting two sides of a controversial issue. This invariably led the producers to frame pressing social issues "as various kinds of misunderstanding, ignorance, and lack of experience with different groups and communities."[14]

Reminiscent of his take on *The Cosby Show*, Gray concludes his discussion of *A Different World* with both criticism and praise. He accepts Mark Crispin Miller's negative observation that the program was overburdened with "cinematic and televisual happy endings."[15] His praise for the program's strengths display a tendency to give a personalized assessment, which is perfectly alright, but only invites all of us to do likewise. "In the end, the real joy of *A Different World* was the weekly televisual ride into this black world, the small pleasures it afforded, the identification it invited, and the memories of black college life it activated for me."[16]

I for one have great difficult in accepting Debbie Allen's vision of black college life because, for me, black colleges largely represent a world of privilege for middle-class African Americans. I will never forget attending my brother's graduation from Howard's Medical School with my mother. We sat at a table across from another mother (and her son) who boasted about having graduated her fourth doctor in the family – all from Howard. When I watched Whitley and Dwayne take center stage week after week I sensed that the black middle class (some of whom have a pathological need to invoke status over less-fortunate African Americans) were being celebrated at the expense of the masses of black people whose parents could never afford to send their children to a private school. Gray indicates how the program attempted to include a wide variety of characters, but he does not discuss the fact that they occupied a world dominated by Whitley and Dwayne. Whitley's character strikes me as a rather shameful perpetuation of Diahann Carroll's earlier *Julia* (with the added sass of a black southern belle) and Dwayne is the penultimate nerd constructed from a Spike Lee image of the b-boy. Unlike Gray, the casting was a major stumbling block for me, simply because my working-class background prevents me from identifying with middle-class African Americans who, in my experience, have demonstrated the ability to be as oppressive to other blacks as any white racist. It is worth noting that my disagreement with Gray's assessment of *A Different World* actually confirms his theory, according to which the same image can have relational meanings for different audiences.

Where the writers for *A Different World* largely relied on B-plot narratives to recode the conventions of situation comedy, Gray argues that the producers of *Frank's Place* employed a strategy of appropriating existing formal and aesthetic elements in the general commercial culture, as well as in television, to construct an alternative image of black life. The two producers, Hugh Wilson and Tim Reid, were committed to achieving a certain look, and feel that required special attention to how the program was shot. Although their use of a film style to produce the show was not cost effective, the technique of shooting scenes out of order allowed them to avoid network control. The use of music, rather than a laugh track, to indicate changing moods made *Frank's Place* seem more like a dramatic series than a situation comedy. This recoding of the comedic format was punctuated by the use of endings that lack resolution – certainly a noticeable step up from *A Different World*.

Gray has a lot of good things to say about the black cultural sensibilities that structured the world of *Frank's Place*. Unlike the fictitious Hillman college (the oldest Huxtable daughter went to Princeton), New Orleans is a well-known specific locale with its own particular history. Another contrast with *A Different World* is the program's focus on black working-class experience, even while it explored tensions among various class positions. Gray cites several episodes devoted to the exploration of African-American experiences that are usually absent from commercial television. For example, there was an episode on the hybrid relationship between the music, cultures, foods, and customs of African Americans and Africans. There was also an episode about the college recruitment of a black high-school All-American basketball player which raised issues pertaining to sports, education, and masculinity as a critique of the recruitment process.

Gray provides a fairly solid assessment of the achievement of *Frank's Place*, but his criticism is a bit confusing. He speaks of its "muted commercial appeal," which resulted in low ratings and ultimate cancellation after the first 20 episodes.[17] Presumably this was because of the manner in which the program "challenged conventional boundaries." Yet, according to Gray, "the show's critical insights were often contained and limited." He notes that the program operated within a structure of containment by relying on the character of Frank to express critical insight and moral outrage. For example, the issue of homelessness is presented in terms of a sympathetic portrait of a homeless person, but the complex social issues it raises are reduced to Frank's moral problem. Gray objects to the program's tendency to rely on Frank's moral character instead of presenting a strategy for social change. This objection, however, does not square completely with Gray's claim that "The narrative structure, thematic approach, and cinematic look of the show disturbed the normal television experience."[18] It is not clear how the program can exhibit containment and still disturb the normal television experience. If *Frank's Place* operated within a structure of containment, then the explanation of its commercial failure cannot be attributed to its being uncontained, threatening, and unfamiliar.

Unlike the other programs Gray discusses, *In Living Color* is not a situation comedy, a difference in genre that goes largely unremarked. Instead, Gray focuses on the program's underlying political orientation. To some extent, the hierarchy of values I attributed to Gray's theory is complicated by his assessment of *In Living Color*. He is much less supportive of this program, even though he places it in the category of a multiculturalist discourse. The program's use of irreverence, satire, and spectacle to engage issues of diversity within black culture is problematic for Gray because it settles around a politics of ambivalence. He asks, "Does this ambivalence contest hegemonic assumptions and representations of race in general and blacks in particular, or does it simply perpetuate troubling images of blacks?" His own answer to this question is expressed in terms of a worry about the program's bimodal appeal to black and to white audiences. The program's crossover success relied heavily on its use of the trope of race to reconfigure audiences that are differently positioned socially. Hence, ambivalence was employed to meet the demands of television's commercial imperative, but at the expense of black women, gays, and poor and working-class people.

The concern Gray expresses regarding *In Living Color*'s indulgence of the politics of ambivalence must be well taken. He points out that the available social positions from which to make sense of the show are not equivalent in some pluralist sense. The representations are influenced mostly by the power of the white viewer.

Following Norma Schulman, he surmises that "Within television's own discourse some viewing positions are simply more socially privileged, more economically valuable, more culturally legitimate than others."[19] Gray's theory is important to consider in this regard, for his point is that the determination of whether the images of race, gender, and sexuality in programs of this sort are complicitous with domination, critical of it, or just harmless fun rests not so much with the images, especially with regard to the historic and contemporary meanings they carry, but must be understood in terms of their alignment with the three discourses he identifies. Hence, the multiculturalist discourse instituted by *The Cosby Show* allowed the program to present an often troubling rendering and interrogation of the complex social relations that characterize black life.

Everyone knows that *In Living Color* presented a really problematic image of black people, but the reason often given by the positive-image police has always missed the mark. Gray smartly employs his theory to put his finger on the problem. This program depended on differently positioned audiences and the political discourses to which they subscribe for its meanings. If we choose either to praise or to condemn it we come up short because the program's representations are not inherently progressive nor reactionary. Depending on who reads the images, and from what standpoint, there is a potential for them to be both. Filled with contradictions, the program's political potential is determined by its ability to articulate black popular discourses as well as Reaganism. Gray accepts the fact that the program intervened in television constructions of blackness while it also provided the cultural terms through which racial subordination was legitimated.

How was *In Living Color* different from other black comedy-variety shows that were assimilationist and pluralist? Gray quotes Keenan Wayans and the show's producer, Tamara Rawitt, to present the intention with which they operated in using parody and satire. Without privileging their intentions, he credits the program's use of the comedy-variety genre to explore African-American culture. He urges us to read the cultural politics of the program beyond the closed system of the text. The program's treatment of sexuality (homophobia), class, and gender were deliberately constructed to produce an ambivalence through which the subject position of the viewer and the characters is addressed. Hence, many of the sketches on black women, gays, and the underclass can be read as trivializations *and* as acknowledgments. Gray levels a scathing criticism of the program's politics of ambivalence.

For a segment of the black community on which so many different kinds of claims are made, including uncritical nationalist celebrations and racist demonizations, this ambivalence makes it hard to construct a critical space from which to speak, especially because it so effectively and cleverly organizes several different social positions. In the end, I fear that the hegemonic balance tilts far too dramatically and decidedly in the direction of object-ification and derision. For all their high jinks, clever deconstructive turns, and transgressive hipness, *In Living Color's* sketches about the black poor more often than not seem simply to chump out, leaving the black poor exposed and positioned as television objects of middle-class amusement and fascination.[20]

Despite this criticism, Gray thinks *In Living Color* cannot be dismissed along with other problematic images of black people on television.

There is an obvious parallel between *In Living Color* and other black comedy-variety programs (mostly specials) produced by Richard Pryor and Robert Townsend. Gray does not discuss any of these programs, but he does mention the influence of *Saturday Night Live* and *Second City Television*. The mainstream audience for *In Living Color* was undoubtedly a carry-over from *Saturday Night Live*, with its history of black tokenism and white comedians performing in blackface. I do not think *In Living Color* should be credited with innovation, given that it can be viewed as a black version of *Saturday Night Live* with black comedians doing blackface, along with reverse white tokenism. In the program's last season, after the departure of the Wayans, the reversion to minstrelsy escalated beyond any hope of redemption.

I wonder why Gray chose not to discuss *True Colors*, a knock-off of *The Cosby Show* that appeared on Sunday evening on the FOX channel just prior to *In Living Color*. To a great extent, *True Colors* is on par with *A Different World*, presenting an image of the black middle class that Bill Cosby proclaimed he would not touch. While *The Cosby Show* and *True Colors* operated within an assimilationist discourse, *True Colors* was much more transgressive than *The Cosby Show*, or any of the other *Cosby Show* imitators. Neither *A Different*

World, nor *Fresh Prince of Bel Air*, for example, were able to transcend the assimilationist discourse, whereas *True Colors*, in its treatment of the socially taboo subject of interracial marriage, picks up where Sidney Poitier left off in *Guess Who's Coming to Dinner* to push this discourse to its logical conclusion. Unlike the constant critique of the white male-black female couple in *The Jeffersons*, *True Colors* presented an image of a black male-white female couple that challenged the separate-but-equal social order that George Jefferson sought to legitimate.

I raise this issue mainly because the multiculturalist discourse within the black community includes a debate between nationalists and so-called mixed-race people (but what African American isn't?) regarding the racial status of the offspring of interracial parents. *True Colors*, in fact, skirted this devilish issue by not presenting any mixed-race children, while Bill Cosby used a self-identified mixed-race actor (Lisa Bonet) to portray one of his non-mixed-race kids who just happened to be light skinned. Lisa Bonet's problematic standing in the black community can be offered as a reason for the abortion of her role on *A Different World*. Her character required a white room-mate because, by her own admission, in the real world, she cannot fit into an all-black social setting. The representation of diversity (of complexions) on *The Cosby Show* in fact plastered over a battery of issues related to the program's penchant for color coding. This feature of the program was the source of heated debates between African Americans. This matter is not so much a criticism of Gray as it is an insert, for it is a point that he can easily accommodate within his analysis. Gray's account of black-oriented commercial television provides a much needed theory that addresses the complexities we face whenever we attempt to voice our approval of, or dissatisfaction with, the black image on television.

Notes

Introduction

1 W. E. B. Du Bois, "The Conservation of Races" in Howard Brotz (ed.), *Negro Social and Political Thought: 1850–1920* (New York: Basic Books, 1966), 483–92.

2 See Molefi Asante, *Afrocentricity* (Trenton, N.J.: Africa World Press, 1988).

3 Paul Gilroy, *The Black Atlantic* (Cambridge, MA: Harvard University Press, 1993).

4 See Gerda Lerna (ed.), *Black Women in White America: A Documentary History* (New York: Pantheon Books, 1972), Bettina Aptheker, *Women's Legacy* (Amherst: University of Massachusetts Press, 1982), Angela Y. Davis, *Women, Race, and Class* (New York: Random House, 1981), and Paula Giddins, *When and Where I Enter: The Impact of Black Women on Race and Sex in America* (New York: Bantam Books, 1985).

5 Susan Brownmiller, *Against Our Will: Men, Women and Rape* (New York: Harper and Row, 1988), Angela Davis, "The Myth of the Black Rapist" in Davis, *Women, Race and Class*, Alice Walker, "Advancing Luna and Ida B. Wells" in *Midnight Birds*, ed. Mary Helen Washington (Garden City, NY: Anchor Books, 1980), Valerie Smith, "Split Affinities" in *Conflicts in Feminism*, eds, Marianne Hirsch and Evelyn Fox Keller (New York: Routledge, 1990), and Joy James, *Transcending the Talented Tenth: Black Leaders and American Intellectuals* (New York: Routledge, 1997).

6 See Abby Arthur Johnson and Ronald Maberry Johnson (eds), *Propaganda and Aesthetics: The Literary Politics of Afro-American Magazines in the Twentieth Century* (Amherst: University of Massachusetts Press, 1979).

Kobena Mercer revisits this debate in his discussion of the black artists' burden of representation. See his *Welcome to the Jungle* (New York: Routledge, 1994), 233–58.

7   See William Julius Wilson, *The Truly Disadvantaged* (Chicago: University of Chicago Press, 1987).

8   For an interview with Suge Knight, one of the most successful corporate executives managing a company responsible for producing so-called "gangsta" rap music, see Steven Ivory, "Family Matters," *Source* 84 (September 1996): 124–78.

9   Wilson calls for a return to government-sponsored work projects on the model of the WPA. William Julius Wilson, *When Work Disappears* (New York: Knopf-Random House, 1996).

10 Manthia Diawara (ed.), *Black American Cinema* (Bloomington: Indiana University Press, 1993), Ed Guerrero, *Framing Blackness* (Philadelphia: Temple University Press, 1993), Herman Gray, *Watching Race* (Mineapolis: University of Minnesota Press, 1995), Jannette Dates and William Barlow (eds), *Split Image: African Americans in the Mass Media* (Washington, D.C.: Howard University Press, 1990), Tricia Rose, *Black Noise: Rap Music and Black Culture in Contemporary America* (Middletown, Conn.: Wesleyan University Press, 1994), Eric Perkins (ed.), *Droppin' Science: Critical Essays on Rap Music and Hip-Hop Culture* (Philadelphia: Temple University Press, 1996), and David Toop, *The Rap Attack: African Jive to New York Hip-Hop* (London: Pluto Press, 1984).

Chapter 1   Racist Discourse and the Negro-ape Metaphor

1   Winthrop D. Jordan, *White over Black: American Attitudes Toward the Negro 1550–1812* (Baltimore: Pelican, 1968).

2   Charles Darwin, *The Descent of Man*, 1871, 201. Cited in Stephen Jay Gould, *The Mismeasure of Man* (New York: Norton, 1981), 36.

3   Franz Boas, "Human Faculty as Determined by Race" in George W. Stocking, Jr, *Race, Culture, and Evolution* (New York: The Free Press, 1968), 225.

4   Francis Moran III, "Between Primates and Primitives: Natural Man as the Missing Link in Rousseau's *Second Discourse*," *Journal of the History of Ideas*, 54.1 (January 1993): 48.

5   Ibid.

6   George M. Frederickson, *White Supremacy* (New York: Oxford University Press, 1981), 15.

7   Cited in L. Perry Curtis Jr. *Apes and Angels* (Washington, D.C.: Smithsonian Institute Press, 1971), 1.

8   Donna Haraway, *Primate Visions* (New York: Routledge, 1989), 160; Paul Hoch, *White Hero Black Beast* (New York: Pluto Press, 1979), 48.
9   Trudier Harris (ed.), *Selected Works of Ida B. Wells-Barnett* (New York: Oxford University Press, 1991).
10 James Verniere, *Boston Herald* (September 23, 1988): S10.
11 Chandra Talpado Mohanty, Ann Russo, and Lourdes Torres (eds), *Third World Women and the Politics of Feminism* (Bloomington: Indiana University Press, 1991), 84.
12 James Bernard, "The LA Rebellion: Message Behind the Madness," *The Source* 35 (August 1992), 38–48.
13 Sam Dennison, *Scandalize My Name* (New York: Garland Publishers, 1982), 414–15.

Chapter 2   Slavery, Modernity, and the Reclamation of Anterior Cultures

1   Thomas Hobbes, *Leviathan*, ed. Richard Tuck (Cambridge: Cambridge University Press; 1978), John Locke, *An Essay Concerning Human Understanding*, ed. Peter H. Nidditch (Oxford: Clarendon Press, 1975), and Jean-Jacques Rousseau, *On the Social Contract*, ed. Roger D. Masters and trans. Judith R. Masters (New York: St Martin's Press, 1978).
2   Paul Gilroy, *The Black Atlantic* (Cambridge, MA: Harvard University Press, 1993). Subsequent page references to this work will appear in parentheses in the text with the abbreviation BA.
3   See Winthrop D. Jordan, *White over Black: American Attitudes toward the Negro, 1550–1812* (Baltimore: Penguin, 1968), 430–6.
4   Jurgen Habermas, *The Philosophical Discourse of Modernity* (Cambridge: Polity Press, 1987), 37–41.
5   I do not mean to suggest that Hegel had no well-formed view of the enslavement of Africans. Given that Montesquieu was his chief Enlightenment influence, the parable's historically specific meaning seems to be, as Gilroy suggests, that slavery is bad, yet a defining characteristic of modernity.
6   Gilroy does not cite any systematic study, but refers instead to the archival material on the practice of slave suicide and the various representations of death as agency in early African-American fiction (such as the chapter in William Wells Brown's *Clotelle*, titled "Death is Freedom") See BA, 63 and 233, note 63.
7   Sterling Stuckey cautions against assuming that the more acculturated house slaves were less African. *Slave Culture: Nationalist Theory and the Foundations of Black America* (New York: Oxford University Press, 1987), 33.

8   "African Civilization Society" (February 1859), in Howard Brotz (ed.), *Negro Social and Political Thought: 1850–1920* (New York: Basic Books, 1966), 265.

9   "The Folly of Colonization" (January 9, 1894), in Brotz, 330.

10   "The Future of The Colored Race" (May 1886), in Brotz, 309.

11   July 12, 1854 in Brotz, 243.

12   "African Civilization Society" (February 1859), in Brotz, 262.

13   "The Call of Providence to The Descendants of Africa in America" (1862), in Brotz, 115.

14   "The African Problem and The Method of Its Solution" (1890), in Brotz, 130.

15   Gilroy cites the example of Ron Kerenga's invention of Kwanza as an African substitute for Christmas (BA, 193).

16   Cf. Stuckey, *Slave Culture*, 35–6.

17   See Richard Price, *First-Time: The Historical Vision of an Afro-American People* (Baltimore: Johns Hopkins University Press, 1983), Sally Price, *Co-wives and Calabashes*, 2nd ed. (Ann Arbor: University of Michigan Press, 1993), and Richard Price and Sally Price, *On the Mall: Presenting Maroon Tradition Bearers at the 1992 FAF* (Bloomington: Indiana University Press, 1994).

Chapter 3   Frederick Douglass on the Myth of the Black Rapist

1   Toni Morrison raised a similar concern in her analysis of the media construction of O. J. Simpson during the trial. "The official story has thrown Mr. Simpson into that representative role. He is not an individual who underwent and was acquitted from a murder trial. He has become the whole race needing correction, incarceration, censoring, silencing; the race that needs its civil rights disassembled; the race that has made trial by jury a luxury rather than a right and placed affirmative action legislation in even greater jeopardy. This is the consequence and function of official stories: to impose the will of a dominant culture." Toni Morrison (ed.), *Birth of a Nation'hood* (New York: Pantheon Books, 1997), xxviii.

2   For a general discussion of antebellum southern sexual mores, see John D'Emilio and Estelle Freedman, *Intimate Matters: A History of Sexuality in America* (New York: Harper and Row, 1988), 85–108 and W. J. Cash, *The Mind of the South* (New York: Alfred Knopf, 1941). For first-hand reports from black victims of rape in the post-Civil War era see Gerda Lerner (ed.), *Black Women in White America: A Documentary History* (New York: Pantheon Books, 1972), 172–97. See also Robert Staples, "Violence and Black America," *Black World* (May 1972): 17–34.

3   See, for instance, Susan Brownmiller, *Against Our Will: Men, Women and Rape* (New York: Harper and Row, 1975); Allison Edwards, *Rape, Racism, and the White Women's Movement: An Answer to Susan Brownmiller* (Chicago: Sojourner Truth Organization, 1979), chap. 7; Angela Davis, "Rape, Racism and the Myth of the Black Rapist" in her *Women, Race and Class* (New York: Random House, 1981), 172–201; Joy James, *Resisting State Violence* (Minneapolis: University of Minnesota Press, 1997), chap. 7; Trudia Harris, *Exorcising Blackness: Historical and Literary Lynching and Burning Rituals* (Bloomington: Indiana University Press, 1984).

4   I refer to Frederick Douglass, "Why is the Negro Lynched?" in *The Life and Writings of Frederick Douglass*, vol. 4, ed. Philip Foner (New York: International Publishers, 1952), 491–523 as the pamphlet, and "Lessons of the Hour: An Address Delivered in Washington, DC, on 9 January 1894" in *The Frederick Douglass Papers*, vol. 5, eds John W. Blassingame and John R. McKivigan (New Haven: Yale University Press, 1992), 575–607 as the lecture. Also reprinted in *The Oxford Frederick Douglass Reader*, ed. William L. Andrews (New York: Oxford University Press, 1996), 340–65.

5   For a discussion of the early European view of black people as apes see Jordan, *White over Black*, 28–42.

6   Several commentators have pointed out this tendency in the O. J. Simpson trial. See David Goldberg, *Racial Subjects* (New York: Routledge, 1997), 149–55 and A. Leon Higginbotham, Jr, Anderson Bellegarde Francois, and Linda Y. Yuch "The O. J. Simpson Trial: Who Was Improperly 'Playing the Race Card'?" in Morrison, *Birth of a Nation'hood*, 31–56.

7   In the trial following the Rodney King incident, the police officers charged with the beating offered what some commentators refer to as the "King Kong" and "Mandingo" defenses. The officers bolstered their claim that King was a physical threat with the statement that he was also a sexual threat to a female officer. See Ishmel Reed, "Bigger and O. J." in Morrison, *Birth of a Nation'hood*, 169–95.

8   Douglass often gave this lecture under the title "The Negro Problem." See Atchison, Kansas, *Blade*, October 7, 1893; Boston, Massachusetts, *Globe* May 11 and 12 and October 26, 1894; Providence, Rhode Island, *New England Light*, November 10, 1894. See also his address delivered at the Annual Meeting of the American Missionary Association on October 25, 1894 in Lowell, Massachusetts and published as a pamphlet titled "A Defense of the Negro Race" (New York, 1894). Cited in Blassingame and McKivigan, *Douglass Papers*, vol. 5, 640.

9   Frederick Douglass, "Why is the Negro Lynched?" in Foner, *Life and Writings*, vol. 4, 503.

10 Frederick Douglass, "Lynch Law in the South," *The North American Review* 155.428 (July 1892): 19.

11 Ibid.

12 Trudier Harris (ed.), *Selected Works of Ida B. Wells-Barnett* (New York: Oxford University Press, 1991), 50–61.

13 Douglass, "Lynch Law," 20–1.

14 Douglass, "Reason Why" in Harris, *Selected Works*, 60.

15 Ibid.

16 Despite their similar emphasis on economic self-help, Washington's accommodationist political orientation later became a source of great friction between his followers and Wells-Barnett. It should be noted that Washington was not completely unknown to have made public statements against lynching. See, for instance, his remarks in "Democracy and Education," September 30, 1896 in Brotz, *Negro Social and Political Thought*, 370; "Address Delivered at Hampton Institute," February 19, 1898, in Brotz, 374; "Is the Negro having a Fair Chance?" in Brotz, 446, 459–60.

17 Foner, *Life and Writings*, vol. 4, 493.

18 Douglass often cited the horrid details of lynchings. My point here is that he considered economically motivated racism, more than the black rapist myth, to be a source of the vengeance expressed through the ritualistic killing of lynch victims. He believed the racism fostered by the black rapist myth was only a catalyst for lynching, the cause of which was class antagonisms between blacks and whites.

19 Foner, *Life and Writings*, vol. 4, 503.

20 Blassingame and McKivigan, *Douglass Papers*, vol. 5, 587.

21 Ibid., 589.

22 Douglass equated the exclusion of educated African Americans from the Chicago World's Fair with the silence about lynching. In a section of his pamphlet devoted to the unfairness of the American exhibition he raised the issue of misrepresentation and pointed out that the reputation of crime is added to an image of African Americans that is already negative. He accused the exhibitioners at the Chicago World's Fair of deliberate distortion. According to Douglass, "It says to the lynchers and mobocrats of the South, go on in your hellish work of Negro persecution. You kill their bodies, we kill their souls." Foner, *Life and Writings*, vol. 4, 508. For an updated version of this critique of the black male image in mass media see Earl Ofari Hutchinson, *The Assassination of the Black Male Image* (New York: Touchstone, 1994/97).

23 Foner, *Life and Writings*, vol. 4, 496–7.

24　As was common in his time, Douglass often used the term "manhood" to speak of what we now would term "human." He has been criticized by Paul Giddings for having succumbed to this practice. See Paula Giddings, *When and Where I Enter: The Impact of Black Women on Race and Sex in America* (New York: Bantam Books, 1985), 5. His discussion of the "manhood rights of the Negro" was ambiguous as between masculinity and humanity. See Foner, *Life and Writings*, vol. 4, 521. But there are several distinct issues involved in his use of this expression. Hazel Carby quotes Pauline Hopkins's claim that "Lynching was instituted to crush the manhood of the enfranchised black" to show the connection between lynching and citizenship. Pauline Hopkins, *Contending Forces: A Romance Illustrative of Negro Life North and South* (1900; Carbondale, Ill., 1978), 270, cited in Hazel Carby "On the Threshold of Woman's Era: Lynching, Empire, and Sexuality in Black Feminist Theory," *Critical Inquiry* 12 (Autumn 1985): 314. But the denial of citizenship is to the group as a whole, not just to men. Because, at that time, only men had the franchise, such claims are sometimes taken also to raise the question of emasculation. For a discussion of this function of lynching and disfranchisement, see Trudier Harris, *Exorcising Blackness: Historical and Literary Lynching and Burning Rituals* (Bloomington: Indiana University Press, 1984), chap. 2.

25　Quoted from the Memphis *Daily Commercial*: cited in "Southern Horrors," Harris (ed.), *Selected Works*, 33.

26　See D'Emilio and Friedman, *Intimate Matters*, xvi and Gerda Lerner, *Black Women in White America: A Documentary History* (New York: Pantheon Books, 1972), 193, cited in Angela Davis, *Women, Race and Class* (New York: Vintage, 1981), 174.

27　E. K. Love, "Lynch-Law and Raping," November 5, 1893, (n.p.): 1–19 in *African-American Pamphlets* 1820–1920 from the *Daniel A. P. Murray Collection*, Library of Congress.

28　Love, "Lynch-Law," 6.

29　Douglass, "Lynch Law," 19.

30　Love, "Lynch-Law," 8.

31　Needless to say, Love's refusal receives little support from black women who have written on this subject. For example, in her novel, *Contending Forces*, Pauline Hopkins writes, "The men who created the mulatto race, who recruit its ranks year after year by the very means which they invoked lynch law to suppress, bewailing the sorrows of violated womanhood! No: it is not rape." *Contending Forces*, 270–1, cited in Carby, "On the Threshold of Woman's Era," 314.

32 For a discussion of the psychology of the guilt-ridden white south-erner see Calvin C. Herton, *Sex and Racism in America* (Garden City, NY: Doubleday, 1965); Joel Kovel, *White Racism: A Psychohistory* (New York: Pantheon Books, 1970), chap. 4; Thomas F. Gossett, *Race: The History of an Idea in America* (New York: Schocken, 1973) and Paul Hoch, *White Hero Black Beast* (UK: Pluto, 1979), chap. 3. See also John W. Blassingame, *The Slave Community: Plantation Life in the Antebellum South* (London: Oxford University Press), 10–11, 140, 163–4.

33 Rev. Love acknowledged cases of false accusations, but with little concern for the innocent victims in such cases. See Love, "Lynch-Law," 7.

34 William McFeely, *Frederick Douglass* (New York: Norton, 1991), 360.

35 Ibid., 361–2.

36 I propose an alternative to this strong reading of her remarks. In the same context she also spoke of herself as having believed the news reports were true, until her first-hand experience with the lynching of her friend, Thomas Moss, on a false rape accusation. See Alfreda M. Duster, *Crusade for Justice: The Autobiography of Ida B. Wells* (Chicago: University of Chicago Press, 1970), chap. 6.

37 "Lessons of the Hour" in Blassingame and McKivigan, *Douglass Papers*, vol. 5, 581–2. For parallel remarks see Douglass's introduction to "The Reason Why," in Harris, *Selected Works*, 57 and Douglass, "Why is the Negro Lynched?" in Foner, *Life and Writings*, vol. 4, 496.

38 Douglass's ambivalence regarding his mother's relationship with her master may be a factor here. Janny Franchot has argued that Aunt Ester, whom Douglass presented in his autobiography as the victim of a severe whipping by her master, was a surrogate figure for Douglass's mother. See "The Punishment of Ester: Frederick Doug-lass and the Construction of the Feminine" in *Frederick Douglass: New Literary and Historical Essays*, ed., Eric J. Sundquist (New York: Cambridge University Press, 1990), 141–65.

39 See Wells-Barnett's comments regarding the negative reception of Douglass's interracial marriage. Duster, *Crusade for Justice*, 71–5.

40 Harris, *Selected Works*, 15–16.

41 Italics added. "Lessons of the Hour," Blassingame and McKivigan, *Douglass Papers*, vol. 5, 581.

42 In her autobiography Wells-Barnett remarked that, "I too, would have preferred that Mr. Douglass had chosen one of the beautiful, charm-ing colored women of my race for his second wife. But he loved Helen Pitts and married her and it was outrageous that they should be crucified by both white and black people for so doing." Duster, *Crusade for Justice*, 73.

43 According to Douglass, "In warning the South that it may place too much reliance upon the cowardice of the negro, I am not advocating violence by the negro, but pointing out the dangerous tendency of his constant persecution. . . . [H]e was not a coward at Harper's Ferry, with John Brown; and care should be taken against goading him to acts of desperation by continuing to punish him for heinous crimes of which he is not legally convicted." Douglass, "Lynch Law," 22–3.

44 "Southern Horrors," Harris, *Selected Works*, 42.

45 Wells-Barnett describes the homicide, for which Charles was pursued and killed, as an act of self-defense against an unprovoked clubbing by a white policeman. See *Mob Rule in New Orleans: Robert Charles and His Fight to the Death* (1900) in Harris, *Selected Works*, 253–322.

46 Mary Helen Washington has discerned a number of fictional devices Wells-Barnett employed for rhetorical purposes. Presented at a colloquium sponsored by the Monroe Trotter Institute, University of Massachusetts/Boston, spring 1988.

47 Foner, *Life and Writings*, vol. 4, 519.

48 In *The Reason Why* Douglass pointed out that in most of the southern states there is a "convict lease system, the chain-gang, vagrant laws, election frauds, keeping back laborers' wages, paying for work in worthless script instead of lawful money, refusing to sell land to Negroes and the many political massacres where hundreds of black men were murdered for the crime(?) of casting the ballot." Harris, *Selected Works*, 62.

49 In "Red Record" Wells-Barnett recommended a similar remedy to lynchings. She instructs her northern readers to "Bring to the intelligent consideration of Southern people the refusal of capital to invest where lawlessness and mob violence hold sway. Many labor organizations have declared the resolution that they would avoid lynch infested localities as they would the pestilence when seeking new homes." Harris, *Selected Works*, 248.

50 See "A Red Record: Tabulated Statistics and Alleged Causes of Lynchings in the United States, 1892–1893–1894" in Harris, *Selected Works*, 139–252.

51 Foner, *Life and Writings*, vol. 4, 518–19.

52 See Paul Hoch, *White Hero Black Beast*, 44.

53 It is worth noting here that Douglass did not connect his earlier critique of racist ethnologists with the rapist myth. See Frederick Douglass, "The Claims of the Negro Ethnologically Considered" (1854) in Foner, *Life and Writings*, vol. 2, 289–309.

54 Harris, *Selected Works*, 15. For arguments that parallel Douglass's see "Southern Horrors," Harris, *Selected Works*, 18, 26–8, 44; "The Reason Why," Harris, 74.

55   "Southern Horrors," in Harris, 19.

56   Frances Willard responded with the assertion "It is my firm belief that in the statements made by Miss Wells concerning white women having taken the initiative in nameless acts between the races she has put an imputation upon half the white race in this country that is unjust, and save in the rarest exceptional instances, wholly without foundation." cited in Wells-Barnett, "A Red Record," in Harris, *Selected Works*, 226–7.

57   Alice Walker, "Advancing Luna and Ida B. Wells" in *Midnight Birds*, ed. Mary Helen Washington (Garden City, NY: Anchor Books, 1980), 63–81 and Valerie Smith, "Split Affinities" in *Conflicts in Feminism*, eds. Marianne Hirsch and Evelyn Fox Keller (Routledge, 1990), 271–87. For a critical discussion of the Walker-Smith interpretation see Joy James, *Transcending the Talented Tenth: Black Leaders and American Intellectuals* (New York: Routledge, 1997), chap. 3, and *Resisting State Violence*, chap. 7.

58   In her autobiography Wells-Barnett stated,

> The many unspeakable and unprintable tortures to which Negro rapists (?) of white women were subjected were for the purpose of striking terror into the hearts of other Negroes who might be thinking of consorting with willing white women.
>
> I found that in order to justify these horrible atrocities to the world, the Negro was being branded as a race of rapists, who were especially mad after white women. I found that white men who had created a race of mulattoes by raping and consorting with Negro women were still doing so whenever they could, these same white men lynched, burned, and tortured Negro men for doing the same thing with white women; even when the white women were willing victims.
>
> Duster, *Crusade for Justice*, 71.

59   "Southern Horrors," Harris, *Selected Works*, 14; In a passage, from "Red Record," that urges the law and order remedy proposed by Douglass she stated, "we demand a fair trial by law for those accused of crime, and punishment by law after honest conviction. No maudlin sympathy for criminals is solicited, but we do ask that the law shall punish all alike." In "A Red Record," published in 1895, Wells-Barnett cites Douglass's pamphlet and incorporated many aspects of his argument against lynching. See Harris, *Selected Works*, 140, 246–52.

60   Wells-Barnett maintained,

It is certain that lynching mobs have not only refused to give the Negro a chance to defend himself, but have killed their victim with a full knowledge that the relationship of the alleged assailant with the woman who accused him, was voluntary and clandestine. . . . The defense has been necessary because the apologists for outlawry insist that in no case has the accusing woman been a willing consort of her paramour, who is lynched because overtaken in wrong.

"A Red Record," Harris, Selected Works, 200.

61 Wells-Barnett included cases of black women raped and lynched by white men. See especially "Southern Horrors," Harris, *Selected Works*, 27–9, 45. As an activist in the women's movement, she lectured in England to garner support for the antilynching campaign, and considered herself a founder of the black women's club movement. The historical significance of Wells-Barnett's social activism is discussed in Joy James, *Resisting State Violence* (Minneapolis: University of Minnesota Press, 1997), chap. 7; Bettina Aptheker, *Women's Legacy* (Amherst: The University of Massachusetts Press, 1982), 60–76, 107–14; Giddings, *When and Where I Enter*, 26–31, 90–4.

62 Cf. Joy James, *Resisting State Violence*, 136 and Rosemarie Tong, *Women, Sex, and the Law* (Totowa, NJ: Rowman & Allanheld, 1984), 167.

63 At the Equal Rights Association convention in New York, May 1869.

64 In a letter to the editor of the *New York Standard* (December 26, 1925) Elizabeth Cady Stanton claimed,

The representative women of the nation have done their uttermost for the last thirty years to secure freedom for the negro, and as long as he was lowest in the scale of being, we were willing to press his claims, but now, as the celestial gate to civil rights is slowly moving on its hinges, it becomes a serious question whether we had better stand aside and see "Sambo" walk into the kingdom first. . . . In fact, it is better to be the slave of an educated white man, than of a degraded, ignorant black one. . . .

quoted in Davis, *Women, Race and Class*, 71. For a satire of white feminist complicity with opponents of affirmative action see Ishmael Reed, *Reckless Eyeballing* (New York: Atheneum, 1988), 26–7.

65 Foner, *Life and Writings*, vol. 4, 43.

66 For a discussion of the history of the women's movement in relation to the earlier abolitionist and later antilynching movements see Bettina Aptheker, *Women's Legacy*, Angela Davis, *Women, Race and Class*; Paula Giddings, *When and Where I Enter*; Gerda Lerner, *Black Women in White America*.

67 Many commentators have noted that it was not until 1930 that Jesse Daniel Ames organized the Association of Southern Women for the Prevention of Lynching. See Tong, *Women, Sex and the Law*, 167–9.

68 "Lessons of the Hour," in Blassingame and McKivigan, *Douglass Papers*, vol. 5, 595.

69 Some black abolitionists, such as Sojourner Truth and Robert Purvis, also opposed ratification. See Aptheker, *Women's Legacy*, 47.

70 Ibid., 48.

71 "Reason Why," Harris, *Selected Works*, 63. Douglass had remarked on miscegenation laws in connection with colonization as early as 1849, "The history of the repeal of the intermarriage law shows that the prejudice against color is not invincible." Frederick Douglass, "The American Colonization Society" in Foner, *Life and Writings*, vol. 1, 396. In 1862 he again addressed the subject of amalgamation and interracial marriage in a discussion of colonization. "And among those who denounce amalgamation most, you often find the fathers of mulatto and quadroon children, men mean enough to take advantage of their absolute power, as masters, to sustain a relation to their black slave women which can only be honorable in marriage, are the men who most loudly and coarsely denounce amalgamation." Frederick Douglass, "The Spirit of Colonization" in Foner, *Life and Writings*, vol. 3, 265. For Douglass's other remarks regarding miscegenation see "The Future of the Colored Race" in Foner, *Life and Writings*, vol. 4, 195.

72 Giddins, *When and Where I Enter*, 38. Carby, *Reconstructing Womanhood*, chap. 2.

73 "Why is the Negro Lynched?" in Foner, *Life and Writings*, vol. 4, 599. Douglass claimed, "But I am not only a citizen by birth and lineage, I am such by choice." See "The Future of the Negro People of the Slave States" in Foner, *Life and Writings*, vol. 3, 213. In his other writings on emigration and colonization, he insisted only upon citizenship by soil. See Foner, *Life and Writings*, vol. 1, 350–2; 387–99; vol. 2, 167–9; 172–3; 243–54; 441–7; vol. 3, 210–25; 260–6; vol. 5, 111–25; 471–2.

74 "Why is the Negro Lynched?" in Foner, *Life and Writings*, vol. 4, 512.

75 Ibid., 595.

76 See Andrew Ross, "If the Genes Fit, How Do You Acquit? O. J. and Science" in Morrison, *Birth of a Nation'hood*, 241–72 and Armond White, "Eye, the Jury" in Morrison, 339–66.

77 Foner, *Life and Writings*, vol. 4, 500. See also Douglass, "Lynch Law," 19–20.

78 For a discussion of "legal lynching" in connection with the Central Park Rape case see James, *Resisting State Violence*, chap. 7.

Chapter 4   *Du Bois on the Invention of Race*

1   W. E. B. Du Bois, "The Conservation of Races" in Brotz, *Negro Social and Political Thought*, 491. All subsequent references to Du Bois will be to this work unless otherwise indicated.
2   Ibid., 491.
3   Bernard R. Boxill, *Blacks and Social Justice* (Totowa, New Jersey: Rowman & Allanheld, 1984), 180.
4   Du Bois, 488.
5   Joseph P. DeMarco, *The Social Thought of W. E. B. Du Bois* (Lanham: University Press of America, 1983), 31–62; Boxill, *Blacks and Social Justice*, 173–85; Anthony Appiah, "The Uncompleted Argument: Du Bois and the Illusion of Race" in *"Race", Writing, and Difference*, ed. Henry L. Gates, Jr (Chicago: University of Chicago Press, 1985), 21–37.
6   In this essay I do not take on the larger task of comparing Du Bois's claims in "The Conservation of Races" with modifications that appeared in his later writings. For useful analyses in this regard see the above cited works by DeMarco and Appiah.
7   Du Bois, 485.
8   Ibid., 485.
9   Ibid., 485.
10   Ibid., 485.
11   Ibid., 486–7.
12   Ibid., 486.
13   Boxill, *Blacks and Social Justice*, 178; Appiah, "The Uncompleted Argument," 28.
14   Du Bois, 487.
15   Boxill, *Blacks and Social Justice*, 183.
16   Du Bois, 491.
17   Ibid., 488. Du Bois leaves open the question of whether Egyptian civilization was "Negro in its origin" and stresses that "the full, complete Negro message of the whole Negro race has not as yet been given to the world" (p. 487).
18   Ibid., 487 and 489.
19   Ibid., 489.
20   Ibid., 489. Du Bois's reference to Negroes in Africa as having "slept, but half awakening" reflects his lack of knowledge of African history at this early stage of his career. He later wrote the following about his reaction to Franz Boas's 1906 Atlanta University commencement address on the topic of black kingdoms south of the Sahara: "I was too astonished to speak. All of this I had never heard. . . ." *Black Folk: Then and Now* (New York: Henry Holt, 1939), vii.

21   Du Bois cites the fact that African Americans have given America "its only American music, its only American fairy tales, its only touch of pathos" (p. 489). Later Du Bois spoke of African-American music as "the greatest gift of the Negro people." *The Souls of Black Folk* (New York: Fawcett World Library, 1961), 181.

22   Du Bois, 489.

23   In a much later work, Du Bois rejects what he calls "the physical bond" but goes on to assert that "the real essence of this kinship is its social heritage of slavery." *Dusk of Dawn: An Essay toward an Autobiography of a Race Concept* (New York: Schocken, 1968/75), 116–17, quoted in Appiah, "The Uncompleted Argument," 33.

24   Appiah, 32.

25   Du Bois, 491.

26   Ibid., 489.

27   DeMarco, *Social Thought of W. E. D. Du Bois*, 33; Appiah, "The Uncompleted Argument," 27.

28   Wilson J. Moses, *Alexander Crummell: A Study of Civilization and Discontent* (Oxford: Oxford University Press, 1989), 262. With regard to the notion of "civilization" Du Bois's European influences must also be acknowledged. Bernard W. Bell maintains that, although there is no documentary evidence of his having read Herder, "it is unlikely that Du Bois remained untouched by the spirit and thought of Herder, Goethe, and Rousseau." *Folk Roots of Contemporary Afro-American Poetry* (Detroit: Broadside Press, 1974), 23. For a discussion of Du Bois's known academic influences see Francis L. Broderick, "German Influence on the Scholarship of W. E. B. Du Bois," *Phylon* 19 (December 1958) and "The Academic Training of W. E. B. Du Bois," *Journal of Negro Education* 27 (Winter 1958).

29   Du Bois, 487.

30   Appiah, 25.

31   Du Bois did acknowledge that "The term Negro is, perhaps, the most indefinite of all" and applies to a wide variety of people, but he does not hesitate to override this consideration with remarks such as "200,000,000 black hearts beating in one glad song of jubilee" (pp. 486–7).

32   Ibid., 491.

33   Ibid., 488.

34   Ibid., 489; Booker T. Washington, "Alanta Exposition Address" in Brotz, *Negro Social and Political Thought*, 359. Du Bois seems even closer to Washington when he implores the Academy to "continually impress the fact upon the Negro people that . . . they MUST DO FOR THEMSELVES . . . that a little less complaint and whining, and a little more

dogged work and manly striving would do us more credit and benefit than a thousand Force or Civil Rights bills" (p. 490).

35 Du Bois, 488.

36 See Dorothy Porter, "The Organized Educational Activities of Negro Literary Societies, 1828–1846," *Journal of Negro Education*, 5 (October, 1936): 556–66.

37 See C. M. Wiltse (ed.), *David Walker's Appeal* (New York: Hill and Wang, 1965); Maria W. Stewart, "An Address Delivered Before the Afric-American Female Intelligence Society of America" and "Mrs. Stewart's Farewell Address to Her Friends in the City of Boston" in *Maria W. Stewart, America's First Black Woman Political Writer*, ed. Marilyn Richardson (Bloomington: Indiana University Press, 1987); Howard H. Bell, "National Negro Conventions of the Middle 1840's: Moral Suasion vs. Political Action," *Journal of Negro History*, 42 (October, 1957): 247–60; Howard H. Bell, *A Survey of the Negro Convention Movement 1830–1861* (New York: Arno Press, 1969).

38 W. H. A. Moore, "The New Negro Literary Movement," *AME Church Review* 21 (1904): 52.

39 Cf. Frances E. W. Harper, *Iola* and Pauline E. Hopkins *Sappho* in *Invented Lives*, ed. Mary Helen Washington (New York: Anchor, 1987), 87–129. For a discussion of why some African Americans choose to pass see James E. Conyers and T. H. Kennedy, "Negro Passing: To Pass or Not to Pass," *Phylon*, 24.3 (fall 1963): 215–23, and Virginia R. Dominguez, *White by Definition* (New Brunswick, N.J.: Rutgers University Press, 1986), 200–4.

40 Du Bois, 488.

41 Cf. Boxill, *Blacks and Social Justice*, 185.

42 For a discussion of the rather tenuous racial basis for ethnicity see R. B. LePage and Andree Tabouret-Keller, *Acts of Identity: Creole-Based Approaches to Language and Ethnicity* (Cambridge: Cambridge University Press, 1985), 207–49. Lucius Outlaw has argued a similar line regarding the social construction of race and ethnicity. See his "Toward a Critical Theory of 'Race'," in David T. Goldberg (ed.), *Anatomy of Racism* (Minneapolis: University of Minnesota Press, 1990), 58–82.

43 Appiah, "The Uncompleted Argument," 27. In this regard Du Bois may have followed the view of Herder. According to Herder, "[Races] belong not, therefore, so properly to systematic natural history, as to the physico-geographical history of man" cited in Cedric Dover, "The Racial Philosophy of Johann Herder," *British Journal of Sociology* 3 (1952): 125. See also Vernon J. Williams, Jr, *From A Caste to A Minority: Changing Attitudes of American Sociologists Toward Afro-Americans, 1896–1945* (New York: Greenwood Press, 1989), 86–7.

44 Boxill, *Blacks and Social Justice*, 178.

45 For an historical account of racial classification see Michael Banton, "The Classification of Races in Europe and North America: 1700–1850," *International Social Science Journal* 111 (February 1987): 45–60. According to Robert E. Park, "In South America and particularly in Brazil, where Negroes and mixed bloods constitute more than 60 per cent of the population, there is, strictly speaking, no color line . . . [although] the white man is invariably at the top, and the black man and the native Indian are at the bottom." *Race and Culture* (Glencoe, IL: The Free Press, 1950), 381. Similarly, Julian Pitt-Rivers reports that "A man who would be considered Negro in the United States might, by traveling to Mexico, become *moreno* or *prieto*, then *canela* or *trigueno* in Panama, and end up in Barranquilla white." "Race, Color, and Class in Central America and the Andes" in *Color and Race*, ed. John Hope Franklin (Boston: Houghton Mifflin Co., 1968), 270. With reference to black people of lighter skin, Philip Mason tells us that " 'The white man' in Jamaica sometimes means a well-to-do person who behaves as though he came from Europe and would often not be classed as 'white' in the United States." "The Revolt Against Western Values" in Franklin, *Color and Race*, 61.

46 See the California State University and University of Massachusetts Application Forms, 1991–92. For a discussion of the definitions of affirmative action categories see David H. Rosenbloom, "The Federal Affirmative Action Policy" in *The Practice of Policy Evaluation*, ed. D. Nachimias (New York: Saint Martin's Press, 1980): 169–86, cited in Dvora Yanow, "The Social Construction of Affirmative Action and Other Categories," a paper presented at the Fifth National Symposium on Public Administration Theory, Chicago, April 9–10, 1992. For a discussion of the political implications of treating the concepts of race and ethnicity as interchangeable see Michael Omi and Howard Winant, *Racial Formation in the United States: From the 1960s to the 1980s*, 2nd ed. (New York: Routledge & Kegan Paul, 1994), 14–37.

47 Frederick Douglass, "The Claims of the Negro Ethnologically Considered" in Brotz, *Negro Social and Political Thought*, 250.

48 S. S. N., "Anglo Saxons and Anglo Africans," *The Anglo African Magazine*, vol. 1, 1859 (New York: Arno Press, 1968), 250.

49 "Anglo Saxons," 250.

50 According to Margot Pepper, "Although *Chicano* has been misused to identify all Mexican Americans, it actually refers to a specific political and cultural attitude; it is not an ethnic category." "Resistance and Affirmation," *The San Francisco Guardian* (June 26, 1991): 33. Velina Hasu Houston, President of the Amerasian League, informs us that

"The term (*Amerasian*) referred to all multiracial Asians, whether their American half was Anglo, African American or Latino." "Broadening the Definition of Amerasians," *Los Angeles Times* (July 11, 1991): E5. Cape Verdians are a mixed Portuguese/African group who speak a creole language but, in Massachusetts, are not classified as either black or Hispanic.

51 Ruth Benedict and Gene Weltfish, *The Races of Mankind*, Public Affairs Pamphlet No. 85 (September 1980), 8.

52 Appiah, "The Uncompleted Argument," 34. DeMarco suggests that Du Bois may have believed that the original world population was divided into the three different races, because he "characterized the growth of racial units as one which proceeds from physical heterogeneity to an increasing physical homogeneity." DeMarco, *Social Thought*, 41. Arnold Rampersad, however, has pointed out that, by 1915, Du Bois shifted more toward a common ancestry view. *The Art and Imagination of W. E. B. Du Bois* (Cambridge, MA: Harvard University Press, 1976), 230–1.

53 Cf. Robert A. Hill and Barbara Bair (eds), *Marcus Garvey Life and Lessons* (Berkeley: University of California Press, 1987), 206, and V. R. H. de la Torre, "Indo-America" and "Thirty Years of Aprismo" in *The Ideologies of the Developing Nations* (New York: Simon and Schuster, 1972), 790–800.

54 In 1885, Croatan Indians in Robeson County, North Carolina sought to distinguish themselves from African Americans, with whom they had mixed, by getting the legislature to pass laws that made them the final judges on questions of genealogy. They adopted the pragmatic definition, "an Indian is a person called an Indian by other Indians." Guy B. Johnson, "Personality in a White-Indian-Negro Community" in *When Peoples Meet*, eds Alain Locke and Bernhard J. Stern (New York: Progressive Education Association, 1942), 577.

55 See, for instance, Harriet A. Jacobs, *Incidents in the Life of a Slave Girl*, ed. Jean Fagan Yellin (Cambridge, MA: Harvard University Press, 1987), 29.

56 In the mid-seventeenth century, Virginia enacted legislation that stipulated that children born of a black woman would inherit her status, even when the father was white. This measure allowed slaveholders to literally reproduce their own labor force. See Paula Giddings, *When and Where I Enter* (New York: Bantam, 1985), 37. Marvin Harris argues that the difference between the United States and Latin America in applying this rule of descent must be understood in terms of it being "materially advantageous to one set of planters, while it was the opposite to another." *Patterns of Race in the Americas* (New York: W. W. Norton, 1964), 81.

57 Indeed, in many cases where phenotypic characteristics are ambiguous with regard to an individual's genotype, self-identification (i.e., cultural criteria) becomes more of a possibility. C. Eric Lincoln informs us that "Reliable estimates on the basis of three hundred and fifty years of miscegenation and passing suggest that there are several million 'Caucasians' in this country who are part Negro insofar as they have Negro blood or Negro ancestry." "Color and Group Identity in the United States" in Franklin, *Color and Race*, 250. To see that the issue of genetic heritage is mostly a matter of politics we need only consider the fact that the Louisiana state legislature recently repealed a 1970 statute that established a mathematical formula to determine if a person was black. The "one thirty-second rule" was changed to "traceable amount". Frances Frank Marcus, "Louisiana Repeals Black Blood Law" *New York Times* (July 6, 1983): A10. For a detailed historical account of the politics surrounding the Louisiana law see Dominguez, Chapters 2 and 3. When Hawaii became a United States Territory in 1990 the "one thirty-second rule" was lobbied against by five large landholding companies. For economic reasons they favored the present law which requires 50 percent native blood to be eligible for a land grant. See Timothy Egan, "Aboriginal Authenticity to Be Decided in a Vote, "*New York Times* (January 1, 1990), A12.

58 See the discussion of Hansen's Law by Werner Sollors in his *Beyond Ethnicity: Consent and Descent in American Culture* (New York: Oxford University Press, 1986), 214–21. For a discussion of its application to Louisiana creoles see Dominguez, chap. 7.

59 Boxill's definition of black people cannot accommodate such cases for he would insist on phenotype and descent as overriding factors such that black Latinos who operate with a primarily cultural identity must be viewed as in some sense "passing."

60 According to Israel's Law of Return, anyone born to a Jewish mother who has not taken formal steps to adopt a different religion has the right to become a citizen of Israel.

61 Benedict and Weltfish, *The Races of Mankind*, 10; Abram Leon Sachar, *A History of the Jews* (New York: Alfred A. Knopf, 1979), 250.

62 According to Louis Wirth "What has held the Jewish community together in spite of all disintegrating forces is . . . the fact that the Jewish community is treated as a community by the world at large." "Why the Jewish Community Survives" in Locke and Stern. *When Peoples Meet*, 493.

63 Cf. Peter Singer, "Is Racial Discrimination Arbitrary?" *Philosophia* 8.2–3 (November 1978): 185. See also Edward W. Said, "Zionism from the Standpoint of Its Victims" in Goldberg, *Anatomy of Racism*, 210–46.

64 Webster's dictionary emphasizes the fact that this term applies primarily to marriage or interbreeding between whites and blacks.

65 See Thomas E. Skidmore, "Racial Ideas and Social Policy in Brazil, 1870–1940" in *The Idea of Race in Latin America, 1870–1940*, ed. Richard Graham (Austin: University of Texas Press, 1990), 7–36 and Parks, *Race and Culture*, 385.

66 For an account of the aboriginal struggle for social equality in Australia see Roberta B. Sykes, *Black Majority* (Victoria, Australia: Hudson Publishing, 1989).

67 Consider, for instance, the following quote:

> Now, a comment about the title of the book and why we have chosen the term "black population." What the immigrants from New Commonwealth and Pakistan (NCWP) and their children born have in common is the material consequences and, in very many cases, the direct experience of discrimination. Discrimination, as the studies, by Political and Economic Planning (PEP) have demonstrated, is based upon colour. Hence, the reference to Britain's black population. It can, of course, be argued that some immigrants and their children do not and would not want to be labelled as *black*. That is not denied, but the defence of this terminology in this context lies with the fact that, irrespective of their own particular beliefs, experiences and the wide range of cultural variations, racism and racial discrimination is a crucial determinant of their economic and social situation.

The Runnymede Trust and The Radical Statistics Race Group, *Britain's Black Population* (London: Heinemann Educational Books, 1980), xii. The following stipulation seems tantamount to Du Bois's revisionist proposal: "The term 'black' has been selected to refer generally to those people, usually of Afro-Caribbean and Indian sub-continent geographical origin, who have black or brown skin colouring. The term focuses on skin colour as the important factor in categorising people as either black or white, a distinction that is of social significance because it is used as a basis for social action." Frank Reeves, *British Racial Discourse* (Cambridge: Cambridge University Press, 1983), 255. See also Lionel Morrison, *As They See It* (London: Community Relations Commission, 1976), 35–49; Brian D. Jacobs, *Black Politics and Urban Crisis in Britain* (Cambridge: Cambridge University Press, 1986), 41–62; Paul Gilroy, *There Ain't No Black In The Union Jack* (London: Hutchinson, 1987).

68 In *Worlds of Color*, written near his ninetieth birthday, Du Bois gave the following description of Jean Du Bignon: "a 'white Black Girl' from New Orleans; that is, a well educated young white woman who was classed as 'Colored' because she had a Negro great-grandfather."

Worlds of Color (Millwood, N.Y.: Kraus-Thomson, 1976), 9. It should be noted here that Du Bois treats his own blood tie with his Dutch ancestors as inessential. Most likely this is because of his *cultural* identification with black people, as well as with his commitment to the "census" definition of a black person – namely, that a black person is a person who passes for a black person in the community where he lives. See Parks, *Race and Culture*, 293.

69   In the nineteenth century black Americans sometimes referred to themselves nonpejoratively as "Anglo-Africans." With a similar reference to a white cultural influence, Nathan Hare's book, *The Black Anglo Saxons* (New York: Collier Books, 1965), was meant to be a criticism of the assimilationist mentality of certain segments of the black middle class.

70   One notable exception is the white rap group, *Young Black Teenagers,* who explain their appropriation of this title (along with tunes such as, "Proud To Be Black" and "Daddy Kalled Me Niga Cause I Likeded To Rhyme") as an expression of their having grown up in a predominately black youth culture in New York City. See Joe Wood, "Cultural Consumption, From Elvis Presley to the Young Black Teenagers," *Village Voice Rock & Roll Quarterly*, 10–11.

71   Quoted in L. Perry Curtis, Jr, *Apes and Angels: The Irishman in Victorian Caricature* (Washington, D.C.: Smithsonian Institution Press, 1971), 1.

72   In his very interesting documentary film, *The Black and The Green*, St Claire Bourne explores the theme of black consciousness in the Irish Catholics' struggle for social equality.

73   See Norman Mailer's "The White Negro" in his *Advertisements for Myself* (New York: Andre Deutsch, 1964).

74   Kobena Mercer cites a passage from Arthur Rimbaud's "A Season in Hell" (1873) in which the claim is made: "I am a beast, a Negro". Mercer, "1968" in his *Welcome to the Jungle* (New York: Routledge, 1994), 432.

75   With regard to his discussion of Du Bois's concept of race, Anthony Appiah was sharply criticized by Houston Baker for downplaying the role of color discrimination in everyday affairs. See Baker's essay, "Caliban's Triple Play" in Gates, *"Race," Writing, and Difference*, 384–5 and Appiah's reply "The Conservation of 'Race'", *Black American Literature Forum*, 23.1 (Spring 1989): 37–60.

76   Cf. Morris Lounds, Jr, *Israel's Black Hebrews: Black Americans in Search of Identity* (Washington, D.C.: University Press of America, 1981), 209–13.

77   See Ozzie L. Edwards, "Skin Color As A Variable in Racial Attitudes of Black Urbanites," *Journal of Black Studies*, 3.4 (June, 1972): 473–83; Robert E. Washington, "Brown Racism and the Formation of a

World System of Racial Stratification," *International Journal of Politics, Culture, and Society*, 4.2., 1990, and Lincoln, "Color and Group Identity," 249–63.

78 With regard to the "self-questioning," "hesitation," "vacillation," and "contradiction" faced by mulattoes, Du Bois remarked that "combined race action is stifled, race responsibility is shirked, race enterprises languish, and the best blood, the best talent, the best energy of the Negro people cannot be marshalled to do the bidding of the race." (p. 488).

Chapter 5   Black Consciousness in the Art of Sargent Johnson

1   Douglas Daniels, *Pioneer Urbanites* (Berkeley: University of California Press, 1980/90) and Albert Broussard, *Black San Francisco* (Lawrence, KS: University Press of Kansas, 1993).
2   Daniels, *Pioneer Urbanites*, xiv.
3   Broussard, *Black San Francisco*, 15.
4   Alain Locke (ed.), *The New Negro: An Interpretation* (Boston: Atheneum, 1925/68).
5   Langston Hughes, *The Big Sea* (New York: Farrar, Straus & Giroux, 1940).
6   Verna Arvey, "Sargent Johnson", *Opportunity* 17 (July 1939): 213–14.
7   "San Francisco Artists," *San Francisco Chronicle* (October 1935): D3.
8   Alain Locke, "Advance on the Art Front", *Opportunity* 27.5 (May 1939): 132–6.
9   Alain Locke, "The Art of the Ancestors", *Survey Graphic* 6.6 (March 1925): 673.
10 Arvey, "Sargent Johnson," 214.
11 James A. Porter, *Modern Negro Art* (Washington D.C.: Howard University Press 1943/92) 95; Arvey 1939, 214.
12 James A. Porter, "The New Negro and Modern Art" in *The New Negro Thirty Years Afterwards*, eds Rayford W. Logan, Eugene C. Holmes, and G. Franklin Edwards (Washington D.C.: Howard University Press, 1955), 105.
13 Alain Locke, *Negro Art: Past and Present* (Salem, NH: Ayer, 1936/1991).
14 "San Francisco Artists," *San Francisco Chronicle* (October 1935): D3.
15 Dick Hebdige, *Hiding in the Light: On Images and Things* (London: Comnedia, 1988).
16 Knute Stiles, "San Francisco," *Artforum* 8 (May 1971): 84.
17 Cedric Dover, *American Negro Art* (New York: Graphic Society, 1960).

18 Beniamino Benvenuto Bufano, "For the Present We Are Busy" in Francis V. O'Connor (ed.), *Art for the Millions* (Greenwich, Conn.: New York Graphic Society Ltd., 1973), 108.
19 Romare Bearden and Harry Henderson, *A History of African-American Artists: From 1792 to the Present* (New York: Pantheon Books, 1993).
20 Richard D. McKinzie, *The New Deal for Artists* (Princeton University Press, 1973). Bufano's biographers claim that "He was also accused of carving the features of Harry Bridges, the labor leader, and of Russia's Lenin into the frieze." H. Wilkening and Sonia Brown, *Bufano: An Intimate Biography* (Berkeley: Howell-North Books, 1972), 148.
21 "Art Commission, WPA Tangle, 'Bufano' Frieze Causes First Class Fight," *San Francisco Chronicle* (14 November 1940): 1.
22 Bufano, "For the Present We Are Busy" in O'Connor, *Art for the Millions*.
23 O'Connor, *Art for the Millions*, 110.
24 Arvey, "Sargent Johnson," 214.
25 Lizzetta LeFalle-Collins and Shifra M. Goldman, *In the Spirit of Resistance: African-American Modernists and the Mexican Muralist School* (New York: The American Federation of Arts, 1996), 46.
26 *San Francisco Chronicle* (November 14, 1940): 1.
27 Abdias do Nascimento, *"Racial Democracy" in Brazil: Myth or Reality?* (Chicago: Third World Press, 1977).
28 O'Connor, *Art for the Millions*, 110.

Chapter 6 Black Vernacular Representation and Cultural Malpractice

1 "Blacks Fail to See Humor in Ted Danson's Blackface Tribute to Whoopi Goldberg", *Jet*, 84.1 (November 1, 1993): 56–9.
2 See Deborah Gray White, *Ar'n't I A Woman* (New York: W. W. Norton, 1985) and bell hooks, *Ain't I A Woman: Black Women and Feminism* (Boston: South End Press, 1982); but also see the rendering of some of Sojourner Truth's speeches in standard English in *Black Women in White America: A Documentary History*, ed. Gerda Lerner (New York: Vintage, 1972), 566–72, and in conventional southern black dialect in Olive Gilbert, comp., *Narrative of Sojourner Truth, A Bondwoman of Olden Time* (New York: Arno, 1968). For a critical discussion of the ideological orientation of Sojourner Truth's transcribers, see Nell Irvin Painter, "Sojourner Truth in Feminist Abolitionism: Difference, Slavery, and Memory," in *An Untrodden Path: Antislavery ad Women's Political Culture*, eds, Jean Fagan Yellin and John C. Van Horne (Ithaca: Cornell University Press, 1993).

3   Arthur Fauset criticized the earlier authors for inaccurately transcribing Truth's speech. "[W]hen in the following pages quotations are made from these later sources, it may seem that her English was normal at the beginning of her life and degenerated as she grew older. This, of course, is not the case. In her childhood she spoke a Dutch jargon, which, even if we knew the language, we probably could not transcribe." Arthur Huff Fauset, *Sojourner Truth: God's Faithful Pilgrim* (Durham, N.C.: University of North Carolina Press, 1938), vii.

4   Sterling A. Brown, "On Dialect Usage," in *The Slave's Narrative*, eds, Charles T. Davis and Henry Louis Gates, Jr (New York: Oxford University Press, 1985), 37–9.

5   Ibid., 35.

6   Warren Miller, *The Cool World* (New York: Fawcett World Library, 1969).

7   A similar suspicion was raised by June Jordan with regard to Miller's book and to Shirley Clarke's film version of the story. See June Jordan, *Civil Wars* (Boston: Beacon Press, 1981), 3–15.

8   According to Dillard, "Virtually every articulate Black critic has argued that the white writer ignores the meaning of the Negro's language, as well as of his experience in general." J.L. Dillard, *Lexicon of Black English* (New York: Seabury Press, 1977). Conversely, the charge of racism against Mark Twain has to be rethought in the light of new evidence that the voice of Huck Finn (and, hence, his use of the term "nigger") may have been influenced by a ten-year-old black servant. Anthony DePalma, "Huck Finn's Voice is Heard As Twain Meets Black Youth," *New York Times* (July 7, 1992), A1, A9.

9   Anna Julia Cooper, "The Negro's Dialect" in Anna Julia Cooper Papers, Folder #35, (Washington, D.C.: Moorland-Spingarn Research Center, Howard University), 23–4.

10   In addition to receiving her doctorate from the Sorbonne, Cooper published in both Latin and French. For a biographical account, see Louis Daniel Hutchinson, *Anna Julia Cooper: A Voice from the South* (Washington D.C.: Smithsonian Institution Press, 1982).

11   According to Dillard, "Zora Neale Hurston's writings come close to being the ultimate source for a rural Black lexicon." J. L. Dillard, "Can We Trust Literary Sources," in his *Lexicon of Black English*, 153.

12   Gale Jones remarked, "the problem with Hurston is how does one write of ordinary people without making the story seem trivial, without making the writer's concerns seem likewise?" "Breaking Out of the Caricatures of Dialect," in *Zora Neale Hurston*, eds, Henry L. Gates, Jr and Kwame A. Appiah (New York: Amistad, 1993), 147. Richard Wright claimed, "Miss Hurston seems to have no desire whatever to move in the direction of serious fiction. . . . Her dialogue manages to

catch the psychological movements of the Negro folk-mind in their pure simplicity, but that's as far as it goes. Miss Hurston voluntarily continues in her novel the tradition which was forced upon the Negro in the theater, that is the minstrel technique that makes the 'white folks' laugh." "Review of *Their Eyes Were Watching God*" in *Zora Neale Hurston*, 17.

13   Alain L. Locke, "Jingo, Counter-Jingo and Us" in *the Critical Temper of Alain Locke*, ed. Jeffrey C. Stewart (New York: Garland, 1983), 260.
14   Alain L. Locke, "Dry Fields and Green Pastures" in ibid., 288.
15   See, for instance, Roger Abrahams, *Deep Down in the Jungle* (Chicago: Aldine Publishing Co., 1970), 3; John W. Roberts, *From Trickster to Badman* (Philadelphia: University of Pennsylvania Press, 1989), 35. For an interesting debate about the African origins of African-American folklore, see Daniel J. Crowley, (ed.) *African Folklore in the New World* (Austin: University of Texas, 1977).
16   Henry L. Gates, Jr, *The Signifying Monkey* (New York: Oxford University Press, 1988), xxii.
17   See R. D. G. Kelley, "Notes on Deconstructing 'The Folk'", *American Historical Review* (December 1992), 1400.
18   Alain L. Locke, "The Drama of Negro Life," Locke Papers, Box 107, 14, Moorland-Springarn Research Center, Howard University. Locke wrote several somewhat different versions of this paper under the same title, some of which were never published, or were slightly altered for publication. In subsequent notes, reference will be made to: Locke Papers, "The Drama of Negro Life," followed by a designation of his five-page version, his 16-page typescript version, or his published version appearing in Stewart, *Critical Temper*, 87–91. See also Locke's essay, "The Negro and the American Theatre," in *Theatre: Essays on the Arts of the Theatre*, ed. Edith J. R. Isaacs (Freeport, NY: Books for Libraries Press, 1927), 249–56.
19   Locke queried, "Is the dance hall in the city as innocent an amusement as the plantation dance in the corn crib?" Paul Laurence Dunbar Lecture delivered at Fisk University, date unknown, Locke Papers, Box 125, File #46, 15.
20   Alain Locke, "The Negro and the American Stage" in Stewart, *Critical Temper*, 85. Alain Locke, "The Negro and The American Theatre," *Theatre: Essays on the Arts of the Theatre*, 301. Locke co-authored a scenario for a Negro folk play in which the opening scene is set in the African jungle and the closing scene is set in a New York concert hall: Nokomis Cobb and Alain L. Locke, *Scenario Outline of a Negro Folk Play for Dramatic and Motion Picture Presentation*, 1933 in Locke Papers, miscellaneous file.

21 Locke-Hurston Correspondence, June 13–16, 1929, Locke Papers, Folder 163, File #28. Later Locke criticized Hurston's published field work, *Tell My Horse*, as "anthropological gossip." Locke, "The Negro: 'New' or Newer. A Retrospective Review of the Literature of the Negro for 1938," Stewart, *Critical Temper*, 279.

22 See, for instance, Locke's review of N. N. Puckett, *Folk Beliefs of the Southern Negro*, date unknown, Locke Papers, Box 164–133, Folder 33 in which he criticized Puckett's inability to ascertain "genuine survivals." Similarly, he criticized the conclusions of a report by the Virginia WPA: "In their present shape they suggest a little too strongly the thesis of straight African survivals, and need to be gone over carefully from the acculturation angle as composite folkways and folk-lore, which in the main they seem to represent." Alain Locke, "Of Native Sons: Real and Otherwise," Stewart, *Critical Temper*, 306.

23 Locke Papers, Dunbar Lecture, 6.

24 Locke Papers, "The Drama of Negro Life", five-page version, 4.

25 Locke Papers, "The Drama of Negro Life," 16-page version, 5.

26 Locke, 6.

27 See Locke Papers, Dunbar Lecture, 12–13. Locke presents a fuller account of his sociohistorical view of race in Alain LeRoy Locke, *Race Contacts and Interracial Relations*, ed. Jeffrey Stewart (Washington, D.C.: Howard University Press, 1992) and in the editorial sections of Alain L. Locke and Bernard J. Stern (eds), *When Peoples Meet* (New York: Progressive Education Association, 1942).

28 Locke Papers, Dunbar Lecture, 13.

29 It is worth noting that Locke's authorized interpreter, Margaret Just Butcher, presented a more evenhanded assessment of Hurston. According to Butcher, "The work of such present-day writers as Guy Johnson, Julia Peterkin and Zora Neale Hurston (to name but three out of many) has done a great deal to establish the folk tale in legitimate perspective." *The Negro in American Culture* (New York: New American Library, 1956), 45.

30 Locke Papers, "Folk Tale lecture," Locke Papers, Box 164–133, 2–3.

31 Locke Papers, "The Drama of Negro Life," 16-page version, 7.

32 Locke, 7.

33 Locke, 16.

34 Locke papers, "The Drama of Negro Life," five-page version, 4.

35 Locke, 5.

36 Alain Locke, "Dry Fields and Green Pastures," Stewart, *Critical Temper*, 288.

37 Alain Locke, "Jingo, Counter-Jingo and Us," Stewart, *Critical Temper*, 260.

38 See, for instance, Alain Locke, "The Negro and the American Theatre," Stewart, *Critical Temper*, 297 and 58; Alain Locke, "The Eleventh Hour of Nordicism: Retrospective Review of the Literature of the Negro for 1935," Stewart, 229; Alain Locke, "The Negro: 'New' or Newer," Stewart, 274, and Alain Locke, "From *Native Son to Invisible Man*: A Review of the Literature of the Negro for 1952" in Stewart, 385. For Locke's main argument against propaganda, see Alain Locke, "Art or Propaganda?" in Stewart, 27–8 and Alain Locke, "Propoganda – or Poetry?" in Stewart, 55–61.

39 Locke Papers, "The Drama of Negro Life," five-page version, 4.

40 According to Locke, "And a test of the achievement of such a point of view will not only be the changed position of the Negro in the picture but the altered values – as the painters say, with which he will have to be painted." Locke Papers, "The Drama of Negro Life," five-page version, 4.

41 Alain Locke, "The Eleventh Hour of Nordicism," Stewart, *Critical Temper*, 230.

42 Locke complained of "an unfortunate insistence of proletarian poetry on being drab, prosy and inartistic, as though the regard for style were a bourgeois taint and an act of social treason." Alain Locke, "Propaganda – or Poetry?" Stewart, *Critical Temper*, 57. He included some of the poetry of Langston Hughes and Richard Wright among this propagandistic proletarian school. While speaking favorably about the successful run of the play *Stevedore*, he remarked that "Only a driving, pertinent theme could carry such amateurish dialogue and technique. . . ." Alain Locke, "The Eleventh Hour of Nordicism" in Stewart, 231–2. And, after giving Wright's *Native Son* a favorable review, Locke cited Wright's communist ideology as a major flaw. Alain Locke, "From *Native Son to Invisible Man*: A Review of the Literature of the Negro for 1952" in Stewart, 385.

43 Locke Papers, "The Drama of Negro Life," 16-page version, 7.

44 Locke, 7.

45 Alain Locke, "The Negro and the American Theatre," Stewart, *Critical Temper*, 300.

46 Stewart, *Critical Temper*, 302. Elsewhere Locke states this point in relation to his general theory of folk art. According to Locke, "it [Negro drama] learns how to beautify the native psychological idioms of our folk life and recovers the ancestral folk tradition, it will express itself in a poetic and symbolic style of drama that will remind us of Synge and the Irish Folk Theatre or Ansky and the Yiddish Theatre. There are many analogies both of temperament, social condition and cultural reactions, which suggest this." Alain Locke, "The Drama of Negro Life" in Stewart, 90.

47 Alain Locke and Sterling A. Brown, "Folk Values in a New Medium" in *Black Films and Film-makers*, ed. Lindsay Patterson (New York: Dodd, Mead & Co., 1975), 26–7.

There is a typescript of Locke's contribution to this joint article in the Locke Papers. Apparently he wrote the section on *Hearts in Dixie* and Sterling Brown wrote the section on *Hallelujah*. Locke Papers, Box 65. In his review of the play, *Cabin in the Sky*, Locke wrote in a similar praiseworthy fashion. He claimed that it "does convey an authentic and characteristic Negro feeling" and that "Its comedy is inoffensive . . . and its tempo and emotional tone are set true to real folk values." Alain Locke, "Of Native Sons: Real and Otherwise" in Stewart, *Critical Temper*, 305. He also spoke highly of the play, *The Rider of Dreams*, as "showing for the first time a way of poetizing humble folk characters and extracting comedy without farce." Locke Papers, "The Drama of Negro Life," 16-page version, 4. It is worth noting that Locke wrote a letter agreeing to be a consultant on *Song of the South* with Disney Studios. See Locke's letter to Walter Wanger, September 4, 1944, Locke Papers, Box 164–133.

48 Locke and Brown, "Folk Values in a New Medium," 26.
49 Ibid., 26.
50 Ibid., 26.
51 Gary Null, *Black Hollywood* (Secaucus, N.J.: Citadel Press, 1975), 27.
52 Saunders Redding, "The Negro Writer and American Literature" in Anger, and Beyond, ed. Herbert Hill (New York: Harper and Row, 1968), 7.
53 Ibid., 4.
54 Saunders Redding, "The Problems of the Negro Writer" in *Black & White in American Culture*, eds. Jules Chametzky and Sidney Kaplan (Amberst: University of Massachusetts Press, 1969), 363. For a discussion of the link between apes and the Sambo image, see Joseph Boskin, *Sambo* (New York: Oxford University Press, 1986), 123.
55 Saunders Redding, *To Make A Poet Black*, (College Park, MD: McGrath Publishing Company, 1968), 52.
56 The term "signifying" derives its meaning from African-American folklore, specifically the trickster tale, "The Signifying Monkey and the Lion." According to Roger Abrahams, "The name 'signifying' shows the monkey to be a trickster, signifying being the language of trickery, that set of words or gestures achieving Hamlet's 'direction through indirection' and used often, especially among the young, to humiliate an adversary." *Deep Down in The Jungle* (Chicago: Aldine Publishing Company, 1963/70), 66–7. In his well-received attempt "to lift the discourse of Signifyin[g] from the vernacular to the discourse of literary criticism" Henry Louis Gates offers the following revision of the term: "When one text Signifies upon another text, by tropological

revision or repetition and difference, the double-voiced utterance allows us to chart discrete formal relationships in Afro-American literary history. Signifyin[g], then, is a metaphor for textual revision." Henry Louis Gates, Jr, *The Signifying Monkey* (New York: Oxford University Press, 1988), xi and 88.

57 Cf. Robert C. Toll, *Blacking Up: The Minstrel Show in Nineteenth-Century America* (Oxford: Oxford University Press, 1974), 268–248; and Joseph Boskin, "The Life and Death of Sambo: Overview of an Historical Hang-Up" in *Remus, Rastas, Revolution*, ed. Marshall Fishwich (Bowling Green, OH: Bowling Green Popular Press, n.d.), 147.

58 See, for instance, Howard McGary, "Resistance and Slavery", in Howard McGary and Bill E. Lawson, *Between Slavery and Freedom* (Bloomington: Indiana University Press, 1992), 38–9. Pierson has cautioned against using this conceptual dichotomy. According to Pierson, "A more African perspective, on the other hand, would permit us to understand that the black bondsmen intended their musical satire as a basic and primary weapon in their arsenal of resistance against oppression." William D. Piersen, *Black Legacy: America's Hidden Heritage* (Amherst: University of Massachusetts Press, 1993), 54.

59 This interpretation of Dunbar's work was originally maintained by George W. Ellis in his early essay, "The Mission of Dunbar," *The Boston Citizen*, 2 (1915) but has been supported recently by John Brown Childs, *Leadership, Conflict, and Cooperation in Afro-American Social Thought* (Philadelphia: Temple University Press, 1981), 92; Marcellus Blount, "The Preacherly Text: African American Poetry and Vernacular Performance," *Proceedings Modern Language Association*, 107.3 (May 1992): 586; and Gossie Harold Hudson, "Paul Laurence Dunbar: Dialect Et La Negritude," *Phylon*, 4.3 (September 1973): 242.

60 J. L. Dillard, *Lexicon of Black English*, 148.

61 William J. Mahar, "Black English in Early Blackface Minstrelsy: A New Interpretation of the Sources of Minstrel Show Dialect," *American Quarterly* (1984): 284.

62 Joseph V. Tirella, "Video Vigilante," *Vibe*, 2.3 (April 1994): 23.

63 John Michael Spencer refers to the white audience for rap as "resentment listeners." See "The Emergency of Black and the Emergence of Rap," *Black Sacred Music*, 5.1 (spring 1991): 5. David Samuels proclaimed gangsta reppers to be nothing more than cartoonish minstrels entertaining white kids. See "The Rap on Rap," *The New Republic* (November 11, 1991): 24–6. See also J. D. Considine, "Fear of a Rap Planet," *Musician* (February 1992): 57.

64 Sterling Brown justified his interpretation of Dunbar as an accommodationist by reference to "his omission of the hardships that

the Negro folk met with." *Negro Poetry and Drama,* (New York: Atheneum, 1978), 36. See also Saunders Redding, "Negro Writer," 6.

65 Sterling Brown cites the testimony of Dunbar's friends to show that it is not clear what Dunbar thought of his dialectal poetry. Brown also cites Dunbar's well-known autobiographical line from "The Poet" in which he expressed regret that his non-dialectal verse had been ignored. *Negro Poetry and Drama,* 47.

66 Although Dunbar was sometimes criticized for not speaking out against racial injustice, he wrote a letter on race riots and lynchings that was widely published. "Negro Author Voices Protest," *Chicago Tribune,* (July 10, 1903): 3. Revell points out that Dunbar risked the goodwill of his editor to get his poem on lynching, "The Haunted Oak," printed in the *Century.* See Peter Revell, *Paul Laurence Dunbar* (Boston: Twayne Publishers, 1979), 172.

67 See, for instance, Revell, *Paul Laurence Dunbar,* 168.

68 Sterling Brown noted that "When Dunbar dealt with the harsher aspects of Negro life, he discarded not only dialect, but also directness and simplicity." Brown, *Negro Poetry and Drama,* 48. Locke argued that Dunbar's race consciousness extended to his poetry written in standard English as well. Locke Papers, Dunbar Lecture, 9–11.

69 Frederick Douglass is reported to have been pressured by white abolitionists to speak in a dialect to prove that he had really been on a plantation. See Leon F. Litwack, *North of Slavery: The Negro in the Free States, 1790–1860* (Chicago: University of Chicago Press, 1961).

70 Vincent Harding, "Religion and Resistance among Antebellum Negroes 1800–1860," in *The Making of Black America,* vol. 1, eds, August Meier and Elliot Rudwick (New York: Atheneum, 1969), 179–97; Raymond Bauer and Alice Bauer, "Day to Day Resistance to Slavery," in *Old Memories, New Moods,* ed. Peter I. Rose (New York: Atherton, 1970), 5–29.

71 John Brown Childs is quite critical of this feature of the New Negro movements. John Brown Childs, *Leadership, Conflict, and Cooperation,* 69–80. Gates's claim "that dialect ceased to be a major form in the Harlem Renaissance" should not be taken to imply that Locke's advocacy of folk art went unheralded. See Henry Louis Gates, Jr, *Figures in Black* (New York: Oxford University Press, 1987), 180.

72 Gates seems to want to deny this. He states, "Afro-American dialects exist between two poles, one English and one lost in some mythical linguistic kingdom now irrecoverable." *Figures in Black,* 172.

73 David Toop, *Rap Attack 2 African Rap to Global Hip Hop* (London: Serpent's Tail, 1991). See also Cornel West, "On Afro-American Popular Music: From Bebop to Rap," *Black Sacred Music,* 6.1 (Spring 1992): 292.

74 See Melvin Patrick Ely, *The Adventures of Amos 'n' Andy* (New York: The Free Press, 1991), 194–244 and Thomas Cripps, "Amos 'n' Andy and the Debate over American Racial Integration" in *American History/ Amrican Television*, ed. John E. O'Connor (New York: Frederick Ungar Publishing Co., 1983), 33–54.

75 Ice Cube gave the following response to an interviewer's question of whether he aimed to educate whites as well: "Yeah, if they're educated too, then that's fine; if they're not, that's fine too. . . . As long as I get to *my* brothers and sisters who are spilling blood on the streets." Lisa Anthony, "Lyrics of Fury," *Hip-Hop Connection*, 36 (January 1992): 15.

76 Frank Owen, "Hanging Tough," *Spin*, 6.1 (April 1990): 34.

77 Kierna Mayo Dawsey, "Caught Up in the (Gangsta) Rapture," *The Source*, 57 (June 1994): 58–62. See also Clarence Lusane, "Rap, Race and Politics," *Race and Class*, 35.1 (July–September, 1993): 52–5.

78 Ras Baraka, "Mo' Dialogue," *The Source*, 24 (September 1991): 32.

79 Lisa Anthony, "Lyrics of Fury", 15.

80 Paul Gilroy, *There Ain't No Black in the Union Jack* (London: Hutchinson, 1987): 209–17 and Tricia Rose, *Black Noise: Rap Music and Black Cultural Resistance in Contemporary American Popular Culture* (Middletown, Conn.: Wesleyan University Press, 1994).

81 See Lusane, "Rap, Race and Politics," 44.

82 Lusane, "Rap, Race and Politics," 49–55; and Robin D. G. Kelly, "Kickin' Reality, Kickin' Ballistics: The Cultural Politics of Gangsta Rap in Post-industrial Los Angeles," in his *Race Rebels: Culture, Politics, and the Black Working Class* (New York: The Free Press, 1994), 183–227.

83 See, for instance, Cornel West, "On Afro-American Popular Music: From Bebop to Rap," *Black Sacred Music*, 6.1 (Spring 1992): 294; Michael E. Dyson, *Reflecting Black* (Minnepolis: University of Minnesota Press, 1993), 15; James Barnard, "The Rise of Rap: Reflections on the Growth of the Hip Hop Nation," *African Commentary* (June 1990): 50, cited in Spencer, "The Emergency of Black and the Emergence of Rap," 7.

84 For a defense of the claim that motives are irrelevant, see Michael Philips, "Racist Acts and Racist Humor," *Canadian Journal of Philosophy* 26.1 (March 1984): 82.

85 With regard to the social meaning of "bitch" and "whore" a similar line of thought has been argued by members of the female gangsta rap group, Hoez With Attitude. See Rob Marriott, "Studio Hoez," *The Source*, 56 (May 1994): 46.

86 Ice Cube illuminates what it means to be a "sellout" in the following remarks: "I think you compromise your integrity to sell records to a pop crowd, that's when you've gone pop. . . . I'm on the pop charts,

but I ain't poppin' shit!" Cleo H. Choker, "Down for Whatever," *The Source*, 53 (February 1994): 62.

87 Clarence Lusane makes this point in his statement that "[t]he commodification of black resistance is not the same as resistance to a society built upon commodificaton." Lusane, "Rap, Race and Politics," 45.

88 Ibid., 42.

89 For a selection of these narratives see Daryl Cumber Dance, *Shuckin' and Jivin'* (Bloomington: Indiana University Press, 1978), 224–46. See also H. Nigel Thomas, *From Folklore to Fiction: A Study of Folk Heroes and Rituals in the Black American Novel* (New York: Greenwood Press, 1988), 71–9.

90 I owe this point to Ronald Judy.

91 See Thomas, *From Folklore to Fiction*, 71–2.

92 Quoted in Stewart, *Critical Temper*, 300.

93 For Locke's references to Zola, see Stewart, *Critical Temper*, 299–300, 323, 329–30 and 332.

94 According to Ezy-E, "The way I see it, as long as you're being talked about, people still remember you. All publicity is good publicity whether it's bad or good." Carter Harris, "Easy Street", *The Source*, 58 (July 1994): 89. Ezy-E is the owner of Ruthless Records, a company that has sold over 20 million records since 1986. A recent dispute with Dr. Dre led Ezy-E to make the following remarks: "Dr. Dre's claimin' he's from a place he ain't really from. . . . He ain't never gang-banged or sold dope. Never, never in his life. All of a sudden he know gankin' and robbin' and all this chronic and low ridin'. He ain't never done that shit in his life." Carter Harris, "Easy Street," *The Source*, 58 (July 1994): 76.

95 MC Ren is reported to have converted to Islam.

96 Spencer, "The Emergency of Black and the Emergence of Rap," 7.

97 Snoop Dogg and Dr. Dre, for instance.

98 See James Bernard, "The L. A. Rebellion: Message Behind the Madness", *The Source*, 35 (August 1992): 38–48.

Chapter 7   *Marooned in America: Black Urban Youth Culture and Social Pathology*

1 Daniel P. Moynihan, "Employment, Income, and the Ordeal of the Negro Family," in *The Negro American*, eds Talcott Parsons and Kenneth B. Clark (Boston: Beacon Press, 1965), 157.

2   For an analysis of the rise of neoconservative thought regarding race and social policy, see Cornel West, "Race and Social Theory: Towards a Genealogical Materialist Analysis" in *The Year Left 2: An American Socialist Yearbook*, eds M. Davis, M. Marable, F. Pfeil, and M. Sprinker (London: Verso, 1987).

3   William Julius Wilson, *The Truly Disadvantaged* (Chicago: University of Chicago Press, 1987).

4   Leonard Harris, "Agency and the Concept of the Underclass" in *The Underclass Question*, ed. Bill E. Lawson (Philadelphia: Temple University Press, 1992), 33–54.

5   Some of Wilson's more recent overtures in this direction are plagued by his use of misguided concepts such as "hyperghettoization." Loïc J. D. Wacguant and William J. Wilson, "The Cost of Racial and Class Exclusion in the Inner City" in *Annals*, AAPSS, 501 (January, 1989). In response to criticisms of his use of the term "underclass" Wilson reluctantly proposed to substitute the term "ghetto poor," although he professed a preference for the "subtle theoretical meaning" of the former. The term "ghetto," however, has become a post-1960s media reference term for the black community which is equally pejorative, if not overtly racist, in some contexts. Clearly the problem stems from a major shortcoming of Wilson's theoretical orientation, namely, his failure to provide an analysis of culture. See his "Studying Inner City Social Dislocations: The Challenge of Public Agenda Research," *American Sociological Review*, 56 (February 1–14, 1991). In this regard, Paul Gilroy has introduced a much more fruitful methodology for understanding the conceptual scheme embedded in black expressive cultures. See his *There Ain't No Black in the Union Jack* (London: Hutchinson, 1986).

6   I use the term "assimilation" to refer specifically to the claim that black people ought to acquire the values, that is, cultural practices, of the dominant European groups at the expense of retaining any such values, that is, cultural practices, that are derived from their own African heritage. For a discussion of the variety of meanings attached to this notion, see Milton M. Gordon, *Assimilation in American Life* (New York: Oxford University Press, 1964).

7   Orlando Patterson denounces recent scholarship for overlooking the historical persistence since slavery of the so-called "underclass" problem. See his "Toward A Study of Black America", *Dissent* (fall 1989).

8   See, for example, Thomas Sowell, *Ethnic America: A History* (New York: Basic Books, 1981); and Walter Williams, *The State Against Blacks* (New York; McGraw-Hill, 1982).

9   Martin Delany, "The Condition, Elevation, Emigration and Destiny of the Colored People of the United States" (1852) in *Negro Social and Political Thought, 1850–1920*, ed. Howard Brotz (New York: Basic Books, 1966), 37–101.

10 Edward Blyden, "The Call of Providence to the Descendents of Africa in America" (1862) in Brotz, 112–26.

11 See Valentin Y. Mudimbe, *The Invention of Africa* (Bloomington: Indiana University Press, 1988), chap. 4.

12 Frederick Douglass, "The Present and Future of the Colored Race in America" (1863) in Brotz, *Negro Social and Political Thought*, 267–77.

13 Booker T. Washington, "Atlanta Exposition Address" (September 18, 1895) in Brotz, 356–9 and "Address Delivered at Hampton Institute" (November 15, 1895) in Brotz, 371–2.

14 Laurence Thomas explores the ethical implications of Washington's social philosophy in his "Rawlsian Self-Respect and the Black Consciousness Movement," *The Philosophical Forum* 9 (1978): 303–14.

15 Washington, "Address Delivered at Hampton Institute," 372.

16 Louis R. Harlan, "Booker T. Washington and the Politics of Accomodation," in *Black Leaders of the Twentieth Century*, ed. John Hope Franklin and August Meier (Chicago: University of Illinois Press, 1982).

17 Du Bois, "The Conservation of Races," Brotz, 488.

18 Nathan I. Huggins, *Voices from the Harlem Rennaissance* (New York: Oxford University Press, 1976).

19 Alain Locke, "The New Negro," in *The New Negro*, ed. Alain Locke (New York: Albert and Charles Boni, 1925).

20 See, for example, Hazel Carby, *Reconstructing Womanhood* (New York: Oxford University Press, 1987), chaps 4 and 5; and Mary Helen Washington, (ed.) *Invented Lives* (Garden City, NJ: Doubleday, 1987), part 2.

21 See Huggins, *Voices from the Harlem Renaissance*; and John Brown Childs, "Concepts of Culture in Afro-American Political Thought, 1890–1920," *Social Texts* 4.28 (1982): 28–43.

22 Du Bois's strongest anti-assimilationist views were expressed around the turn of the century, especially in "The Conservation of Races." His position was modified considerably in his later writings. See for instance, his *Dusk of Dawn: An Essay Toward an Autobiography of a Race Concept* (1940; reprint, New York: Schocken, 1968).

23 Henry Louis Gates, Jr has questioned the arbitrariness of this alleged connection between cultural production as a sign of civilization and the elimination of race prejudice. See his *Figures in Black* (New York: Oxford University Press, 1987), xxiii.

24 See Williams, *The State against Blacks*; and Thomas Sowell, *Civil Rights: Rhetoric or Reality?* (New York: William Morrow, 1984).

25 Marcus Garvey, "Race Assimilation" (1922), in Brotz, *Negro Social and Political Thought*, 553–4.

26 Julianne Malveaux, "Race, Class and Black Poverty," *Black Scholar* 19.3 (May/June 1988): 19.

27 Stephen Steinberg, *The Ethnic Myth*, 2nd ed. (Boston: Beacon Press, 1989).

28 In his much-neglected book, *The Black Underclass* (San Francisco: Jossey-Bass, 1980), Douglas G. Glasgow argued for structural change that would address chronic unemployment in black neighborhoods.

29 James Jennings, "Escaping from the Poorhouse of Ideas," *In These Times*, 17–23 February 1988.

30 Jack L. Daniel and Anita L. Allen, "Newsmagazines, Public Policy, and the Black Agenda," in *Discrimination and Discourse*, ed. Geneva Smitherman-Donaldson and Teun A. Van Dijk (Detroit: Wayne State University Press, 1988).

31 See Herman Gray, "The Reemergence of 'Culture' in Public Discourse about Racial Inequality and Poverty: The Instance of Media Coverage of the Urban Underclass," paper presented at the Annual Meeting of The Society for the Study of Social Problems, Berkeley, California, August, 1989; and Steinbert, *The Ethnic Myth*.

32 Several black independent film-makers, including Haile Gerima (*Bush Mama and Ashes and Embers*), Billy Woodberry (*Bless Their Little Hearts*), and Charles Burnett (*Killer of Sheep*), have made films that present the perspective of black urban poor people.

   Unfortunately, however, their films have not been widely distributed and, consequently, are relatively unknown to either black or white audiences.

33 The class status of rap is indicated most significantly by the linguistic style and paralinguistic behavior of rap artists. Although there are many middle-class suburban rappers, as well as a growing number of white artists, they must be viewed as participating in a black urban art form.

34 Playthell Benjamin refers to rap artists as "cultural deviates, sociopaths who are leading the way to self-destruction." "Miles of Heart," *Village Voice* (November 6, 1990), 85. See also Nathan Hare and Julia Hare, *Bringing the Black Boy to Manhood: The Passage* (San Francisco: The Black Think Tank, 1985), 17.

35 For an analysis of the historical significance of this myth, see Angela Y. Davis, *Women, Race and Class* (New York: Random House, 1981), chap. 11.

36 See Rene Girard, "Generative Scapegoating" in *Violent Origins: Ritual Killing and Cultural Formation*, eds. Walter Burkert, Rene Girard, and Jonathan Z. Smith (Stanford: Stanford University Press, 1987), 73–105.

37 In a recent editorial supporting the police against a public outcry over the Rodney King beating, Christopher Matthews asks, "Who separates the innocent from the guys with the automatic weapons? Who must stalk and restalk the murderers and muggers the courts cannot hold? Who keeps the underclass under control? The cops." "Sometimes its difficult, but support your local police!" *San Francisco Examiner* (March 24, 1991): A-25.

38 This suggestion has been rejected by Frank Owen, who maintains that "Criminal imagery in rap does not oppose the mainstream at all. It instead creates a vicious, supercilious caricature of mainstream values, with all the liberal cant about honesty and fair play, truth and justice, brutally shorn off." *Spin* 4.7 (October 1988): 52. Similarly, Kevin Mattson has argued that rap artists "take up the tradition of black protest not as politics but as style." "The Dialectic of Powerlessness: Black Identity Culture and Affirmative Action," *Telos* (summer 1990): 178. But clearly, if rap were only a matter of style and not politics, then why would it provoke various authorities to engage the state apparatus to suppress it, as in the case of the State of Florida's prosecution of 2 Live Crew and the FBI's investigative report to Congress on rap music and its effect on national security. See Lisa Jones, "The Signifying Monkees," *Village Voice* (November 6, 1990): 43–7, 171, and Houston A. Baker Jr, "Handling 'Crisis,' " *Callaloo*, 13.2 (spring 1990): 177.

39 A remark made by Chuck D of Public Enemy in an interview with John Leland, "Armageddon in Effect," *Spin*, 4.6 (September 1988): 48. Brand Nubian's Derek X claimed: "It's our mass media for getting our message across," "Brand Nubian," *Rap Masters Presents Wanted: Rap's 25 Most Hardcore* (April 1991): 48. See also, Jon Pareles, "How Rap Moves to Television's Beat," *New York Times* (January 14, 1990): Sec. 2, 1.

40 See Gilroy, *There Ain't No Black in the Union Jack*, chap. 5.

41 Robin Hoffman, "Digital Sampling – Lawyers Debate the Legal Realities of an Emerging New Art Form," *Backstage* (October 27, 1989): 34.

42 The expression "criminal minded" was coined by KRS-One as an album title and discussed at length on the liner notes of Boogie Down Production's *By All Means Necessary* album.

43 Nancy Guevara arrives at a similar conclusion. See her article, "Women Writin' Rappin' Breakin' " in *The Year Left 2*, eds M. Davis,

M. Marable, F. Pfeil, and M. Sprinker, 173. Since the publication of Guevara's article, there has developed a more widespread radical black consciousness movement among rap artists. Isis, Brand Nubian, Paris, and many other younger-generation rappers have begun to exert considerable influence on the political content of music by older-generation rappers such as Daddy Kane and Kool Moe D.

44   Jack Beatty attributes to Glen Loury the claim that the success of the black middle class "lies precisely in their euthanasia of the memory of the ghetto." "The Self-Discovery of the Black Middle Class," *The Boston Globe Magazine* (November 17, 1985): 49.

45   See, for instance, Louis Kraar, "The Drug Trade," *Fortune* 117.13 (June 20, 1988): 26–38; and Peter T. White, "Coca – An Ancient Herb Turns Deadly," *National Geographic* 175.1 (January 1989): 3–47.

46   Terry Williams, *The Cocaine Kids* (Reading, MA: Addison-Wesley, 1988).

47   Orlando Patterson insists that there is a distinction between problems that are cultural continuities and those that are socioeconomically conditioned persistences. "Study of Black America," 477.

48   Michel Foucault, *Discipline and Punish* (New York: Pantheon, 1977).

49   Bill Lawson, "Crime, Minorities and the Social Contract," *Criminal Justice Ethics*, 9.2 (Summer/Fall 1990): 16–24.

50   This recoding of negative images is reflected in many of the names adopted by rap artists, such as Intelligent Hoodlum, Public Enemy, Special Ed, Hoes With Attitude, Bitches With Problems, and Niggas With Attitude.

51   The stringent measure taken to suppress rap music cannot but remind us of the earlier slave codes that aimed to outlaw African drum practices.

52   E. Franklin Frazier, *Black Bourgeoisie* (New York: Free Press, 1957).

53   Thomas Sowell, *Race and Economics* (New York: Longman, 1975).

Chapter 8   Black Marxist in Babylon: Bayard Rustin and the 1968 UFT Strike

References to Rustin's Writings

PP "From Protest to Politics: The Future of the Civil Rights Movement," *Commentary* (February 1964), 111–22.

IRL "The Influence of the Right and Left in the Civil Rights Movement." An address to the Negro Leadership Conference, New York City (January 30–31, 1965), 123–31.

BPCP " 'Black Power' and Coalition Politics," *Commentary* (February 1965): 154–65.

MHM "Making His Mark," [Review of *The Autobiography of Malcolm X*] *Sunday Herald Tribune*, "Book Week" (November 14, 1965): 132–9.

MR "The Watts 'Manifesto' and the McCone Report," *Commentary* (March 1966): 140–53.

GBB "Guns, Bread, and Butter," *War/Peace Report* (March 1967), 166–8.

KPD "Dr. King's Painful Dilemma," *New Amsterdam News* (March 3, 1967): 169–70.

WOEG "A Way Out of the Exploding Ghetto," *New York Times Magazine* (August 13, 1967): 178–86.

LLHS *"The Lessons of the Long Hot Summer,"* *Commentary* (October 1967): 187–99.

MBM "The Mind of the Black Militant." An address to the Conference on the Schoolhouse in the City, Stanford University (July 10, 1967), 206–12.

ID "Integration within Decentralization," Rustin's John Dewey Award acceptance speech, addressed to members of the United Federation of Teachers (April 6, 1968), 213–21.

MLK "Reflections on the Death of Martin Luther King, Jr.", *AFL-CIO American Federationist* (May 1968), 222–9.

AF "The Anatomy of Frustration." An address to the Anti-Defamation League of B'nai B'rith (May 6, 1968), 230–7.

SCSC "Soul Searching vs. Social Change," *New York Amesterdam News* (May 18, 1968): 238–9.

SE "Separate is Not Equal," *New York Amsterdam News* (February 13, 1969): 253–4.

BC "What about Black Capitalism," *New York Amsterdam News* (March 8, 1969): 259–60.

APR "The Total Vision of A. Philip Randolph," *The New Leader* (April 14, 1969): 261–6.

NMG "No More Guns," *New York Amsterdam News* (April 24, 1969): 267–8.

RNMC "The Role of the Negro Middle Class," *Crisis* (June–July 1969): 271–6.

TB "An Exchange with Daniel Moynihan and Thomas A. Billings," *The New Leader* (December 22, 1969): 280–7.

FBS "The Failure of Black Separatism," *Harper's Magazine* (January 1970): 291–308.

BN "Benign Neglect: A Reply to Daniel Moynihan," *Long Island Press* (March 15, 1970): 309–15.

VSS "Violence and the Southern Strategy," *New York Amsterdam News* (April 23, 1970): 316–17.

DBW "Death in Black and White," *New York Amsterdam News* (May 21, 1970): 318–19.

BU "The Blacks and the Unions," *Harper's Magazine* (May 1971): 335–49.
All page references to the above sources are in Bayard Rustin, *Down the Line: The Collected Writings of Bayard Rustin* (Chicago: Quadrangle Books, 1971).

1   Daniel Perlstein, "The Case against Community: Bayard Rustin and the 1968 New York School Crisis," *Educational Foundation* (Winter 1994) and "The Question is Race," a roundtable on racism, hosted by Phil Donahue that was aired on PBS in spring 1993.
2   Robert Gore reported having mixed feelings after hearing a debate between Rustin and Malcolm X. Gore's remarks are cited in August Meier and Elliott Rudwick, *CORE* (New York: Oxford University Press, 1973), 206.
3   See BPCP, 158 and WOEG, 184.
4   Perlstein, "The Case against Community," 56.
5   Although Rustin presents this as his official view in his Radner Lectures, it should be noted that he sometimes identified only two phases of the civil rights struggle. See his *Strategies for Freedom* (New York: Columbia University Press, 1976) and BU, 335.
6   Rustin's conception of this coalition varied depending on the context of his discussion. He generally included only three core groups vaguely identified as the liberal-labor-civil rights coalition. His emphasis on commonly shared interests, however, does not seem to match his occasional inclusion of religious groups and business organizations as members of this coalition. In the early 1970s he began to urge African Americans to join with labor and the Democratic party to form a coalition.
7   William Julius Wilson, *The Declining Significance of Race* (Chicago: University of Chicago Press, 1978) and *The Truly Disadvantaged* (Chicago: University of Chicago Press, 1987). Several features of Rustin's analysis are reflected in Wilson's work. Rustin argued for a class analysis on the basis of which he employed the term "underclass" to refer to black urban poor people who were experiencing the impact of urban deindustrialization and increased social dislocation because of the exodus of black middle-class professionals from black neighborhoods. See Bayard Rustin, *Strategies for Freedom: The Changing Patterns of Black Protest* (New York: Columbia University Press, 1976), 59; BPCP, 163–4; RNMC, 276, and BU, 336. He pointed out that, once legal barriers were removed, African Americans were stymied by more deeply rooted economic obstacles such as automation and urban decay. These problems are "the result of the total society's failure to meet not only the Negro's needs but human needs generally" and hence will not

vanish after the demise of legal segregation (PP, 115). They require progressive measures derived from a social vision based on class rather than race. See Rustin, *Strategies for Freedom*, 55 and FBS, 299, Moreover, given the conservative climate of the Nixon era, only a political strategy with the color-blind objective of eradicating poverty will gain the support of a majority liberal-civil-rights-labor coalition. See FBS, 307–8.

8 Perlstein, "The Case against Community," 54.

9 Ibid., 60.

10 Ibid., 53.

11 Ibid., 56.

12 See especially BU, 349.

13 Perlstein cites the criticisms of other black unionists to indicate the inadequacy of Rustin's application of Marxist theory to the Ocean Hill-Brownsville situation. See Perlstein, "The Case against Community," 58–60. Rustin's willingness to work behind the scenes to reach a compromise, however, provides some reason to believe that he was aware of these weaknesses in his view. Moreover, his Marxist justification was constrained by certain implications of his own account of the history of the civil rights movement. According to Rustin, "the previous period was a period of protest; the present period must be one of politics" (LLHS, 197). In his Radner Lectures he maintained that, to achieve the economic objectives of the later phase of the civil rights movement, coalition politics must become less absolute and more willing to arrive at political compromises. See SF, 53. Even in his Dewey Award acceptance speech to the UFT he had spoken of "the need for flexibility" with community activitists while remaining faithful to integrationist values (ID, 218).

14 BPCP, 164. See also Rustin, *Strategies for Freedom*, 75; APR, 264; WOEG, 185–6; AF, 235–6; PP, 118; LLHS, 191–2; RNMC, 275; BU, 346; ID, 216; and MR, 153.

15 Cf. BU, 346.

16 In his discussion of the frustration motivating black nationalism, Rustin distinguished between "America's ability" and "her willingness" to respond to the aspirations of African Americans (FBS, 292). He questioned the willingness of the conservative Nixon administration and of members of interracial political coalitions. In an earlier address to B'nai B'rith he had already flatly acknowledged that coalition politics had become ineffective. See AF, 232–3.

17 For citations of Rustin's various remarks regarding his economic proposals, see above Note 14. Although he spoke generally of a "comprehensive" program to address housing, education, and health care,

he consistently included on his economic agenda specific measures to deal with full employment, minimum wage, guaranteed income, and public works programs, but occasionally included others such as mass transportation and environmental polution.

18 Rustin meant this literally. He proclaimed: "We must create new towns and destroy the ghettos" (AF, 237).

19 Rustin, *Strategies for Freedom*, 62. See also FBS, 304; AF, 237; LLHS, 195; BPCP, 162; PP, 116; and MM, 137.

20 Rustin claimed that Malcolm X's economic program was "petty bourgeois" (MM, 139). It is worth noting that, in his discussion of black capitalism, Rustin never mentioned the economic viability of Elijah Muhammed's Nation of Islam. See, for instance, BC, 259–60. He also carelessly lumped the Black Panther Party (which espoused a Marxist ideology) together with black nationalist groups such as the US organization. See FBS, 294.

21 See Rustin, *Strategies for Freedom*, 57; SSSC, 238 and AF, 235.

22 MBM, 211, his emphasis.

23 Cf. FBS, 295.

24 BPCP, 156, his emphasis. See also Rustin's claim that "The demand for black power" is "a demand for black middle class power" (RNMC, 275).

25 BPCP, 155, but see also Rustin, *Strategies for Freedom*, 73–4; BU, 338; FBS, 305; and RNMC, 276.

26 Perlstein, "The Case against Community," 56.

27 See Rustin, *Strategies for Freedom*, 27–8 and APR, 261–6. In a discussion of his involvement with the War Resisters League, Rustin claimed that "nonviolence was not simply a philosophical stance for the peace movement, but was indeed a fundamental way of life" (GBB, 166). His position on United States involvement in the war in Viet Nam was inconsistent with this claim. He boldly confronted peace activists with the idea that the military provided job opportunities that impoverished African Americans cannot forego for the sake of morality. See GBB, 168. In a rather polite disagreement with Martin Luther King's anti-war speech on Vietnam, he maintained that "I would consider the involvement of the civil rights organizations as such in peace activities distinctly unprofitable and perhaps even suicidal" (KPD, 170). He argued that peace activists should support the civil rights struggle to provide alternative opportunies for African Americans who join the military out of economic necessity. According to Rustin, "we can have guns and butter . . . we can pursue our course in Vietnam and still make progress at home" (WOEG, 186).

28 SF, 21.

29 Rustin claimed: "To many Americans, in fact, it appeared that the transition was not from protest to politics, but from nonviolent civil disobedience to violent disruption and rioting." Rustin, *Strategies for Freedom*, 57.

30 Cf. Rustin's claim that "the phrase designates fundamental changes in social and economic class relations resulting from mass political action" (WOEG, 180).

31 Rustin's rather conservative remarks about having "the courage to defend and maintain those principles which are indispensible to the survival of civility" can be interpreted as an allusion to the "ignorant armies" who are bent on turning the class struggle into a violent revolution (ID, 215).

32 Rustin even expressed fear of a race war that might result from Nixon's southern strategy to reverse the integration of schools. See VSS, 316–17.

33 See MBM, 206; FBS, 298; and WOEG, 179.

34 See also MR, 153 and MBM, 209–10 for Rustin's remarks regarding his own frustration as an activist.

35 MR, 152.

36 After pointing out the need to transform social and economic relations by changing central institutions, Rustin claimed that neither the church nor the banking system are central institutions. Rather, 'it is the trade union movement and the Democratic party which offer the greatest leverage to the black struggle' FBS, 306).

Chapter 9   A No-theory Theory of Contemporary Black Cinema

1 Thomas Cripps, *Black Film as Genre* (Bloomington: Indiana University Press, 1979), 3–12.

2 Phyllis Klotman (ed.), *Frame by Frame: A Black Filmography* (Bloomington: Indiana University Press, 1979) and James R. Parish and George H. Hill (eds), *Black Action Films* (Jefferson, N.C.: McFarland, 1989).

3 With regard to Klotman's black filmography, Gladstone Yearwood registered the following objection, "to identify a black film *as any film with black faces* is to trivialize or nullify a definition of black film." "Towards a Theory of a Black Cinema Aesthetic" in Gladstone L. Yearwood (ed.), *Black Cinema Aesthetics: Issues in Independent Black Filmmaking* (Athens: Ohio University Center for Afro-American Studies, 1982), 68–9. In his review of *Black Action Films*, Roland Jefferson takes Parish and Hill to task for including *Rocky I-IV* as black films. *Black Film Review* 5.4 (Fall, 1989): 22.

4   Teshome H. Gabriel "Third Cinema as Guardian of Popular Memory:
    Towards a Third Aesthetics" in *Questions of Third Cinema*, eds. Jim Pines
    and Paul Willemen (London: British Film Institute, 1989), 53–64;
    Kobena Mercer, "Diaspora Culture and the Dialogic Imagination:
    The Aesthetics of Black Independent Film in Britain" in *Blackframes:
    Critical Perspectives on Black Independent Cinema*, eds. Mbye B. Cham and
    Claire Andrade-Watkins (Cambridge, MA: The MIT Press, 1988), 50–61.

5   August Wilson, "I Don't Want to Hire Nobody Just 'Cause They're
    Black'," *Spin* 6.7 (October 1990): 71.

6   Various periodizations have been offered by other commentators. See,
    for instance, James Snead, "Images of Blacks in Black Independent
    Films: A Brief Survey" in Cham and Andrade-Watkins, *Blackframes*,
    16–25; and Clyde Taylor, "The L. A. Rebellion: A Turning Point in
    Black Cinema." Circular for *The New American Filmmakers Series 26* (New
    York: Whitney Museum of American Art, 1986).

7   Cf. Renee Ward, "Black Films, White Profits," *The Black Scholar* (May
    1976): 13–24; Jim Pines, *Blacks in Films* (London: Studio Vista, 1975),
    chap. 8; James A. Miller, "From Sweetback to Celie: Blacks on Film
    into the 80s" in Mike Davis, et al., *The Year Left 2*, 139–59.

8   In this sense, Fred Williamson's independently produced films (which
    have been continuous since his participation in the earlier phase of
    Hollywood blaxploitation) would count as a perpetuation of this style.
    Eddie Murphy's recent *Harlem Nights* is a throwback to Williamson's
    Black Caesar and *Hell Up in Harlem*. I would also include the recent
    spate of hip-hop movies as a neo-blaxploitation genre, although, within
    this genre, we must again distinguish, "positive-image" films, such as
    Harry Belafonte's *Beat Street*, from more violence-laden films such as
    Run DMC's *Tougher Than Leather*.

9   Mark Reid, "The Black Action Film: The End of the Patiently Endur-
    ing Black Hero," *Film History* (1988); 25.

10 Several commentators have noted the inherent dangers of using
    the black hero image as a narrative strategy. For a discussion of the
    co-optational use of black heroic characters to legitimate oppression
    see Gladstone Yearwood's "The Hero in Black Film," *Wide Angle* 5.2
    (1982): 42–51. David E. James provides a wise bit of cautionary reflec-
    tion on the *Bildungsroman* narrative of *Sweetback* as a self-defeating
    contributor to the film's commodification into blaxploitation. See
    his "Chained to Devilpictures: Cinema and Black Liberation in the
    Sixties" in *The Year Left 2*, eds Davis, et al., 135–7. Clyde Taylor takes
    issue with the master narrative in all of its various guises. See his
    "We Don't Need Another Hero: Anti-theses on Aesthetics" in Cham
    and Watkins, *Blackframes*.

11 For instance, there is a need to examine more fully the transition period in the late 1960s as a precursor to blaxploitation-era film-making, especially with regard to independently produced films about black people. Some attention should also be given to the carry-over effect of blaxploitation-era films on the image of black people in mass-audience films and to the intertextual influences of blaxploitation on television programming.

12 There were several factors operating in various ways to shape the movie industry's multifarious output of blaxploitation-era films, but most outstanding was the market orientation of each film. Given that some of the larger-budgeted productions (e.g., *100 Rifles, The Great White Hope,* and *The Learning Tree*) were intended for a mainstream audience, whereas low-budget productions (e.g., *Superfly, Blacula,* and *Coffey Brown*) were limited to box-office showing in black communities, it would be a serious oversight to ignore the guerrilla tactics employed by Melvin Van Peebles to produce *Sweetback* and Bill Gunn to film *Ganja and Hess.* The avant-garde styles mastered by Van Peebles and Gunn owe much to the clandestine context in which their projects were pursued, and contrasts sharply with the more standard approaches displayed in mainstream productions such as *Claudine, A Hero Ain't Nothing But A Sandwich, The River Niger, Brothers, The Spook Who Sat by the Door,* and *Gordon's War.* These latter films, nonetheless, were a far cry from the more typical black action movies of the period.

13 Cf. Michael Ryan and Douglas Kellner, *Camera Politica* (Bloomington: Indiana University Press, 1988), 121–9.

14 Cf. Miller, "From Sweetback to Celie," 149.

15 Reid, "The Black Action Film," 29.

16 Ibid., 30.

17 Pearl Bowser, "Sexual Imagery and the Black Woman in Cinema" in Yearwood, *Black Cinema Aesthetics,* 51.

18 Reid makes the former claim (Reid, "The Black Action Film," 26) and Pines makes the latter (Pines, *Blacks in Films,* 123).

19 Circular for *The New American Filmmakers Series 23* (New York: Whitney Museum of American Art, 1985), 2.

20 Reid, "The Black Action Film," 30.

21 On this point see Clyde Taylor, "We Don't Need Another Hero," 84–5.

22 A panel discussion on *Sweetback,* with Melvin Van Peebles, St Clair Bourne, Haile Gerima, and Pearl Bowser, was held at a conference on independent black film-making at Ohio State University in 1981. This discussion was published in Yearwood, *Black Cinema Aesthetics,* 53–66.

23   This point was brought to my attention at a lecture at Northeastern University (Fall 1987) during which Clyde Taylor presented an analysis of the class differences in audience reactions to *Sweetback* as a methodological device by which to interpret the film. See the very interesting discussion of this issue by Mercer in his "Recoding Narratives," but also see, Mercer and Julien, "De Margin and De Centre," *Screen* 29.4 (1988): 2–10; and Paul Willemen, "The Third Cinema Question: Notes and Reflections," *Framework* 34 (1987): 1–29.

24   In a similar vein, Keenan Ivory Wayans's *I'm Gonna Git You Sucka* and his television show, *In Living Color*, present a black-oriented variety of post-Eddie Murphy humor that relies heavily on the ridicule of white stereotypes of black people.

25   The social taboo against public statements regarding the media hype of Larry Bird as the greatest basketball player ever was quite deliberately violated by Lee in *She's Gotta Have It*. Lee seemed to rail against the *de facto* censorship of what many black people believe about Larry Bird by having his character, Mars Blackman, flaunt anti-Bird jokes in the face of the audience that had witnessed Isiah Thomas being coerced on national television to demeaningly recant his truthful comments regarding the racist commentary in sports broadcasting.

26   For a pointed discussion of this dilemma facing independent black film-makers see Clyde Taylor, "Black Films in Search of a Home," *Freedomways* (Fourth Quarter, 1983): 226–33, "The Paradox of Black Independent Cinema," *Black Film Review*, 4.4 (Fall 1988), and Paul Gilroy, "Nothing But Sweat inside My Hand: Diaspora Aesthetics and Black Arts in Britain" in Mercer, *Black Film British Cinema*, 44–6. See also Larry Rohter's discussion of Charles Burnett's *To Sleep With Anger*. "An All-Black Film (Except for the Audience)," *New York Times* (November 20, 1990): B1.

27   Prince's films remain closer to Hollywood's assimilationist paradigm of the "crossover" black film-maker, while Spike Lee entered the crossover market with black-oriented films that are closer to the black independent tradition.

28   I have in mind here, specifically, films such as *The Killing Floor, Minstrel Man, Autobiography of Miss Jane Pittman, Go and Tell It On the Mountain*, and *The Women of Brewster Place*.

29   Some rap artists have characterized their cultural practice as "black America's TV station." See John Leland, "Armageddon in Effect," *Spin*, 4.6 (September 1988): 48.

30   Cf. Alan Fountain, "Channel 4 and Black Independents" in Mercer, *Black Film British Cinema*, 42–4, and Jim Pines, "The Cultural Context

of Black British Cinema" in Cham and Andrade-Watkins, *Blackframes*, 26–36.
31 He argued for a socially constructed concept of black identity that black people should "invent" to advance themselves. W. E. B. Du Bois, "The Conservation of Races" in Brotz, *Negro Social and Political Thought*, 483–92.
32 Within the unspoken norms of African American culture, black people with a Caucasian appearance generally bear the burden of proving their loyalty, given that they have an option to "pass," despite their known biological heritage.
33 See the alternative accounts of Kobena Mercer, "Third Cinema at Edinburgh," *Screen*, 27.6, 1986; David Will, "Report on the Third Cinema Conference at Edinburgh," *Framework* 32/33 (1986): 197–209; Paul Willemen, "The Third Cinema Question," *Framework* 34 (1987); and Clyde Taylor, "Eurocentrics vs. New Thought at Edinburgh," *Framework* 34 (1987): 140–8.
34 Willemen displays this tendency when he attempts to utilize Bakhtin's thesis regarding sociohistorical specificity to reconstruct Gabriel's internationalist account of third-cinema practice. See his "The Third Cinema Question: Notes and Reflections" in *Questions of Third Cinema*, eds, Jim Pines and Paul Willemen (London: British Film Institute, 1989), 23 ff.
35 While it would be inaccurate to attribute this view to Willemen, some of his declarations lend themselves to an interpretation along these lines. For instance, he maintains that "the question of the national cannot be divorced from the question of Third Cinema" (p. 20), and that those engaged in black film practices must refuse "to homogenise every non-Euro-American culture into a globalised other" (p. 29). But surely Willemen does not mean to deny the possibility of new social formations, perhaps international in scope, which stand opposed to neocolonial structures that are ultimately rationalized on biological notions of national identities.
36 Stuart Hall has advocated an extreme version of the nonessentialist view of cultural practice. See his "Cultural Identity and Cinematic Representation," *Framework* 36 (1989): 68–81, and "New Ethnicities" in Mercer, *Black Film British Cinema*, 27–30.
37 Cf. Julio Garcia Espinosa, "For an Imperfect Cinema" in *Communications and Class Struggle: 2 Liberation, Socialism*, ed., Armand Mattelart (New York: International General, 1979–83), 295–300.
38 For a critical discussion of how black films that are modernist in style have gained a greater currency than those that are steeped in realism, see Judith Williamson, "Two Kinds of Otherness" and Coco Fusco,

"The Other is In" in Mercer, *Black Film British Cinema*. See also Valerie Smith's insightful commentary on what counts as an "experimental" black film, in her "Reconstituting the Image: The Emergent Black Woman Director," *Callaloo* 11.4 (Fall, 1988).

Chapter 10   Prime-time Blackness

1   Herman Gray, *Watching Race: Television and the Struggle for "Blackness"* (Minneapolis: University of Minnesota Press, 1995).
2   Ibid., 5.
3   See Douglass Kellner, *Television and the Crisis of Democracy* (Boulder, Colo.: Westview Press, 1990); John Fiske, *Television Culture* (London: Methuen, 1987); and *Media Matters* (Minneapolis: University of Minnesota Press, 1995); Todd Gitlin (ed.), *Watching Television* (New York: Pantheon, 1986) and *Inside Prime Time* (New York: Pantheon, 1983).
4   Gray, *Watching Race*, 7 and Stuart Hall, "Cultural Identity and Cinematic Representation," *Framework* 36 (1989): 68–82.
5   Gray, *Watching Races*, 111.
6   Ibid., 36.
7   Ibid., 56.
8   Ibid., 58.
9   J. Fred MacDonald, *Blacks and White TV: African Americans in Television since 1948*, 2nd ed. (Chicago: Nelson-Hall, 1992).
10   Gray, *Watching Race*, 78.
11   Cf. Michael Dyson, "Bill Cosby and the Politics of Race," *Z Magazine* (September 1989): 26–30. For discussions of debates surrounding *The Cosby Show* see Sut Jhally and Justin Lewis, *Enlightened Racism: The Cosby Show, Audiences, and the Myth of the American Dream* (Boulder, Colo.: Impact, and Implications* (Westport, Conn.: Greenwood Press, 1992).
12   Gray, *Watching Race*, 101.
13   Ibid., 101.
14   Ibid., 111. Mark Crispin Miller, "End of Story" in Miller (ed.) *Seeing through Movies* (New York: Pantheon, 1990), 186–247.
15   Gray, *Watching Race*, 111.
16   Ibid., 112.
17   Ibid., 125.
18   Ibid., 125.
19   Ibid., 132.
20   Ibid., 144.

Select Bibliography

Abrahams, Roger, *Deep Down in the Jungle* (Chicago: Aldine Publishing Co., 1970).

Andrews, William L. (ed.), *The Oxford Frederick Douglass Reader* (New York: Oxford University Press, 1996).

Aptheker, Bettina, *Women's Legacy* (Amherst: The University of Massachusetts Press, 1982).

Arvey, Verna, "Sargent Johnson," *Opportunity* 17 (July 1939): 213–14.

Asante, Molefi, *Afrocentricity* (Trenton, NJ: Africa World Press, 1988).

Banton, Michael, "The Classification of Races in Europe and North America: 1700–1850," *International Social Science Journal* 111 (February 1987): 45–60.

Bearden, Romare and Henderson, Harry, *A History of African-American Artists: From 1792 to the Present* (New York: Pantheon Books, 1993).

Bell, Bernard W., *Folk Roots of Contemporary Afro-American Poetry* (Detroit: Broadside Press, 1974).

Bell, Howard H., "National Negro Conventions of the Middle 1840's: Moral Suasion vs. Political Action," *Journal of Negro History*, 42 (October, 1957): 247–60.

Bell, Howard H., *A Survey of the Negro Convention Movement 1830–1861* (New York: Arno Press, 1969).

Blassingame, John W. and McKivigan John R. (eds), *The Frederick Douglass Papers*, 6 vols (New Haven: Yale University Press, 1979–92).

Blassingame, John W., *The Slave Community: Plantation Life in the Antebellum South* (New York: Oxford University Press, 1974).

Blount, Marcellus, "The Preacherly Text: African American Poetry and Vernacular Performance," *Proceedings Modern Language Association*, 107.3 (May 1992).

Boas, Franz, "Human Faculty as Determined by Race," in *Race, Culture, and Evolution*, ed. George W. Stocking, Jr (New York: The Free Press, 1968).

Boskin, Joseph, *Sambo* (New York: Oxford University Press, 1986).

Boxill, Bernard R., *Blacks and Social Justice* (Totowa, New Jersey: Rowman & Allanheld, 1984).

Broderick, Francis L., "German Influence on the Scholarship of W. E. B. Du Bois," *Phylon* 19 (December 1958).

— "The Academic Training of W. E. B. Du Bois," *Journal of Negro Education* 27 (winter 1958).

Brotz, Howard (ed.), *Negro Social and Political Thought: 1850–1920* (New York: Basic Books, 1966).

Broussard, Albert, *Black San Francisco* (Lawrence, KS: University Press of Kansas, 1993).

Brown, Sterling, *Negro Poetry and Drama* (New York: Atheneum, 1978).

Brownmiller, Susan, *Against Our Will: Men, Women and Rape* (New York: Harper and Row, 1975).

Burkert, Walter, Girard, Rene and Smith, Jonathan Z., (eds), *Violent Origins: Ritual Killing and Cultural Formation* (Stanford: Stanford University Press, 1987).

Butcher, Margaret Just, *The Negro in American Culture* (New York: New American Library, 1956).

Carby, Hazel, *Reconstructing Womanhood* (New York: Oxford University Press, 1987).

Cash, W. J., *The Mind of the South* (New York: Alfred Knopf, 1941).

Childs, John Brown, *Leadership, Conflict, and Cooperation in Afro-American Social Thought* (Philadelphia: Temple University Press, 1981).

Conyers, James E. and Kennedy, T. H., "Negro Passing: To Pass or Not to Pass," *Phylon*, 24.3 (Fall 1963): 215–23.

Cripps, Thomas, *Black Film as Genre* (Bloomington: Indiana University Press, 1979).

Crowley, Daniel J., (ed.), *African Folklore in the New World* (Austin: University of Texas, 1977).

Curtis, L. Perry Jr., *Apes and Angels: The Irishman in Victorian Caricature* (Washington, D.C.: Smithsonian Institution Press, 1971).

D'Emilio, John and Freedman, Estelle, *Intimate Matters: A History of Sexuality in America* (New York: Harper and Row, 1988).

Dance, Daryl Cumber, *Shuckin' and Jivin'* (Bloomington: Indiana University Press, 1978).

Daniels, Douglas, *Pioneer Urbanites* (Berkeley: University of California Press, 1980/90).

Davis, Angela Y., *Women, Race and Class* (New York: Random House, 1981).

Davis, Manning M., Pfeil, F. and Sprinker, M. (eds), *The Year Left 2* (London: Verso, 1987).

DeMarco, Joseph P., *The Social Thought of W. E. B. Du Bois* (Lanham: University Press of America, 1983).

Dennison, Sam, *Scandalize My Name* (New York: Garland Publishers, 1982).

Dillard, J. L., *Lexicon of Black English* (Seabury Press, 1977).

Dominguez, Virginia R., *White by Definition* (New Brunswick, N.J.: Rutgers University Press, 1986).

Dover, Cedric, "The Racial Philosophy of Johann Herder," *British Journal of Sociology* 3 (1952).

— *American Negro Art* (New York: Graphic Society, 1960).

Du Bois, W. E. B., *Black Folk: Then and Now* (New York: Henry Holt, 1939).

— *Dusk of Dawn: An Essay toward an Autobiography of a Race Concept* (New York: Schocken, 1968/75).

— *The Souls of Black Folk* (New York: Fawcett World Library, 1961).

— *Worlds of Color* (Millwood, N.Y.: Kraus-Thomson, 1976).

Duster, Alfreda M., *Crusade for Justice: The Autobiography of Ida B. Wells* (Chicago: University of Chicago Press, 1970).

Dyson, Michael E., *Reflecting Black* (Minneapolis: University of Minnesota Press, 1993).

Edwards, Allison, *Rape, Racism, and the White Women's Movement: An Answer to Susan Brownmiller* (Chicago: Sojourner Truth Organization, 1979).

Edwards, Ozzie L., "Skin Color As A Variable in Racial Attitudes of Black Urbanites," *Journal of Black Studies*, 3.4 (June, 1972): 473–83.

Ely, Melvin Patrick, *The Adventures of Amos 'n' Andy* (New York: The Free Press, 1991).

Espinosa, Julio Garcia, "For an Imperfect Cinema," in *Communications and Class Struggle: 2 Liberation, Socialism*, ed., Armand Mattelart (New York: International General, 1983).

Fauset, Arthur Huff, *Sojourner Truth: God's Faithful Pilgrim* (Durham, N.C.: University of North Carolina Press, 1938).

Foner, Philip (ed.), *The Life and Writings of Frederick Douglass*, 6 vols (New York: International Publishers, 1952).

Foucault, Michel, *Discipline and Punish* (New York: Pantheon, 1977).

Franklin, John Hope (ed.), *Color and Race* (Boston: Houghton Mifflin Co., 1968).

Frazier, E. Franklin, *Black Bourgeoisie* (New York: Free Press, 1957).

Gates, Henry L. Jr. (ed.), *"Race", Writing, and Difference* (Chicago: University of Chicago Press, 1985).

Gates, Henry L., Jr, *Figures in Black* (New York: Oxford University Press, 1987).

— *The Signifying Monkey* (New York: Oxford University Press, 1988).

Giddings, Paula, *When and Where I Enter: The Impact of Black Women on Race and Sex in America* (New York: Bantam Books, 1985).

Gilbert, Olive (comp.), *Narrative of Sojourner Truth, A Bondwoman of Olden Time* (New York: Arno, 1968).

Gilroy, Paul, *There Ain't No Black in the Union Jack* (London: Hutchinson, 1987).

— *The Black Atlantic* (Cambridge, MA: Harvard University Press, 1993).

Glasgow, Douglas G., *The Black Underclass* (San Francisco: Jossey-Bass, 1980).

Goldberg, David T. (ed.), *Anatomy of Racism* (Minneapolis: University of Minnesota Press, 1990).

— *Racial Subjects* (New York: Routledge, 1997).

Gordon, Milton M., *Assimilation in American Life* (New York: Oxford University Press, 1964).

Gossett, Thomas F., *Race: The History of an Idea in America* (New York: Schocken, 1973).

Graham, Richard (ed.), *The Idea of Race in Latin America, 1870–1940* (Austin: University of Texas Press, 1990).

Habermas, Jurgen, *The Philosophical Discourse of Modernity* (Cambridge: Polity Press, 1987).

Hall, Stuart, "Cultural Identity and Cinematic Representation," *Framework* 36 (1989).

Hare, Nathan, *The Black Anglo Saxons* (New York: Collier Books, 1965).

Hare, Nathan and Hare, Julia, *Bringing the Black Boy to Manhood: The Passage* (San Francisco: The Black Think Tank, 1985).

Harris, Marvin, *Patterns of Race in the Americas* (New York: W. W. Norton, 1964).

Harris, Trudier, *Exorcising Blackness: Historical and Literary Lynching and Burning Rituals* (Bloomington: Indiana University Press, 1984).

— (ed.) *Selected Works of Ida B. Wells-Barnett* (New York: Oxford University Press, 1991).

Herton, Calvin C., *Sex and Racism in America* (Garden City, NY: Doubleday, 1965).

Hill, Robert A. and Bair, Barbara (eds), *Marcus Garvey Life and Lessons* (Berkeley: University of California Press, 1987).

Hirsch, Marianne and Keller, Evelyn Fox (eds), *Conflicts in Feminism* (Routledge, 1990).

Hoch, Paul, *White Hero Black Beast* (UK: Pluto, 1979).

hooks, bell, *Ain't I a Woman: Black Women and Feminism* (Boston: South End Press, 1982).

Hopkins, Pauline, *Contending Forces: A Romance Illustrative of Negro Life North and South* (1900; Carbondale, Ill., 1978).

Hudson, Gossie Harold, "Paul Laurence Dunbar: Dialect Et La Negritude," *Phylon* 4.3 (September 1973).

Huggins, Nathan I., *Voices from the Harlem Rennaissance* (New York: Oxford University Press, 1976).

Hughes, Langston, *The Big Sea* (New York: Farrar, Straus & Giroux, 1940).

Hutchinson, Earl Ofari, *The Assassination of the Black Male Image* (New York: Touchstone, 1994/97; Indiana University Press, 1979).

Jacobs, Brian D., *Black Politics and Urban Crisis in Britain* (Cambridge: Cambridge University Press, 1986).

Jacobs, Harriet A., *Incidents in the Life of a Slave Girl*, ed. Jean Fagen Yellin (Cambridge, MA: Harvard University Press, 1987).

James, Joy, *Resisting State Violence* (Minneapolis: University of Minnesota Press, 1997).

— *Transcending the Talented Tenth: Black Leaders and American Intellectuals* (New York: Routledge, 1997).

Jennings, James, "Escaping from the Poorhouse of Ideas," *In These Times*, 17–23 (February 1988).

Jordan, June, *Civil Wars* (Boston: Beacon Press, 1981).

Jordan, Winthrop, *White over Black: American Attitudes toward the Negro, 1550–1812* (Baltimore: Penguin Books, 1968).

Kelly, Robin D. G., *Race Rebels: Culture, Politics, and the Black Working Class* (New York: The Free Press, 1994).

Klotman, Phyllis (ed.), *Frame by Frame: A Black Filmography* (Bloomington: Indiana University Press, 1979).

Kovel, Joel, *White Racism: A Psychohistory* (New York: Pantheon Books, 1970).

Lawson, Bill, "Crime, Minorities and the Social Contract," *Criminal Justice Ethics* 9.2 (Summer/Fall 1990): 16–24.

LeFalle-Collins, Lizzetta and Goldman, Shifra M., *In the Spirit of Resistance: African-American Modernists and the Mexican Muralist School* (New York: The American Federation of Arts, 1996).

LePage, R. B. and Tabouret-Keller, Andrée, *Acts of Identity: Creole-Based Approaches to Language and Ethnicity* (Cambridge: Cambridge University Press, 1985).

Lerner, Gerda (ed.), *Black Women in White America: A Documentary History* (New York: Pantheon Books, 1972).

Litwack, Leon F., *North of Slavery: The Negro in the Free States, 1790–1860* (Chicago: University of Chicago Press, 1961).

Locke, Alain and Stern, Bernard J. (eds), *When Peoples Meet* (New York: Progressive Education Association, 1942).

Locke, Alain L., "The Art of the Ancestors," *Survey Graphic* 6.6 (March 1925): 673.

Locke, Alain L. (ed.), *The New Negro: An Interpretation* (Boston: Atheneum, 1925/68).
— "Advance on the Art Front," *Opportunity* 27.5 (May 1939): 132–6.
— *Negro Art: Past and Present* (Salem, NH: 1936/1991).
— *Race Contacts and Interracial Relations*, ed. with an introduction by J. Stewart (Washington, D.C.: Howard University Press, 1992).
Lounds, Morris, Jr, *Israel's Black Hebrews: Black Americans in Search of Identity* (Washington, D.C.: University Press of America, 1981).
McFeely, William, *Frederick Douglass* (New York: Norton, 1991).
McGary, Howard and Lawson, Bill E., *Between Slavery and Freedom* (Bloomington: Indiana University Press, 1992).
McKinzie, Richard D., *The New Deal for Artists* (Princeton University Press, 1973).
Mahar, William J., "Black English in Early Blackface Minstrelsy: A New Interpretation of the Sources of Minstrel Show Dialect," *American Quarterly* (1984).
Mailer, Norman, *Advertisements for Myself* (New York: Andre Deutsch, 1964).
Meier, August and Rudwick, Elliott, *CORE* (New York: Oxford University Press, 1973).
Mercer, Kobena, "Third Cinema at Edinburgh," *Screen*, 27.6 (1986).
Miller, Warren, *The Cool World* (New York: Fawcett World Library, 1969).
Mohanty, Chandra Talpado, Russo, Ann and Torres, Lourdes (eds), *Third World Women and the Politics of Feminism* (Bloomington: Indiana University Press, 1991).
Moore, W. H. A., "The New Negro Literary Movement," *AME Church Review* 21 (1904).
Moran, Francis, III, "Between Primates and Primitives: Natural Man as the Missing Link in Rousseau's *Second Discourse*," *Journal of the History of Ideas*, 54.1 (January 1993).
Morrison, Lionel, *As They See It* (London: Community Relations Commission, 1976).
Morrison, Toni (ed.), *Birth of a Nation'hood* (New York: Pantheon Books, 1997).
Moses, Wilson J., *Alexander Crummell: A Study of Civilization and Discontent* (Oxford: Oxford University Press, 1989).
Mudimbe, Valentin Y., *The Invention of Africa* (Bloomington: Indiana University Press, 1988).
Nachimias, D. (ed.), *The Practice of Policy Evaluation* (New York: Saint Martin's Press, 1980).
Nascimento, Abdias do, *"Racial Democracy" in Brazil: Myth or Reality?* (Chicago: Third World Press, 1977).

Null, Gary, *Black Hollywood* (Secaucus, N.J.: Citadel Press, 1975).

O'Connor, Francis V., *Art for the Millions* (Greenwich, Conn.: New York Graphic Society Ltd., 1973).

Omi, Michael and Winant, Howard, *Racial Formation in the United States: From the 1960s to the 1990s* (New York: Routledge, 1994).

Parish, James R. and Hill, George H. (eds), *Black Action Films* (Jefferson, N.C.: McFarland, 1989).

Park, Robert E., *Race and Culture* (Glencoe, IL: The Free Press, 1950).

Perlstein, Daniel, "The Case Against Community: Bayard Rustin and the 1968 New York School Crisis," *Educational Foundation* (Winter 1994).

Philips, Michael, "Racist Acts and Racist Humor," *Canadian Journal of Philosophy* 26.1 (March 1984).

Piersen, William D., *Black Legacy: America's Hidden Heritage* (Amherst: University of Massachusetts Press, 1993).

Pines, Jim, *Blacks in Films* (London: Studio Vista, 1975).

Pines, Jim and Willemen Paul, (eds), *Questions of Third Cinema* (London: British Film Institute, 1989).

Porter, Dorothy, "The Organized Educational Activities of Negro Literary Societies, 1828–1846," *Journal of Negro Education*, 5 (October, 1936): 556–66.

Porter, James A., *Modern Negro Art* (Washington, D.C.: Howard University Press 1943/92).

Redding, Saunders, "The Negro Writer and American Literature," in *Anger, and Beyond*, ed. Herbert Hill (New York: Harper and Row, 1968).

— *To Make A Poet Black* (College Park, MD: McGrath Publishing Company, 1968).

Reed, Ishmael, *Reckless Eyeballing* (New York: Atheneum, 1988).

Reeves, Frank, *British Racial Discourse* (Cambridge: Cambridge University Press, 1983).

Reid, Mark, "The Black Action Film: The End of the Patiently Enduring Black Hero," *Film History* (1988).

Revell, Peter, *Paul Laurence Dunbar* (Boston: Twayne Publishers, 1979).

Richardson, Marilyn (ed.), *Maria W. Stewart, America's First Black Woman Political Writer* (Bloomington: Indiana University Press, 1987).

Roberts, John W., *From Trickster to Badman* (Philadelphia: University of Pennsylvania Press, 1989).

Rose, Tricia, *Black Noise: Rap Music and Black Cultural Resistance in Contemporary American Popular Culture* (Middletown, Conn.: Wesleyan University Press, 1994).

Rustin, Bayard, *Down the Line: The Collected Writings of Bayard Rustin* (Chicago: Quadrangle Books, 1971).

— *Strategies for Freedom: The Changing Patterns of Black Protest* (New York: Columbia University Press, 1976).

Ryan, Michael and Kellner, Douglas, *Camera Politica* (Bloomington: Indiana University Press, 1988).

Sachar, Abram Leon, *A History of the Jews* (New York: Alfred A. Knopf, 1979).

Singer, Peter, "Is Racial Discrimination Arbitrary?", *Philosophia* 8.2–3 (November 1978).

Smith, Valerie, "Reconstituting the Image: The Emergent Black Woman Director," *Callaloo*, 11.4 (fall, 1988).

Sollors, Werner, *Beyond Ethnicity: Consent and Descent in American Culture* (New York: Oxford University Press, 1986).

Sowell, Thomas, *Race and Economics* (New York: Longman, 1975).

— *Ethnic America: A History* (New York: Basic Books, 1981).

Steinberg, Stephen, *The Ethnic Myth*, 2nd ed. (Boston: Beacon Press, 1989).

Stewart, Jeffrey C. (ed.), *The Critical Temper of Alain Locke* (New York: Garland, 1983).

Stiles, Knute, "San Francisco," *Artforum* 8 (May 1971): 84.

Stuckey, Sterling, *Slave Culture: Nationalist Theory and the Foundations of Black America* (New York: Oxford University Press, 1987).

Sundquist, Eric J. (ed.), *Frederick Douglass: New Literary and Historical Essays* (New York: Cambridge University Press, 1990).

Sykes, Roberta B., *Black Majority* (Victoria, Australia: Hudson Publishing, 1989).

Taylor, Clyde, "Black Films in Search of a Home," *Freedomways* (Fourth Quarter, 1983).

— "Eurocentrics vs. New Thought at Edinburgh," *Framework* 34 (1987).

— "The Paradox of Black Independent Cinema," *Black Film Review* 4.4 (fall 1988).

Thomas, H. Nigel, *From Folklore to Fiction: A Study of Folk Heroes and Rituals in the Black American Novel* (New York: Greenwood Press, 1988).

Thomas, Laurence, "Rawlsian Self-Respect and the Black Consciousness Movement," *Philosophical Forum* 9 (1978): 303–14.

Toll, Robert C., *Blacking Up: The Minstrel Show in Nineteenth Century America* (Oxford: Oxford University Press, 1974).

Toop, David, *Rap Attack 2: African Rap to Global Hip Hop* (London: Serpent's Tail, 1991).

Ward, Renee, "Black Films, White Profits," *The Black Scholar* (May 1976).

Washington, Mary Helen (ed.), *Midnight Birds* (Garden City, NY: Anchor Books, 1980).

— (ed.) *Invented Lives* (Garden City, NY: Anchor, 1987).

Washington, Robert E., "Brown Racism and the Formation of a World System of Racial Stratification," *International Journal of Politics, Culture, and Society*, 4.2 (1990).

West, Cornel, "On Afro-American Popular Music: From Bebop to Rap," *Black Sacred Music* 6.1 (spring 1992).

White, Deborah Gray, *Ar'n't I a Woman* (New York: W. W. Norton, 1985).

Will, David, "Report on the Third Cinema Conference at Edinburgh," *Framework* 32/33 (1986).

Willemen, Paul, "The Third Cinema Question," *Framework* 34 (1987).

Williams, Vernon J., Jr, *From a Caste to a Minority: Changing Attitudes of American Sociologists toward Afro-Americans, 1896–1945* (New York: Greenwood Press, 1989).

Williams, Walter, *The State against Blacks* (New York: McGraw-Hill, 1982).

Wilson, William Julius, *The Declining Significance of Race* (Chicago: University of Chicago Press, 1978).

— *The Truly Disadvantaged* (Chicago: University of Chicago Press, 1987).

Wiltse, C. M. (ed.), *David Walker's Appeal* (New York: Hill and Wang, 1965).

Yearwood, Gladstone L. (ed.), *Black Cinema Aesthetics: Issues in Independent Black Filmmaking* (Athens, Ohio: Ohio University Center for Afro-American Studies, 1982).

— "The Hero in Black Film," *Wide Angle* 5.2 (1982).

Index

A Different World, 5, 160
abolitionist movement, 11, 99
aboriginals, of Australia, 63
aesthetics, 1, 82, 140, 145–6, 148
Africa, 8, 18, 54
African American identity, 49,
    65
African Americans, 27, 39, 56
African art, 69, 82, 114
African Civilization Society, 53
African culture, 114, 161
African identity, 121
African retentions, 2, 15, 20, 22,
    25, 51, 89–90; *see also*
    Africanisms
African tradition, 15, 21
African worldview, 17
African-American art, 73
Africanisms, 22, 90; *see also*
    African retentions
Africans, 9, 10, 14
Afrocentricism, 2, 20, 102
Ali, Muhammed, 13
Allen, Debbie, 160
American Negro Academy, 1, 47,
    51, 53

Amos 'n' Andy, 101
Anglo-African Magazine, 58
animal rights, 11
anterior culture, 2, 15, 19, 25
Anthony, Susan B., 41
anti-Semitism, 63
antilynching campaign, 2
ape, 7
Appiah, Anthony, 52, 53, 59
Aptheker, Bettina, 3, 43
Aristotle, 7, 16
Arnold, Matthew, 136
Asanti, Molefi, 2, 20
assimilation, 126
assimilationism, 116
assimilationist discourse, 153
authenticity, 47
autonomy, 14

Barthé, Richmond, 73
Beeckman, Daniel, 8
Benjamin, Walter, 15, 22
biological essentialism, 5, 59, 141,
    145, 150
black Atlantic, 20
black cinema, 5, 139, 146

black dialect, 85–8, 95, 101; *see also* black speech
black identity, 1, 5, 88, 149–50, 155
black middle class, 115, 116, 118
black popular culture, 112
black power movement, 133
black rapist myth, 2, 28
black social thought, 1, 113
black speech, 97; *see also* black dialect
black underclass, 4, 112
black urban poor people, 4, 111, 120
black urban youth, 4, 102, 124
black vernacular culture, 21, 85
blackface, 97
blackface comedy, 84
blackness, 5
blaxploitation films, 5, 142, 145, 149
Blyden, 19, 20, 53, 54, 114
Boas, Franz, 8
Bodin, Jean, 8
Bonet, Lisa, 165
Boxill, Bernard, 51, 57
Boyce, Sonia, 12
Brazil, 82
Broussard, Albert: *Black San Francisco*, 67
Brown, Sterling, 86
Brownmiller, Susan, 3
Bufano, Beniamino, 75, 78–9
Buffon, 8
Burnett, Charles: *To Sleep with Anger*, 148
Bush, George, 120

Caliban, 9, 16
Cape Verdians, 59
caricature, 91–2
Central Park rape, 120; trial, 33

Charles, Robert, 37
chattel slavery, 14
Chicanos, 59
Chow, Rey, 12
civil rights movement, 135
civilization, 15, 20, 51, 53
class struggle, 135
coalitions, 128, 131–2, 135
color stratification, 64
conquest, 16
consent theory, 14; *see also* social contract theory
Cooper, Anna Julia, 3, 55, 87
Cosby, Bill, 146, 165
Cosby Show, The, 5, 119, 122, 152, 154, 164
Cripps, Thomas, 139
Crummell, Alexander, 53
cultural imperative, 50
cultural malpractice charge, 85, 96
cultural mission, 51–2
cultural pluralism, 52
cultural resistance, 100; *see also* right of resistance
cultural self-determination, 54
cultural studies, 3
culture of poverty, 119, 126

Da Lench Mob, 8, 110
Daniels, Douglas: *Pioneer Urbanites*, 67
Dapper, Olfert, 9
Darwin, 8
Davis, Angela, 3
De Laurentiis, Dino, 11
Delany, Martin, 19–20, 113, 114
Dillard, J. L., 88
disfranchisement, 39
double consciousness, 15, 47, 68
Douglass, Frederick, 2, 4, 14, 17, 18, 26, 28–9, 31, 33, 35–8, 41–2, 53, 54, 55, 58, 99, 114

Du Bois, 1, 4, 47–8, 53, 55, 62, 117, 149
Du Chaillu, 10
Dubose, Heywood, 3, 91, 95, 97–100

economic reform, 135
education, 133
Egyptians, 18
Enlightenment, 8, 14, 20
Equal Rights Association, 41
Eurocentric worldview, 17
Europeans, 10
Ezy-E, 101–2, 109

feminist thought, 2
Fetchit, Stepin, 94
First Amendment, 106
folk art, 4
folk culture, 3
Frank's Place, 161
Frazier, E. Franklin, 125
Fredrickson, George, 9

Gabriel, Teshome, 140
gangsta rap, 104, 106, 108; *see also* hardcore rap
Garner, Margaret, 17, 25
Garnet, Henry Highland, 53
Garvey, Marcus, 117
Gates, Daryl, 97
Gates, Jr., Henry L.: *The Signifying Monkey*, 89
George, Nelson, 148
ghetto culture, 111
Gilroy: *The Black Atlantic*, 14, 24–6
Goldberg, Whoopi, 84
gorillas, 7, 85
Gray, Herman, 5, 152
Greek mythology, 39

Habermas, Jurgen, 14, 15
Hall, Arsenio, 146
Hall, Stuart, 152
hardcore rap, 102–4; *see also* gangsta rap
Harlem Renaissance, 3, 5
Harmon Foundation, 74
Harper, Frances, E. W., 55, 116
Harris, Joel Chandler, 91
Hearts in Dixie, 94
Hebdige, Dick, 75
Hegel, 14–16
Herbert, Sir Thomas, 9
hip-hop culture, 4, 121
Hobbes, Thomas, 14, 16
Hopkins, Pauline E., 3, 55, 116
Horton, Willie, 27, 120, 154
Hottentots, 8–9
House Party, 146
Huggins, Nathan, 67
Hughes, Langston, 69, 71, 100
Hurston, 90, 100
Hurston, Zora Neale, 3, 88

Ice Cube: *The Predator*, 101, 103, 109, 110, 125
Ice T: *Body Count*, 105, 109, 125, 154
imperialism, 151
In Living Color, 5, 152, 163
independent black film, 145
intentionalist criteria, 96
interracial marriage, 36
interracial sexual relations, 44
interracial sexual taboo, 27

Jackson, Jesse, 7
Jacobs, Harriet, 99
James, Joy, 3
Jefferson, Thomas, 14
Jewish identity, 62
Johnson, Sargent, 4, 69–71, 74
Jones, Grace, 12

Kerner Commission Report, 132
King Kong (1933), 10, 12
King Kong (1976), 11
King, Rodney, 7, 12

L. L. Cool J, 124
Latinos, 61
Lee, Spike, 148
LeFalle-Collins, Lizzetta, 80
legal segregation, 114
Leguat, François, 8
Linnaeus, 8
Locke, Alain: *The New Negro*, 4,
    69–70, 71, 89, 91, 93, 107,
    116
Locke, John, 8, 14, 16
Love, E. K., 33
lynching, 2, 10, 11, 29, 35, 46,
    68, 120

MacDonald, J. Fred, 155
McFeely, William, 35
Malcolm X, 129, 132, 143
Maroons, 118
mass media, 101, 119
Mayfield, Percy, 23
Mercer, Kobena, 140
Mexico, 81
Mighty Joe Young (1948), 11
Miller, Mark Crispin, 160
Miller, Warren: *The Cool World*, 87
minstrel image, 3, 109
minstrelsy, 91, 94, 96–8, 101,
    146, 164
Miranda, 9, 11
miscegenation, 31, 34, 36, 39–40,
    44
misogyny, 103
mixed blood, 64
mixed-race people, 165
modernization, 19–20
Modigliani, Amedeo, 82

Molinari, Gustave, 10, 65
Monboddo, Lord, 8, 9
Morrison, Toni: *Beloved*, 25
Moses, Wilson J., 53
Moynihan, Daniel, 111, 132
mulattoes, 116
multiculturalist discourse, 153
Murphy, Eddie, 146
myth of racial tolerance, 67, 82

NAACP (National Association for
    the Advancement of Colored
    People), 101
National Woman's Suffrage
    Association, 42
nationalism, 150
natural rights, 16
natural slave, 16
Negritude, 100
Negro art, 70; *see also* African art,
    African-American art
Negro Renaissance, 115; *see also*
    Harlem Renaissance
Negro-ape mythology, 2
neoconservative, 4, 112
Nietzsche, 16
Niggaz With Attitude (NWA), 103,
    122, 124, 154
nihilism, 104, 106, 108
nihilistic values, 102
Null, Gary, 94

obligation, 3
Ocean Hill-Brownsville, 127, 136
Ovington, John, 8

Pan-African nationalism, 63
Pan-Africanism, 60
pan-Indian, 60
pan-Negroism, 52, 54
passing, 57, 116
patriarchy, 28, 43

Perlstein, Daniel, 127
Picasso, Pablo, 82
pluralist discourse, 153
politics of ambivalence, 161
Porter, James A., 73
portraiture, 93–4
poverty, 112, 134
Prevost, 8
Prince, 148
propaganda, 3, 93
Prospero, 9
Pryor, Richard, 146
Public Enemy, 124
public policy, 111

race riots, 68; *see also* riots
race tradition, 91
race uplift, 1, 5, 113, 116
race-class debate, 1
race, definition of, 47–8
racial amalgamation, 64
racial antagonism, 30
racial classification, 57, 60–1
racial intermingling, 63
racial invisibility, 68
racial subordination, 163
racism, in women's movement,
    42
racist discourse, 2, 33
Randolph, A. Philip, 135
rap artists, 112
rap music, 3, 100, 101, 104,
    120–2
rape accusation, 31–2, 35
Redding, Saunders, 95
Reid, Mark, 142, 144
representation, 1, 85, 154
right of resistance, 14; *see also*
    cultural resistance
riots, 137; *see also* race riots
Rivera, Diego, 77, 81
Roberts, John, 108

Robeson, Paul, 88
Roots, 156
Rousseau, Jean-Jacques, 14
Rustin, Bayard, 4, 127

Saramaccas, 25
savages, 10
scientific racism, 65
self-determination, 126
Shakespeare: *The Tempest*, 9, 16
Simpson, O. J., 27
slave narratives, 99
slave trade, 14
slavery, 2, 16, 17, 22, 30, 38, 156
slaves, 15
Smith, Valerie, 3, 40
Snead, James, 144
social contract theory, 16; *see also*
    consent theory
social elevation, 20, 31
social equality, 2, 48, 52, 116
social memory, 23
social pathology, 4
Spence, Jon Michael, 108
spirituals, 100
Stanton, Elizabeth Cady, 41
stereotype, 71, 88, 109, 144
Stewart, Maria W., 55
Superfly, 148
Survey Graphic, 72

Third Cinema, 150
tradition, 16, 21, 22
Trespass, 109
True Colors, 164–5
Truth, Sojourner, 86
Tyson, Edward, 8
Tyson, Mike, 12

Van Peebles, Melvin: *Sweet
    Sweetback's Baaadasssss Song*,
    143–4

Vanishing Family, The, 119
violence, 102, 135
visual aesthetic, 5

Walker, Alice, 3, 40
Walker, David, 55
Washington, B. T., 30, 31, 53–4, 115, 117–18
Weems, Carrie Mae, 12
Wells-Barnett, Ida B., 2, 4, 28, 32, 35–8, 40–1, 43
West, Cornel, 127

white negroes, 65
white woman, 10, 11
Wilson, August: *Fences*, 141
Wilson, William Julius, 4, 111–13, 119
WPA, 76, 86
Wray, Fay, 10
Wright, Richard, 21, 88, 107

xenophobia, 7, 11, 12

Zapotec Indians, 81